STRATEGIES
for
E-BUSINESS SUCCESS

STRATEGIES
for
E-BUSINESS SUCCESS

Erik Brynjolfsson
Glen L. Urban

Editors

Center for
eBusiness@MIT
http://ebusiness.mit.edu

JOSSEY-BASS
A Wiley Company
www.josseybass.com

Published by

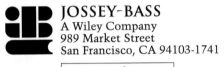

JOSSEY-BASS
A Wiley Company
989 Market Street
San Francisco, CA 94103-1741

www.josseybass.com

Jossey-Bass books and products are available through most bookstores. To contact Jossey-Bass directly, call (888) 378-2537, fax to (800) 605-2665, or visit our website at www.josseybass.com.

Substantial discounts on bulk quantities of Jossey-Bass books are available to corporations, professional associations, and other organizations. For details and discount information, contact the special sales department at Jossey-Bass.

We at Jossey-Bass strive to use the most environmentally sensitive paper stocks available to us. Our publications are printed on acid-free recycled stock whenever possible, and our paper always meets or exceeds minimum GPO and EPA requirements.

Library of Congress Cataloging-in-Publication Data
Strategies for e-business success / Erik Brynjolfsson, Glen
L. Urban, editors.— 1st ed.
    p. cm. — (The Jossey-Bass business & management series)
Includes bibliographical references and index.
  ISBN 0-7879-5848-4 (alk. paper)
  1. Electronic commerce. 2. Internet marketing. I. Title:
Strategies for ebusiness success. II. Brynjolfsson, Erik. III.
Urban, Glen L. IV. Series.
  HF5548.32 .S77 2002
  658.8'4—dc21   2001005786

FIRST EDITION
   10 9 8 7 6 5 4 3 2 1

The Jossey-Bass
Business & Management Series

CONTENTS

PART TWO IMPLEMENTATION

MARKETING

COMMUNITY

STRATEGIES
for
E-BUSINESS SUCCESS

ERIK BRYNJOLFSSON
GLEN L. URBAN
EDITORS

The first generation of e-business has passed into history, and a second generation is now being born. The first generation was marked by high hopes, a landgrab for market opportunities, an infatuation with technology for its own sake, and a disregard for traditional performance metrics. Speed was the generation's defining characteristic, and traditional firms—slower by nature than start-ups—found themselves at a comparative disadvantage. As excitement about the possibilities promised by the Internet's disruptive technology mounted, dot-com stock prices rose to unsustainable levels. A crash inevitably followed, and the Internet economy was confronted with the need to deliver real value to customers and profits to investors.

This boom-and-bust pattern involving disruptive technologies is not new, of course. Although it's hard to imagine today, General Motors was once a fast-growing start-up. Between 1914 and 1920, GM's share price increased 5,500 percent as motor vehicle production surged. By the early 1920s, however, the stock had lost two-thirds of its value as profit expectations clashed with the reality of an overcrowded marketplace. Similarly, the pioneer in radio broadcasting, RCA, saw its share price rise twentyfold between 1923 and 1929 only to plummet thereafter. Then as now, the crashes had the healthy effect of winnowing out unsustainable business models. And a crash in itself is not a comment on revolutionary change in business; the troubles experienced by GM and RCA earlier in the century did nothing to lessen the economic and social impact of the automobile and radio industries. Today, too, swings in the pendulum of investor sentiment shouldn't blind people to those aspects of e-business that are both revolutionary and sustainable.

We believe—and the contents of this book support our belief—that the fundamentals are in place for a second generation of e-business that will overwhelm the economic impact of the first. In the coming decade, the performance of computer chips will improve thirtyfold, and communication and storage capacity will experience even bigger improvements. The number of businesses and consumers connected to the Internet will easily surpass one billion. The application of technology, however, will not drive the new generation of e-business. Instead, it will be powered by the transformational possibilities created when traditional companies successfully incorporate e-business practices.

In the first generation of e-business, traditional companies were derided as hopelessly behind the times; they were charged with "not getting" the Internet. Most of the attention was focused on start-ups and on the companies that provided the hardware and software to power the Internet. Now, however, old-line companies such as General Electric, FleetBoston, Wal-Mart, UPS, and Merrill Lynch have begun to take tremendous advantage of the efficiencies and new markets made available by e-business. Such companies often have built-in advantages over pure e-commerce firms. Start-ups cannot quickly duplicate the assets of large firms: a substantial customer base, brand recognition, knowledge capital, physical plant, solid supplier relationships, and overall market power. Successful large companies also have processes, policies, and people in place that have been built up over time and therefore complement one another. Despite the existence of these advantages, the steps to e-business transformation can be rocky if companies don't follow through on the systemic changes that they must make.

Consider that most executives today have a vision of where they want their companies to be with e-business. They can imagine the benefits of successfully integrating the Internet throughout their entire value chain. They can see the advantages of e-business transformation: reduced costs, increased productivity, accelerated business processes. But the myriad changes in business practices that they need to make are blurry and out of focus, and so they can't make their vision a reality. Many executives suffer from the all-too-common ailment of technological presbyopia—the belief that having a clear view of something means it is only a short distance away. They become impatient when success doesn't arrive overnight, and they are tempted to skip certain steps that are necessary to create a stable and profitable business.

In a time of radical uncertainty, managers have made all manner of mistakes in their attempt to extrapolate next year's growth from last year's buzz. But the era of unfocused experimentation and speed to market above all else is over. The only way to distinguish passing fads from lasting trends is by returning to business fundamentals. To be successful in the second generation, managers must understand the fundamentals—and then execute by running their businesses on that basis. A common thread in the articles we selected for this book—first published as articles in the *Sloan Management Review* in 2000 and 2001—is their respect for business fundamentals.

The chapters of this book provide a road map of the fundamental principles and tools that executives will need if they are to guide their companies successfully in the second generation of e-business. The first six chapters cover strategy. John M. de Figueiredo takes on the most critical strategic issue for companies in the second generation: how to build profitability and earn a solid rate of return on investment. David Feeny then constructs a platform of the opportunities within operations, marketing, and customer service. In Chapter Three, Subramanian Rangan and Ron Adner warn executives against being seduced by popular half-truths about e-business that can lead to critical strategic errors. N. Venkatraman follows by providing help on the best way to steer clear of such trouble: a step-by-step guide on the fundamentals of a Web strategy. Leslie P. Willcocks and Robert Plant then demonstrate that companies should concentrate on achieving market leadership, not technology leadership. In the final chapter on strategy, Clayton M. Christensen makes it clear that the concept of competitive advantage will be just as important to e-business as it has been in the bricks-and-mortar world.

The second six chapters focus on strategic implementation in marketing, organization, and technology. Glen L. Urban, Fareena Sultan, and William J. Qualls begin by discussing the importance of winning customers' trust on the Web and the three-stage process companies must follow to build that trust. Thomas H. Davenport, Jeanne G. Harris, and Ajay K. Kohli then describe the best practices of companies that really get to know their customers. Two chapters—by Gil McWilliam and by Ruth L. Williams and Joseph Cothrel—discuss the importance of Internet communities, which can have strategic value if they are built and run carefully. The last two chapters deal with technology, as Alan MacCormack discusses the merits of an evolutionary approach to the development of software solutions, and M. Lynne Markus, Brook Manville, and Carole E. Agres examine the organizational implications of an open-source world.

Solving customers' needs and delivering real profits to investors will be the hallmark of the second generation of e-business. For senior managers in both start-ups and established companies, the articles we have drawn together for this volume provide some of the best research on how to achieve those goals. They provide many of the tools needed to build and carry out an effective e-business strategy.

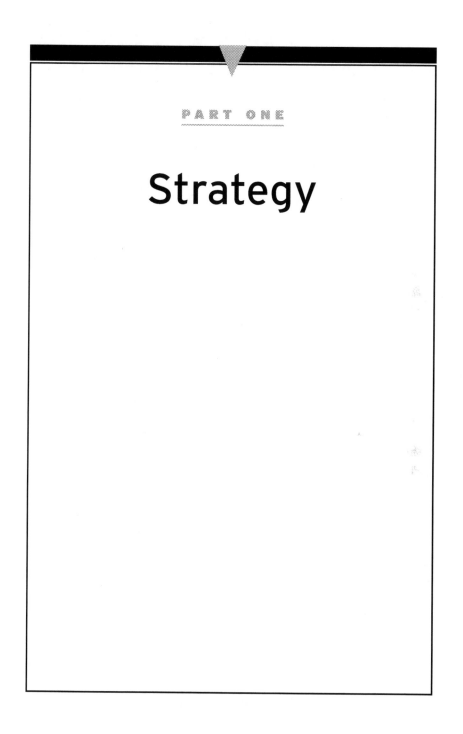

PART ONE

Strategy

CHAPTER ONE

Finding Sustainable Profitability in Electronic Commerce

JOHN M. DE FIGUEIREDO

arren Buffett, the president of Berkshire Hathaway Inc. and one of America's most storied investment managers, remarked last year that if he were teaching an M.B.A. class on finance, the final exam would have one question: How do you value an Internet company? He said anyone who turned in an answer would fail.

Clearly, it is extremely difficult to value e-commerce companies on their assets or profits, because most of these companies have little of either. Indeed, even multipliers of revenue are difficult to assimilate into any sensible financial valuation model. Yet the price appreciation of e-commerce stocks in the past two years has been phenomenal, reaching a one-year gain of nearly 100 percent and a five-year gain of 1,100 percent, creating market capitalizations surpassing even some of the most widely held and admired growth and retail companies on the New York Stock Exchange.[1]

As of April 20, 2000, the market capitalization of Amazon.com Inc. was a stunning $18.3 billion—even though the company claims merely $1.6 billion in annual revenue and has never earned a profit. eBay Inc.'s market value was $19.6 billion, despite its unremarkable $11 million profit on merely $225 million in 1999 revenue. To put these dot-com valuations in perspective, consider the mere $14.2 billion market value of Sears, Roebuck and Co., which last year garnered more than $1.3 billion in net income on annual revenue exceeding $32 billion. Similarly, Federal Express Corp., a traditional "heavy asset" company, was valued at only $10.9 billion, even though it boasts almost $700 million in profits on nearly $18 billion in sales and will almost certainly earn more by delivering the goods ordered up during the dot-com revolution.

Indeed, these market data suggest that even after this spring's market shakeout, investors would prefer to own a small and unprofitable e-commerce company such as Amazon rather than Sears—a profitable company twenty times the size of Amazon and one of the world's most respected retail outlets.

It is easy for managers to ignore such stock valuations as whims of the market, venture capitalist hype, and day-trader craziness. However, billions of dollars are riding on such whims, hype, and craziness. Moreover, thousands of the nation's brightest business and engineering minds have chosen to ride the dot-com wave. Given this investment of money and human capital, will e-commerce take over retailing and make traditional merchandising a thing of the past? Are current brands dying—soon to be displaced by new e-commerce brands? Or is this all just a passing fad?[2] After all, new technologies have created bubbles in the market before. In the 1880s, companies built upon the harnessing of a new technology, electricity, saw their stock prices explode 1,000 percent. But it soon became evident to investors that the promise of electricity would take years or decades to offer a return to these companies. Within two years of reaching their peak, electric company share prices fell to between 5 and 15 percent of their former values.

How can business strategists discriminate between types of e-commerce that will likely be attractive and profitable and those that will end up in a commodity market structure? Understanding the role of product quality, information transmission, reputation, and risk in the context of industry structure and company capabilities can help us answer these nagging questions. A market segmentation analysis of the on-line retail trade can shed light on the industry and product characteristics that drive profitability. These findings lead to a set of segment-specific strategies that companies can employ to reach above-industry-average profits and, presumably, high and sustainable market valuations.

THE E-COMMERCE PRODUCT CONTINUUM

On the Web, all goods are not equal. Products possess different attributes and different levels of the same attributes. For example, one important dimension on which goods differ is in the ability of consumers to ascertain the quality of products in cyberspace. On one end of the spectrum are commodity products, where quality can be clearly and contractually articulated and conveyed. Products such as oil, paper clips, and stock shares all fall under this category. On the other end of the continuum are products for which the perception of quality differs from consumer to consumer and product to product, such as produce, used cars, and works of art. Understanding how difficult it is for retailers to convey quality, reliability, or consistency for certain classes of products over the Web enables businesspeople to think strategically about the likely long-term success of different types of e-commerce ventures. Let us take four points on the continuum between barrels of oil and original oil paintings and examine each in turn.[3] There are many product points between these four, but these serve as useful references for understanding the dynamics of e-commerce. (See Figure 1.1.)

Commodity Products

Electronic commerce in commodity goods has occurred for decades. Simply open up the *Wall Street Journal* or the *Financial Times* and you will see the vast array of goods in which transactions are consummated electronically or through e-commerce. From

The ability to judge the quality of a product is the biggest differentiator among product categories on the Web.

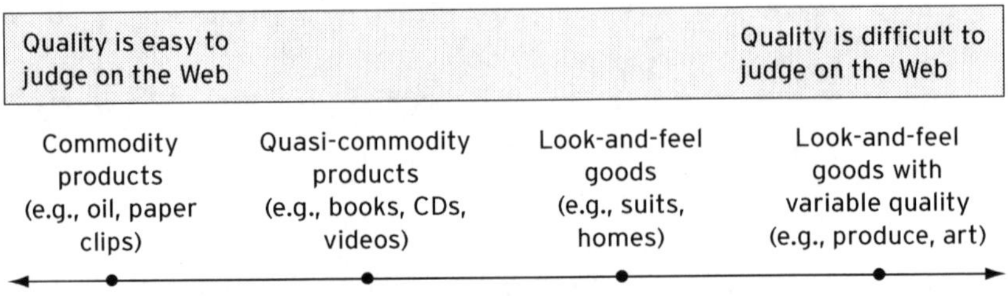

Quality is easy to judge on the Web			Quality is difficult to judge on the Web
Commodity products (e.g., oil, paper clips)	Quasi-commodity products (e.g., books, CDs, videos)	Look-and-feel goods (e.g., suits, homes)	Look-and-feel goods with variable quality (e.g., produce, art)

Figure 1.1. The Dot-Com Retail Continuum.

shares of stocks to pork bellies to ounces of gold, an active e-commerce auction market has existed for decades. Now we see many commodity products being exchanged daily on the Web. Paper clips, nails, and even Internet bandwidth compose this new e-commerce market. Despite a shift in the products, many properties of the market are similar to the more traditional electronic exchange markets.

In these commodity markets, the quality of products can easily be determined by their description. When one specifies a one-inch, galvanized, #6 flathead wood screw, we need little other information to know precisely what the product is or does. Except in extremely high-performance construction situations, the actual maker of the nail is unimportant. The same is true when we specify a barrel of Texas intermediate crude oil, one hundred common shares of MotherNature.com Inc., or seventeen troy ounces of eighteen-karat gold. For commodity products like these, the mere title and its attendant specifications convey complete information about their characteristics and quality. Consumers in these markets care little about the identity of the seller; they only care about the correct characterization of the products, the price, and the terms of delivery.

Quasi-Commodity Products

The biggest increase in e-commerce has occurred in quasi-commodity products. Books, videos, CDs, toys, and new cars all fall into this class of products. Economists consider these differentiated products, as opposed to commodity products—and they are correct. In books, for example, there are classic English plays, romance novels, and do-it-yourself guides. Differentiation exists here even within a product niche: think of the difference between mystery writers such as Arthur Conan Doyle, Tony Hillerman, and Agatha Christie. However, like commodity products, once a book is chosen by a consumer, it is identical across vendors. Any bookseller offering Shapiro and Varian's *Information Rules* carries the same book. There is no difference in the quality of the book, its content, and, if properly shipped, the condition of the book upon arrival. Once a consumer has chosen a title, the competition looks very much like the commodity market competition for oil, gold, and flathead screws.

Thus consumers engage in a two-stage decision-making process. First, the consumer must find a book he prefers among the many different books available. After selecting the title, the consumer cares primarily about its price and the reliability of the e-commerce vendor. That is, the consumer seeks the lowest price, assuming that his credit card transaction is secure, that the book is in stock, and that it will be delivered undamaged and on time.

"Look-and-Feel" Goods

If a company without a well-known brand name advertised a wool suit on the Web, would the suit sell? Even if the size fit perfectly, the color met expectations, and the style was acceptable, would it be bought with regularity if buyers had nothing but a picture to go by? When it comes to cosmetics, suits, upholstered furniture, or model homes, unbranded products have difficulty competing with their branded counterparts on the Web. Consumers need to actually touch, feel, try on, or see these products in person before they buy.

Few would buy a house without actually stepping inside it, getting a "feel" for the neighborhood, and assessing the condition of the house and its surroundings. The words "size two, worsted wool suit" aren't enough for a discerning clothes-shopper. Worsted wool has numerous consistencies and thicknesses, and a suit cut to fit some will not fit others. A size two made by one manufacturer may be classified as a size four or six by another.

"Look-and-feel" goods have a common characteristic—their quality is very difficult to assess from afar. Even something as mundane as bicycle pumps illustrates this concept. Professor Ely Dahan of MIT has conducted experiments with Web-savvy shoppers demonstrating that although the Web could capture many attributes of the product, critical aspects of some pumps were not conveyed. For example, the Web was not able to adequately simulate the quality of an innovative pump. Consumers who received and used the actual pump noted its quality was significantly lower than they had expected based on the Web presentation.

Consumers in this segment may be reluctant to buy a product of unknown or less than fully known quality. But once a consumer has selected a product, there are likely few substitutes. The characteristics of other competing products will probably differ on many dimensions, including quality, look, feel, and reliability. Clearly, this is not a book market. Rather, the "look-and-feel" segment is truly a differentiated market in all respects.

Look-and-Feel Goods with Variable Quality

There is a final class of goods that can be characterized on this continuum as look-and-feel goods with variable quality. These are products where, even if the buyer has completed her search, knows the product, and recognizes the brand, she will need to see and perhaps touch and feel the individual product that will be delivered to her home or business. The distinguishing feature is that each and every individual product is different from every other. Original art, used cars, and fresh produce all fall into this category. The mere names Sunkist orange, Golden Delicious apple, or Chiquita banana convey some information. The phrase "Monet painting," too, provides much information. However, consumers are often more discerning than this. They have preferences over the ripeness of the banana, the color of the orange, the hardness of the apple. They prefer to see, touch, and feel the piece of fruit to be delivered. In order to assess the beauty of a painting, it must be viewed, not only over the Web, but also in its original form under different types of light. Indeed, particularly in the case of an expensive and original Monet, it is necessary to see the work of art in person.

Refinements to the Framework

Two important subtleties of this framework need to be recognized. First, it is important to notice that as you move from left to right on the continuum—from commodity to look-and-feel with variable quality—it is not only the intensity of the consumer "experience" that changes. ("Experience goods" are those that a customer must experience before buying.) In addition, a number of other aspects to the buying process change, such as how much more information the seller has about the product than the buyer, the need of the consumer to engage in a search for optimal goods, and the degree to which seller reputation is important. All of these (and other) aspects of economic and management theory come together in determining this market segmentation scheme.

Second, the purpose of the product and the need to engage in searching might determine the segment to which it belongs. Take books, for example. A textbook assigned to students by a professor takes on a commodity characteristic. The student has a specified title, author, even edition, and then searches for the book at the lowest price. However, if the consumer is searching for a tour guide to London, there exist a host of different book titles to choose from, making "tour books" a quasi-commodity. Rare books and one-of-a-kind used books most closely fit in the look-and-feel-with-variable-quality segment, since each book has been exposed to different wear, which greatly affects its value. A company's choice of which book market to serve and the degree to which consumers must engage in searching will determine which e-commerce segment the firm participates in and, as the next section will show, which on-line strategies it should pursue.

SELECTING MARKETS AND GAINING COMPETITIVE ADVANTAGE

Given this understanding of e-commerce markets, what is the optimal strategy? This framework shows there is not a single optimal strategy, because the sources of competitive advantage differ across product segments. Entrepreneurs pursuing Web opportunities should use the four-segment approach to decide how to invest their time and money; incumbent producers need to carefully consider whether and how to enter the e-commerce fray. Indeed, the market the company serves determines the preferred strategy. (See Table 1.1.)

Commodity Market Strategy

Industry structure in commodity markets is inherently unattractive. Companies are price takers held in check by customers willing and able to seek the lowest price on the same product from many competitors. Thus market power is difficult if not impossible to obtain; customer lock-in and customer loyalty are elusive. Rivalry between firms will make it unlikely for any firm to achieve "supernormal" profits far above the average player in the industry. Entry into commodity markets, although relatively easy, is not very attractive. Profits are whittled away by rivals, leaving little on the table for the entrepreneur. Entry is easy for the e-commerce start-up, but market power cannot be exercised by individual firms, leaving little net income for shareholders. The only strategy available to managers in this market segment is to drive down costs in order to obtain profits.

Quasi-Commodity Market Strategy

The purchase of quasi-commodity products is a two-stage process. In the first stage, consumers conduct a product search in a differentiated product market. In the second stage, consumers conduct a price search for the preferred product. Entry, in theory and in practice, is quite easy in this market. Any individual could list their home library on a Web site and become an on-line book vendor. In practice, despite the infancy of the Internet, thirty-one U.S.-based on-line book vendors last year each carried more than a hundred thousand titles.[4] (Contrast this with eighty thousand titles in the average Barnes & Noble Inc. superstore.) The strategic challenge for companies in these markets is to differentiate themselves on the first dimension (search) and to insulate themselves from price competition in the second dimension.

How is differentiation achieved in search? Amazon.com typifies a potentially successful strategy. A consumer may choose from a broad selection of more than three million book titles or three hundred thousand video titles. In addition, Amazon has developed sophisticated internal search engines to make product search very easy and precise. The on-line bookseller also offers additional search features, such as pointing the customer to related books of interest. Upon logging on to Amazon, a registered user will even find books recommended by the search engine, based on the consumer's preferences and purchase history.

The problem for companies in these markets is that once a book—or any quasi-commodity product—is selected using their powerful search engines, the consumer may purchase it from another e-commerce vendor at a lower price. This is not a big problem in traditional retailing. Consumers have to drive to three or four other bookstores in order to find the same book at a lower price. Search costs, however, are far lower on the Web; consumers are therefore more likely to search for the lowest price. This, in turn, leads to greater price competition among vendors, lowering profits.

Table 1.1. How to Manage E-Commerce for Competitive Advantage: Strategies and Tactics for Maximizing Your Dot-Com Opportunity.

Commodity (e.g., oil, paper clips)	Quasi-Commodity (e.g., books, CDs, videos)	Look-and-Feel (e.g., suits, homes)	Look-and-Feel with Variable Quality (e.g., produce, art)
Low-Cost Strategy	*First Stage: Differentiation*	*Vertically Integrated Firms: Full Differentiation Strategy*	*Customization Strategy*
• Take advantage of economies of scale.	• Use information technology to differentiate Web service.	• Establish equivalent of store brands.	• Keep abreast of and use advances in Web-cam technology.
• Utilize low-cost production technology.	• Develop search engines that match consumer preferences to products quickly and precisely.	• Incorporate latest technologies to convey look and feel to consumers (e.g., virtual model and sizing technologies).	• Combine Web-search technologies with delivery logistics to deliver precise items viewed on Web.
• Achieve efficient distribution and low overhead.	• Employ database management tools that allow real-time data-mining.	• Excel at on-line customer service with both interactive and phone customer support.	• Develop build-to-order technical capabilities.
	• Make Web site "sticky," i.e., include features that encourage Web shoppers to stay on the site.	• Offer industry-leading warranties and return policies.	
	• Offer one-stop shopping.		
	• Seek first-mover advantage.		
	• Establish E-commerce branding.		

Second Stage: Low-Cost and Dif-
ferentiation Strategy

- Take advantage of economies of scale.

- Seek preferential treatment with wholesale suppliers.

- Ensure delivery of product is reliable and timely.

- Offer additional customer services such as chatrooms, affinity programs, and other Web-site "stickiness" technologies.

- Offer site-specific customer loyalty programs.

Additional Differentiation Is
Required for Hybrid Firms

- Employ creative pricing strategies (i.e., time-preference-based pricing).

- Provide showrooms to display merchandise.

- Develop bifurcated back-end logistics and delivery systems to ensure on-time delivery in the showrooms and to the home.

Additional Issues That Can Help
Some of These Firms

- Offer inexpensive products that lend themselves to repeat purchasing.

- Build reputation for quality and reliability.

To make matters worse, Web-based intermediaries are making it even easier to search for the lowest price. Yahoo! Inc., E-Compare, and other search engines will now search ten or more Web bookstores for your title and return to you a list of vendors who have the book and their prices. Even worse, the vendors themselves are entering the fray. At Books.com, after you choose a book, you can compare prices with other vendors. Books.com's own search engine will ping Amazon.com and barnesandnoble.com and tell you their prices for the same book. If the competitors have lower prices, Books.com will lower its price to below those of its competitors.

Given what is potentially fierce price competition in the second stage of this quasi-commodity market, how can companies carve out their own niche positions and retain market power? First movers will have some advantage in this market. Early movers have historically had the highest Web-site "stickiness." In addition, mechanisms that encourage consumers to stay on a site, such as creating virtual communities so consumers can talk to each other, or site-specific customer loyalty and reward programs, will be quite important for attracting repeat purchasers and engendering repeat visits.

Customer loyalty programs will find favor, too. However, since frequent-flier miles will soon become ubiquitous to Web sites, they will not be sufficient to foster consumer loyalty. If barnesandnoble.com and VarsityBooks.com Inc. both offer United Air Lines Inc. frequent-flier miles, frequent-flier programs are no longer a source of differentiation among vendors. Thus, only site-specific loyalty and reward programs will attract repeat purchasers and engender repeat visits. But even site-specific loyalty programs will work well only on those sites where there are repeat purchases to be made. Groceries and toiletries are goods with these characteristics, purchased on a weekly or twice weekly basis. In markets where purchases might be more occasional (such as books), on-line department stores will likely have an advantage. Although a single consumer might not purchase books, hardware, or videos on a weekly or twice weekly basis, combined they may result in significant volume.

Finally, branding will be an important part of any quasi-commodity strategy. Product brands will not be a point of differentiation for the e-commerce vendor, but e-commerce brands will be key. Strong e-commerce brands can signal quality in the reliability of delivery, security of personal information, dependability of the return policy, and customer service in general. Indeed, firms that wish to make above-industry-average margins in this business will have to invest in building e-commerce brands.

Amazon.com is a case in point. As a first-mover to the industry, Amazon invested heavily in broad book choice, powerful search engines, and strong branding. Amazon is now investing in other quasi-commodity businesses, such as over-the-counter drugs, toys, and electronics, to encourage consumers to stay on its Web site. Moreover, Amazon's additional planned investments in Web-site stickiness, such as affinity groups and chat rooms, foster an additional strategic advantage: The company learns an immense amount of information about customer preferences and Web search habits, which, in turn, allows Amazon to further tailor the Web site and its product offerings.

Conversely, it is not surprising that large, established companies such as Merrill Lynch & Co. and Toys "R" Us Inc. have had difficulty leveraging their traditional retail brands in the e-commerce markets. These companies have been second movers in a market where first movers have the advantage. Moreover, their corporate cultures and cost structures are built around traditional retailing rather than faceless interaction. Finally, many incumbents have gone to great pains to avoid cannibalizing their traditional retailing business. However, if traditional incumbents do not establish effective e-commerce ventures to compete with their own core businesses, others will. Fidelity Investments and Charles Schwab & Co. (incumbents unafraid to cannibalize their core businesses and early movers into the e-commerce market) and eToys Inc. (first mover, new entrant) will exploit their competencies in low-cost strategies and electronic know-how to force unbridled competition between e-commerce and traditional retailing in these segments.

The question remains, however, whether the profits that Amazon, eToys, or any quasi-commodity e-commerce venture earns will be dissipated by the fierce, commodity-like competition that occurs in the second stage of competition in these markets. The framework suggests that earnings will be low at best and frequently completely elusive.

Look-and-Feel Market Strategy

The third product point on the continuum, look-and-feel goods, poses a novel question for e-commerce vendors: How can e-commerce retailers provide consumers with look and feel over the Web? While pictures and animation can certainly help, alone they will be insufficient. Alternative technologies such as on-line customization tools will also assist, but unless the consumer feels the swatch of fabric for the suit, the decision to purchase is difficult. In the consumer's quest for information about the quality and characteristics of the product, strong product brands (as opposed to e-commerce brands) will become the kingpins. Established brands like Hugo Boss, Evan Piccone, and Victoria's Secret all provide a substantial amount of information about the product to the consumer. Thanks to past experience, consumers understand the difference between L.L. Bean Inc. duck boots and other duck boots. Brands such as Ann Taylor convey information about the expected product quality, material, and fit. Indeed, this concept suggests that well-branded incumbents, precisely because of their ability to differentiate their products, will be able to wield substantial market power and therefore obtain large profits in this segment of the market.

Given the power of product brands in the look-and-feel market, it is highly unlikely that we will see entrepreneurs successfully inundating this space in quest of profits. More likely, we will see the rise of two forms of distribution, led by traditional incumbents.

The first is a wholly owned vertical distribution system. One example is home furnishings retailer Pottery Barn, which sells its own Pottery Barn furniture exclusively. Such markets will be difficult for e-commerce vendors to penetrate without a strong brand or entry position. The e-commerce vendor must be vertically integrated and must excel at both product creation and product distribution. Building product brands from scratch is still time-consuming and costly, two unattractive features of a strategy when competing on Internet time. Once created, the product brand will then have to compete with products that already have established reputations and considerable brand equity, recognition, and consumer admiration.

However, should an e-commerce company be able to overcome these high hurdles, the market has a number of attractive features, including oligopolistic competition, high entry barriers, and customer loyalty, which are likely to promote profits in the long term. Successful companies in these product classes can retain substantial market power, as price competition is mitigated through substantial product differentiation.

Alternatively, e-commerce vendors like Bluefly Inc., a clothing "mall" on the Web, will arise that sell these branded look-and-feel products on a nonexclusive, widespread basis. Vendors of Broyhill chairs, Evan Piccone suits, and Revlon cosmetics will not need to make investments in the product brands to signal quality. The product manufacturers will do this. Rather, they will have to make investments in merchandising, inventory management, and distribution. Note, however, that these types of e-commerce ventures begin to look increasingly like the quasi-commodity product category. That is, once the search for a chair is complete, price competition can ensue among Web vendors. This suggests that profits will accrue to the branded product manufacturers and profits of e-commerce vendors will soon plummet.

Though the outlook is grim for most start-up or pure-play dot-com companies in this market segment, adopting certain policies can help them compete. For example, liberal warranties and return policies will help attract wavering consumers. Adoption of industry standards can help to allay fears of the wary customer—that is, it's easier to sell a personal computer that runs the Windows operating system than one that uses an obscure flavor of Unix. Unfortunately, such piecemeal approaches that involve warranties and standards are likely to be quickly copied by competitors.

Other solutions may also be available. Vendors can pursue a strategy of rapid or proprietary technological developments to support look-and-feel information over the Web. Alternatively, vendors can attempt to minimize price competition by seeking products that have limited distribution channels. The effective strategic alternatives for the pure e-commerce vendor in this segment of the market are not attractive: either participate in the vertical structure of the market and make the investments in brands, where entry is difficult, or participate in the distribution of branded products, where the specter of price competition raises its head.

Unlike the commodity or quasi-commodity markets, many traditional, incumbent retailers in the look-and-feel segments are likely to survive the transition to an Internet-based economy in large numbers (though some will fail, too). Some will pursue the strong look-and-feel strategy and seek to differentiate their products as "must be worn" and their stores with "outstanding personal service." These successful "pure play" traditional retailers, relying on brick and mortar, will stress the distinctiveness of the clothes and purchasing experience.

Other retailers will rely on showrooms. Rather than carry full inventories of all colors and sizes of clothing, retailers will be able to offer customers samples of clothing sizes and colors—a rack with one of each. Customers will be able to try on clothing, inspect quality and color, and then turn to Web terminals right in the store to order clothes that will be delivered to their home the next day. These hybrid forms of retailing will offer a mechanism for new e-commerce ventures to move into the more traditional retailing channels.

Of course, some consumers may not be able to wait that long, and this opens up opportunities for vendors in these categories, and indeed all categories of products, to tailor pricing to time-based preferences. For customers who cannot wait for delivery of their products, a price premium will be paid. More concretely, a traditional retail vendor can allow the consumer to take it with her for $50, or permit ordering over the Web and delivery tomorrow for $40. Firms make huge margins on their catalog sales because they do not have to carry inventory, buy floor space, or pay sales associates. Catalog margins are as much as 100 percent higher than in the retail stores. In offering this two-tiered pricing option, time preferences can be incorporated into the pricing system to the advantage of both consumers and vendors. A Web-based retailing system can coexist with the traditional system of merchandising.

Eddie Bauer Inc. has implemented somewhat similar systems, integrating its stores and catalogs. An in-store customer who does not find the precise item she wants can order through the catalog using dedicated phones in the stores. Goods are delivered to her home address within a week without a shipping charge. While a start in the right direction, the Eddie Bauer model can be refined to incorporate the technology of the Web, the logistical prowess of a delivery system, and the sophisticated scheme of preference-based pricing. Companies with successful catalogues will likely find the transition to the Web easier than those without.

Look-and-Feel with Variable Quality

In this category, quality is not only difficult to communicate, but it also varies by product, creating large obstacles for e-commerce. Each individual product needs to be inspected by the consumer. Surely, the ability to post product descriptions on the Web mitigates this problem, but it fails to provide a complete solution. One cannot easily sell a used car, three thousand different apples, or original artwork on the Web. Indeed, many firms that have ventured into these segments have found the going difficult. Other firms have recognized this fundamental problem and have shifted to an intermediary function. Usedcars.com informs you of all the used cars available in your area and then tells you how to contact the person who owns the used car. They do not try to sell the used car, fully recognizing the problems of purchasing a used car directly over the Web. Note that the problems with participating in this segment of the market derive not from competition or other economic factors, but from external and technological factors outside managerial control.

In the near future, survival and profitability in this segment will be difficult. However, this situation may not last forever. Research and innovation under way at top universities may enable this segment of the market to grow. Indeed, technology is being developed to allow Web browsers to more finely examine texture and minute details. In addition, software and hardware advancements will soon allow consumers to view the actual products they are selecting in real time and then take quick delivery. Developments like these will help make this product segment accessible to e-commerce vendors, but some product markets, like used cars and homes, will always be difficult to penetrate. In these segments, technological barriers will prevail for years, and intermediaries will need to arise before such problems can be solved.

Until this day arrives, what can managers do? In this segment, and indeed, in the look-and-feel segment more generally, managers must exploit two instruments under their control: price and reputation.

Companies like Peapod Inc., Streamline.com Inc., and Home-Runs.com Inc. have shown that consumers are willing to purchase items such as produce and vegetables over the Web. These companies demonstrate that some look-and-feel products with variable quality might succeed on the Web if they offer inexpensive repeat purchases. Repeat purchases allow the e-commerce vendor to build a reputation for quality by repeated provision of the product to a given consumer. Inexpensive products allow the consumer to mitigate risk. If the consumer does not perceive the products to be of high quality, the loss is relatively low and he can take his future business elsewhere. Thus, inexpensive prices give consumers the incentive to experiment and give the e-commerce vendor the opportunity to build a reputation. A good reputation coupled with low prices will allow some firms to survive in this segment. (See Figure 1.2.)

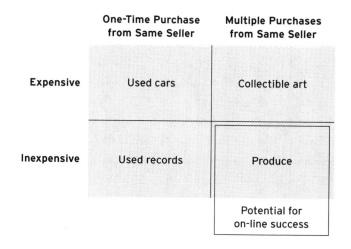

The best opportunities for selling one-of-a-kind products on-line are ventures that can draw repeat business by selling inexpensive products.

Figure 1.2. Used Cars, No; Fresh Fruit, Yes.

INCUMBENTS VERSUS NEW ENTRANTS: WHICH HAS THE ADVANTAGE?

Given this framework and the strategies that companies pursue, can we explain the success and failure of the traditional brick-and-mortar incumbents in various market segments? Here examples may be instructive. Victoria's Secret and Saturn Corp. have found significant sales on the Web. Borders Books and Toys "R" Us, both late movers, have so far failed to succeed. These companies help illustrate a more general pattern and application of market segmentation on the continuum: traditional incumbents have substantial advantage in products that tend toward the look-and-feel end of the spectrum and encounter difficulty in products that tend toward the commodity end of the continuum. That is not to say that traditional incumbents will not succeed in the commodity end of the spectrum, but that they will likely find the playing field more even in those markets, as their brands and brick-and-mortar stores provide little advantage. (See Figure 1.3.)

Consider again the example of individual on-line trading. Charles Schwab and Fidelity Investments have found significant success with their on-line trading services. Merrill Lynch has been slow to launch, and its success is uncertain. Here is a glaring exception to the pattern suggested above. Why might this be? First, Schwab was a very early mover to the on-line trading arena. In addition to the first-mover advantage, the firm built in switching costs. Schwab charges customers substantial financial and transaction fees to close an account before it can be moved to another broker. Second, Schwab has long-held competencies in serving a customer base from a distance. Its telephone trading system was in place long before the Internet existed, and its information and data systems made it relatively easy to make the transition to the Web. Schwab's corporate culture has supported its "serving a customer at a distance" strategy. These in-place competencies and assets transferred efficiently and effectively to the Web, and gave Schwab an advantage over its counterparts.

As the discount brokerage example illustrates, incumbents in the commodity and quasi-commodity segments with first-mover advantage and strong histories in information technology and serving a customer at a distance can become exceptions to this general rule. Such incumbents can reap rewards in these fiercely competitive segments.

SUSTAINING A COMPETITIVE ADVANTAGE

So what about e-commerce? What about these Internet valuations? What about entrepreneurial opportunities for the legions of engineers, M.B.A.s, and venture capitalists entering the e-commerce

Commodity markets are easy to enter, but profit margins are low. Look-and-feel markets are difficult to enter, but they confer high margins.

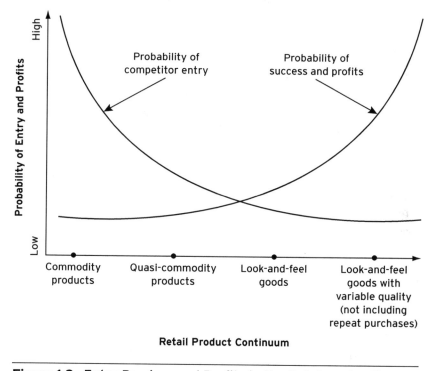

Figure 1.3. Entry Barriers and Profits in the Dot-Com Continuum.

market? The first thing to recognize is that the barriers to entry grow higher as we move across the continuum from commodity to look-and-feel with variable quality. However, precisely because entry will be easy and competition fierce, those companies that enter the commodity and quasi-commodity types of businesses will find small, if any, profits. Nevertheless, companies that are able to "crack the code" and enter successfully into the look-and-feel and look-and-feel-with-variable-quality segments will find substantial profits. It is precisely in these latter segments that bricks will combine with clicks to generate profits.

Companies should not, however, be content with industry

▼

Do On-Line Auctions Have a Future?

Business models that require buyers to trust sellers may have big problems on-line.

eBay, Amazon, and Priceline.com Inc. have all ventured into the on-line auction market. Will they succeed? Will these markets persist? For auctions in new and used products, the framework presented here can help predict the probability of long-term success of auctions over various types of product segments.

In the case of new products, auctions will succeed to the same extent that new ventures will succeed. That is, on-line auctions will succeed in the medium term in "commodities" such as paper clips or barrels of oil, and quasi-commodity segments such as books and CDs, where it is easy to shop for the lowest price. However, on-line auctions will have much more difficulty selling suits or homes, where the look and feel is important in shopping, or in the look-and-feel with variable quality segment, where one-of-a-kind items like original artwork or fresh fruit are sold. Companies selling used products on the Web will have an even harder time being successful, because the difficulty of assessing quality is even greater.

Priceline.com offers the consumer hotel rooms and airline flights on a take-it-or-leave-it basis. The pure sensibility of this format is clear. We need to know little more than the airline and time of departure to obtain all relevant information about our flight. Quality is easy to signal. Likewise, auctions for new books are likely to be successful. The title conveys all information necessary.

On the other hand, a used camera, used piano, or used car requires much closer inspection (even though a new camera, new piano, or new car may not). As in any used product market, the seller has more information about the potential flaws or shortcomings in the product than the purchaser. On the Web, however, the problem becomes even more acute, as an assessment is required at a far distance. The possibility for opportunism by the vendors is enormous, and the anonymity of the parties in the transaction creates numerous potential contractual hazards. This problem becomes even more acute if the products are expensive and the identity of the seller changes from product to product, thus making reputation-creation elusive.

To counter these problems, on-line auctions have recently implemented a "comment" system in which buyers rate sellers. Unfortunately, such ratings fail to address the real concerns of buyers. Since the potential buyer has really no idea who rated the seller, they have no way of knowing how critical or kind that person was in the rating. The seller, too, can sell to her friends for the first ten transactions to "build" reputation that doesn't really exist. (Note, this can also occur with book ratings and reviews on Amazon.com.) Without a measurement and verification mechanism, these ratings are merely what economists call "cheap talk," a message that may be truthful or not and whose accuracy is almost impossible to judge.

Solutions to these cheap-talk problems exist. Impartial consignment or escrow agents can alleviate the risk and permit an inspection period for the buyer. Sellers can offer guarantees and warranties on products in the suspect categories. A strong reputation can also solve these problems. But in the context of the Web, these auction intermediaries and solutions have been slow in coming. Without these types of answers, auction market volumes will suffer in the quasi-commodity and look-and-feel segments of the markets.

Though the economics of these auctions suggest they will encounter problems in some segments, noneconomic forces may actually dominate more clear-headed, strategic thinking. Namely, the utility that buyers obtain from auctions may not be from the goods purchased, but from the satisfaction of the "game" of the auction (much like the "game" of Las Vegas) and "winning" the auction. To this extent, on-line auctioneers' strategies should be oriented toward exploiting these behavioral aspects to their business.

average profits, in whichever segment they choose to compete. They must strive for higher-than-industry profits and recognize that the sources of competitive advantage will differ across segments. Commodity product sellers must strive for low-cost positions. Quasi-commodity sellers must develop strategies to insulate their products from price competition through customer loyalty programs and Web-site stickiness. Look-and-feel sellers must meld their traditional assets with the electronic marketplace to distinguish their products and exploit their current product brands. Look-and-feel-with-variable-quality sellers must either think small and inexpensive to develop a reputation that allows them to grow or invest in both front-end and back-end technologies to facilitate customer purchases.

Finally, branding strategy will be important. In the commodity and quasi-commodity product segments, the actual e-commerce vendor brand is important to the extent that it signals reliability and customer service. In the look-and-feel markets, product brands will dominate as a source of competitive advantage. And both e-commerce brands and product brands are important sources of competitive advantage in the look-and-feel-with-variable-quality segments. An e-commerce start-up's brand strategy will be substantially determined by the markets it serves. Moreover, although even branded retailers in commodity and quasi-commodity products face difficult times ahead, all incumbent brands are not dead. Indeed, product brands will persist, and some retail outlet brands, especially those that cover the look-and-feel segment, will continue to profit. The opportunity for new e-commerce brands has arisen, however, in the commodity and quasi-commodity segments. Hence, we see the rise of Amazon, Buy.com Inc., and Travelocity.com Inc.

This brings us back to the first question: Are these Internet company market valuations justified? If one believes in efficient capital markets, then one must assume that the price of each Internet venture incorporates all information, both past and in expectation, and thus these companies are fairly priced. If capital markets

are not perfectly efficient, and we incorporate the framework proposed, many of these valuations will be called into question. The
majority of entries into the e-commerce market have been in commodity and quasi-commodity markets. The framework suggests
that only a small fraction of these companies will be very successful and generate the supernormal profits their valuations suggest.
But those companies that have invested in capabilities that exploit
the sources of competitive advantage in their particular product
segment will have a much higher probability of justifying their valuations in the long term. (See box, Do On-Line Auctions Have a
Future?, p. 28.)

Acknowledgments

I would like to thank Erik Brynjolfsson, Henry Chesbrough, Ely
Dahan, and participants in the MIT E-Business Research Seminar
for their helpful comments.

ADDITIONAL RESOURCES

The following are classic academic references to the economic and management topics discussed in this article:

G. Akerlof, "The Market for Lemons: Qualitative Uncertainty and the Mar-
    ket Mechanism," *Quarterly Journal of Economics,* 1970, *84,* 488–500.
P. Diamond, "Consumer Differences and Prices in a Search Model," *Quar-
    terly Journal of Economics,* 1987, *102*(2), 429–436.
R. Gibbons, *Game Theory for Applied Economists* (Princeton, New Jersey:
    Princeton University Press, 1992).
H. Hotelling, "Stability in Competition," *Economic Journal,* 1929, 41–57.
M. E. Porter, *Competitive Strategy* (New York: Free Press, 1980).
M. Spence, "Job Market Signaling," *Quarterly Journal of Economics* 1973,
    87(3), 355–374.
D. J. Teece, G. Pisano, and A. Shuen, "Dynamic Capabilities and Strategic
    Management," *Strategic Management Journal,* 1997, *18,* 509–533.

The following are academic references to the Internet ideas proposed:

E. Brynjolfsson and M. Smith, "Frictionless Commerce? A Comparison of Internet and Conventional Retailers," MIT working paper (Cambridge, Massachusetts, 1999).

M. Cusumano and D. Yoffie, *Competing on Internet Time: Lessons from Netscape's Battle with Microsoft* (New York: Free Press, 1998).

C. Shapiro and H. R. Varian, *Information Rules* (Boston: Harvard Business School Press, 1998).

The following Web sites are relevant to this discussion:

www.amazon.com (an example of advanced search engine technology, affinity programs, and ratings that represent what economists call "cheap talk": a message that may or may not be truthful and whose accuracy is almost impossible to judge)

www.arbinet.com (an example of electronic markets for bandwidth)

www.ebay.com (an example of on-line auctions and cheap talk)

www.ecompare.com (an example of Web sites that are able to substantially lower search costs through effective price comparisons)

www.hamquist.com/research/stats/index.html (for the Internet Index and other stock valuation measures)

web.mit.edu/edahan/www/ E. Dahan, "Survey of Portable Bicycle Pumps" (1998) (an example of the success and failure of conveying quality information on the Web)

www.mediametrix.com tracks Web-site stickiness.

www.webtomorrow.com/sticky.htm (a summary of Web-site stickiness strategies)

NOTES

1. Hambrecht & Quist, Internet Index, January 2000. H&Q (www.hamquist.com) tracks a number of Internet stocks, which are placed in its Internet Index. The Chase Manhattan Bank completed a purchase of the San Francisco-based H&Q in December 1999.

2. "Doing Business in the Internet Age," *Business Week,* June 22, 1998, 121–172.
3. Note that these categories are analogous to the production processes outlined fifteen years ago in R. Hayes and S. Wheelwright, *Restoring Our Competitive Edge: Competing through Manufacturing* (New York: John Wiley, 1984). Continuous flow, assembly line, job shop, and project. Another way of thinking about these categories is in a cumulative manner: commodities are differentiated in one attribute (price); quasi-commodities are differentiated in multiple attributes, one of which is price; look-and-feel products are differentiated in multiple attributes, including quality; look-and-feel-with-variable-quality products are differentiated in multiple attributes, including quality, where there are differences within category. Each successive category requires more and more experience with the product.
4. Gomez.com survey from Spring 1999. Gomez.com rates Web sites.

CHAPTER TWO

Making Business Sense of the E-Opportunity

DAVID FEENY

Most corporate executives are convinced by now that the scale and pervasiveness of today's technological change require a fundamental review of business strategy. Web-based technology—through the Internet, intranets, and extranets—offers universal connectivity at astonishingly low cost, with a simple, standardized user interface. The new technology is creating opportunities to rethink business models, processes, and relationships along the whole length of the supply chain in pursuit of unprecedented levels of productivity, improved customer propositions, and new streams of business.

But the scope of the potential for change is daunting. The burgeoning e-business literature bombards executives with ideas competing for their attention. It is hard to make collective sense of it all or to know where to start the strategic analysis. Moreover, e-business ideas are described in unfamiliar terminology—"portals," "infomediaries," and "aggregators" in "B2C-B2B-BTE" settings. Behind the new language, how new are the strategic concepts? To what extent are the old dogs of the established economy required to learn new tricks?

The success of Amazon.com, Dell Computer, eBay, and others served as a wake-up call for many executives. But companies in, say, chemicals, helicopters, or credit-card services are likely to find their strategic opportunity taking a different form.

A first step in confronting the challenges is to construct a coherent map of the e-opportunity. With the mood swings of the financial markets and the faltering fortunes of New Economy icons, the business community at large still feels uncertainty about the future shape and scope of e-business. A comprehensive map of the e-opportunity and its three domains (operations, marketing, and customer services) can become a platform for exploring the new strategic landscape. In each domain, the technology can enable a radical new vision of what a business can accomplish. (See Figure 2.1.)

E-operations opportunities are uses of Web technology that are directed at strategic change in the way a business manages itself and its supply chain, culminating in the production of its core product or service. For example, technology underpins BP Amoco's initiatives to troubleshoot more effectively by sharing the learning of its businesses around the world. General Electric Co. improved its purchasing by posting requirements on a Web site and having suppliers submit bids electronically.

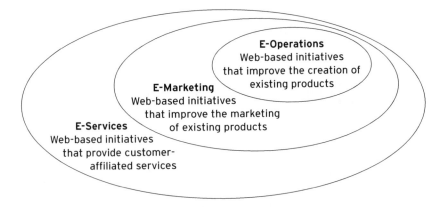

Figure 2.1. Domains of E-Opportunity.

E-marketing opportunities cover Web-based initiatives that are designed to achieve strategic change in downstream activities, either through direct interaction with the customer or through a distribution channel. In e-marketing, a traditional product remains the focus of the business and its revenue generation, but the way the product is delivered or the scope of support services changes. The provider may be a traditional incumbent or a new pure-play entrant: a Barnes & Noble or an Amazon.com, a Toys "R" Us or an eToys. The financial-services sector is illustrative. In that arena, established companies and new competitors are forging links to established intermediary channels, to new intermediaries, and to the customer directly—while continuing to focus on the delivery of traditional financial-services products such as savings accounts, credit cards, and mortgages.

E-service opportunities give companies new ways to address an identified set of customer needs. Rather than promoting proprietary products, the e-service business acts as the customer's agent in achieving a desired outcome. Most current examples are New Economy businesses: Chemdex, the information intermediary in the biosciences sector; OneMediaPlace (formerly Adauction.com), which provides buyers and sellers of advertising space with a radically new set of services; and shopping robots such as mySimon.com, which scour the Internet to find the best deals available. Some Old Economy businesses float an e-service business as a new venture—for example, Overseas Chinese Bank Corporation's Bank of Singapore has a financial-services venture called finatiQ.com. Others may begin to redefine their core business, as Ford Motor Co. is doing in seeking to become "the world's leading consumer company for automotive service."[1]

Defining e-opportunity domains using a business-oriented perspective and language illuminates the role of new technology in competitive advantage. Technology prompts new business practices rather than new business theories. In other words, successful e-strategies translate established strategic concepts into contexts in which they previously were not economically viable. In the 1960s and 1970s, IBM won the loyalty of major corporate customers through highly paid account executives who provided what IBM called "relationship management." That approach to supporting individual consumers is now technologically based.

Distinguishing between the three e-opportunity domains is critical. Each requires its own distinctive framework for identifying ideas that can bring competitive advantage to a given context. Every business should be considering opportunities across all three domains, but the potential significance of each domain, and of individual ideas within it, will vary widely across businesses and industry sectors. Although it is tempting to begin with the excitement of e-service—the Brave New World of the New Economy—in practice, the e-operations and e-marketing layers require the most urgent attention and provide the most certain rewards. As so many dotcoms have demonstrated, if you have e-vision but a single marketing approach and a poor fulfillment capability, you don't really have a business.

THE E-OPERATIONS OPPORTUNITY

Initially, the e-operations applications of most organizations consisted of electronic versions of policy documents and newsletters mounted on an intranet. But the real e-operations opportunity has five potential components. (See Figure 2.2.)

The Shape of the E-Operations Opportunity

The first and most straightforward e-operations-opportunity component is the opportunity for automating administrative processes. Businesses are increasingly using their intranet infrastructure for the low-cost administration of "necessary evils"—enrolling and training new employees, claiming travel expenses, buying pencils, and the like. The improvements in cost efficiency are unlikely to have a competitive impact on cost structures. But as Cisco Systems and

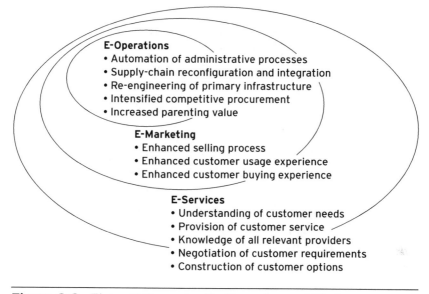

E-Operations
- Automation of administrative processes
- Supply-chain reconfiguration and integration
- Re-engineering of primary infrastructure
- Intensified competitive procurement
- Increased parenting value

E-Marketing
- Enhanced selling process
- Enhanced customer usage experience
- Enhanced customer buying experience

E-Services
- Understanding of customer needs
- Provision of customer service
- Knowledge of all relevant providers
- Negotiation of customer requirements
- Construction of customer options

Figure 2.2. Three E-Opportunity Domains and Their Components.

Schlumberger have demonstrated, such applications create a more IT-literate work force and a more nimble business culture.[2]

A second and more fundamental component is the new technology's ability to trigger a review of the business's primary infrastructure: its core processes and the software base that support them. Web technology may enable a new round of reengineering of the primary infrastructure and lead to faster turnaround of customers' orders, enhanced customer support, improvements in a product's unit-cost structure, and shorter time to market for new products.

The third component, increased parenting value, relates to improving the performance of individual business units through help from other "members of the family."[3] At BP Amoco, for example, an initiative by the center (or parent company) enables each natural-resource-exploration unit (or child) to share learning with its peers (or siblings).[4] At fast-growing Regus, the company intranet is a tool for making the center's view of best operating practice available to the service staff at each office around the world. At Spotless Services, each of the catering units that serve customers across Australasia improves their purchasing through links to groupwide contracts.

The fourth component of the e-operations opportunity is intensified competitive procurement through electronic buying, such as that pioneered by General Electric. Electronic buying can mean a wider supply base, more-competitive prices, and lower administrative costs. Increasingly, electronic-buying initiatives are planned at the sector level rather than the company level. An example is the General Motors–Ford-DaimlerChrysler collaboration that, by one estimate, will enable savings of more than $1,000 per car.

The fifth component, supply-chain reconfiguration and integration, uses technology to enable the virtual enterprise. Companies identify the ideal network of provider partners, arrange for all selected members to have immediate access to relevant information, and give the whole network the advantages of a vertically integrated business (say, focus and response speed at each point in the supply chain) without the disadvantages. Dell Computer's CEO Michael Dell believes that if his company were vertically rather than virtually integrated, it would need five times as many employees and would suffer from a "drag effect."[5] Any business that operates a build-to-order strategy eventually will need to embrace supply-chain-integration concepts.

The e-operations opportunity may look familiar. Businesses have long been accustomed to evaluating the benefits of updating their infrastructure as technology changes. Supply-chain integration represents the logical, economical extension to all suppliers of the electronic-data-interchange links laboriously established with large suppliers in the 1990s. Even the parenting ideas that Regus pursues are similar to the 1980s example of Mrs. Fields Cookies, which sought to embed the operational thinking of its founder into hundreds of small retail outlets across the United States.[6] But the fact that an idea is familiar does not rule out the potential for competitive advantage—particularly if technology now enables radical improvements in the implementation of the idea. For some businesses in some industry sectors, the highest priority should be investment in the components of e-operations. The question is, Which ones?

Identifying the E-Operations Opportunity

The strategic significance of e-operations ideas to a particular business is a function of the role of information within that business.[7] Companies need to examine the role of information on three different dimensions: the information content of the product, information intensity along the supply chain, and information dispersion across the value chain. (See Figure 2.3.)

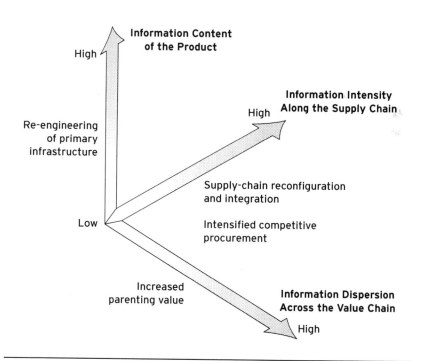

Figure 2.3. E-Operations-Opportunity Model.

Information Content. A high level of information content in the product (found in industries such as financial services and publishing) signals the importance of reengineering the primary infrastructure of the business. An adequate infrastructure is a necessity for every company. But if information content in the product is high, the infrastructure will be central to competitive advantage: it will drive product availability, functionality, and cost structure. In banking, infrastructure is a more fundamental priority than the launch of an Internet banking service. In research-based pharmaceutical companies, too, the information amassed through a product's development process dictates the primacy of infrastructure, which must support discovery, trials, regulatory submission, and product-advice activities.

Information Intensity. Information intensity along the supply chain points to the importance of either intensifying a company's competitive procurement or reconfiguring and integrating the supply chain. Automotive and aerospace companies are examples of enterprises with high levels of information intensity. Often they track hundreds of thousands of the components. In such industries, the availability, quality, and cost of the product are dependent on the way the supply chain is managed. Businesses competing on price will probably favor the intensified-competitive-procurement approach, whereas those stressing some form of differentiation are more likely to find advantage in supply-chain reconfiguration and integration.

Information Dispersion. The opportunity for increased parenting value is greatest when there is a high level of information dispersion across the value chain—for example, when one or more of the company's activities are performed at multiple geographical locations.[8] High levels of information dispersion are becoming more common as even small and midsize businesses become global. A parent-company initiative to coordinate information across replicated activities can lead to shared learning, scale economies, and companywide consistency in the way an activity is performed.

THE E-MARKETING OPPORTUNITY

Businesses differ widely in the scale and scope of their e-operations opportunity. Identifying that opportunity (or the lack of it) is the first task for the strategist, but it is not a predictor of the level of opportunity in the other domains. Even a business that rates low on all three information dimensions in the e-operations-opportunity model may be able to change its competitive fortunes through opportunities in the e-marketing and e-service domains.

The Shape of the E-Marketing Opportunity

E-marketing strategy leverages new technology to get more-effective ways of selling a business's product to existing or new customers. There are three broad categories of e-marketing opportunity:

▼ Enhancing the selling process (making the sales effort more effective through better product and market targeting or by more successfully expressing the characteristics and benefits of the product)

▼ Enhancing the customer's buying experience (providing support services that make the product easier to buy or better matched to the customer's needs)

▼ Enhancing the customer's usage experience (providing support services that increase customer satisfaction over the life cycle of product use)

Although the full potential of those e-marketing-opportunity components is as boundless as marketing creativity, many success stories share features in common. For example, the fastest-source proposition was important in the triumph of category-killer retail chains such as Toys "R" Us back in the bricks-and-mortar days, in the case of American Hospital Supply and its on-line links to corporate customers in the 1980s, and in the success of Amazon.com today. Each of the building blocks of marketing strategy, from customer input to a tailored-support proposition, can be improved with the help of Web technology. (See Table 2.1., pp. 46–47.) A few companies, such as Amazon and Office Depot, have embraced several marketing ideas, but most do not. The objective is not to implement as many ideas as Web technology allows but to identify and pursue the few that will bring competitive advantage to a particular company. Marketing ideas are not sector specific, nor do they come with stickers such as "for business-to-customer use only." For each idea, there may be examples relating to both business customers and consumer customers.

Identifying the E-Marketing Opportunity

Given that Web technology makes many new marketing initiatives technologically and economically viable, strategists must identify which particular initiatives will work for their company. A new framework can pinpoint the business and customer contexts in which a given idea is most likely to bring value to the customer and reward to the business. (See Figure 2.4.) The framework relies on two constructs that are consistently powerful determinants of business and customer contexts: perceived product differentiation and frequency of purchase.[9]

Perceived product differentiation captures the strategic marketing context of a business. For a product with a high level of differentiation, the marketer will want to emphasize enhanced-selling-process ideas—those that promote the creation of distinctive products, the targeting of distribution to customers who will appreciate that distinctiveness, and the successful pre- and post-sale articulation of the benefits of the product. By contrast, providers of products perceived as having a low level of differentiation should select initiatives from

The right e-marketing approach depends on how frequently customers purchase the product and how much differentiation they perceive between competing products.

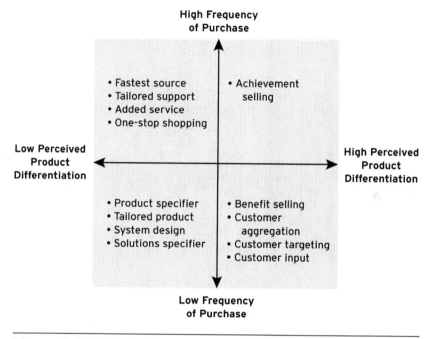

High Frequency of Purchase

- Fastest source
- Tailored support
- Added service
- One-stop shopping

- Achievement selling

Low Perceived Product Differentiation

High Perceived Product Differentiation

- Product specifier
- Tailored product
- System design
- Solutions specifier

- Benefit selling
- Customer aggregation
- Customer targeting
- Customer input

Low Frequency of Purchase

Figure 2.4. E-Marketing-Opportunity Model.

the enhanced-customer-buying-experience and the enhanced-customer-usage-experience categories to create an overall positioning distinct from the competition: "My basic product is no better and no worse than my competitor's, but I provide the customer with additional value by . . ." The logic of such broad prescriptions is that buyers of differentiated products will want to evaluate alternative providers carefully before making a choice, whereas buyers of undifferentiated products will be less inclined to shop around and more likely to settle quickly for an offer that matches their expectations. If a particular customer does not share the provider's view of the product's level of differentiation, however, the logic breaks down.

Table 2.1. Ideas That Fuel E-Marketing Opportunities.

Category	Marketing Idea	Concept	Example
Enhanced selling process	Customer input	The involvement of customers in our development process will lead to better new products.	Ford has put its design studio on-line to obtain the feedback of selected customers.
	Customer targeting	Tracking customer status enables us to offer the relevant product at the relevant time.	Amazon notifies customers of new book-buying options based on a profile of previous purchases.
	Customer aggregation	We have a new ability to reach and serve economically a dispersed customer segment.	eHobbies uses the Internet as a channel to reach model-train enthusiasts around the world.
	Benefit selling	We can improve the way we illustrate to the customer the benefits our product provides.	Timex provides a downloadable simulation of its novel i-Control watch-setting system.
	Achievement selling	Loyalty is strengthened when we show customers our track record of meeting commitments.	W.W. Grainger tracks and documents savings made by its corporate customers for maintenance supplies.

Enhanced customer buying experience	Solutions-specifier proposition	We advise the customer on the types of products required to meet their needs.	Home Depot provides customers with everything they will need to carry out a do-it-yourself project.
	One-stop shopping proposition	Through links with providers of complementary products we meet more of the customer's needs.	Office Depot links to sites such as stamps.com, TelePost to increase its coverage of overall customer needs.
	System-design proposition	Our facilities enable the customer to design the overall system to which our products contribute.	Herman Miller's "room planner" enables design of new furniture for existing office layouts.
	Fastest-source proposition	We offer the customer the best chance of getting what they want quickly, with minimum hassle.	The core of Amazon.com's book-buying proposition and many other Internet offerings.
	Product-specifier proposition	We help customers understand the optimal product specification for their needs.	Lands' End allows the customers to create a "personal model" on which they can test the fit and look of swimwear.
	Tailored-product proposition	We rapidly deliver to the customer's individual product specification.	Chipshot.com allows expert golfers to configure clubs to their own preferred specification.
Enhanced customer usage experience	Added service proposition	As well as providing product, we help improve some aspect of the customer's operational activity.	Lonely Planet publications provides an on-line "travel vault" for storage of travelers' critical information.
	Tailored support proposition	The support services for our products are tailored to reflect the customer's needs and practices.	A Dell corporate customer has a "Premier Page" on-line for employees to access the agreed level of support.

The word "perceived" is key. Differing customer perceptions of product differentiation become the basis for market segmentation.

Frequency of purchase is the other main determinant of buying behavior. Customers who are regularly in the market for a particular product have different requirements from those who are not. The lower the frequency of purchase, the more likely it is that customers will have information needs during the buying process and will respond favorably to a provider whose marketing initiatives help them navigate unfamiliar territory. However, customers who frequently purchase a product have already assimilated the necessary information and are more likely to respond to initiatives that minimize their overall transaction costs. In the frequency-of-purchase dimension, as in the perceived-differentiation dimension, the overall product market may need to be segmented, with different propositions attracting high- and low-frequency buyers.

The quadrant of the e-marketing-opportunity model where high frequency of purchase meets low perceived product differentiation contains four marketing ideas, two from the enhanced-customer-buying-experience category and two from the enhanced-customer-usage-experience category. Each of the four helps reduce hassles for the customer, who is in other respects acquiring a product perceived to be no better or worse than those available from other providers. Many high-profile dot-com "e-tailers" are operating in that quadrant, offering a standard branded product but capitalizing on the new technology's ability to extend product reach and service range.

The quadrant where low frequency of purchase meets low perceived product differentiation also contains four marketing ideas, all from the enhanced-customer-buying-experience category, but this time related to helping the inexperienced buyer to refine choice. The public Web sites of most bricks-and-mortar businesses—referred to dismissively as brochureware—represent first steps. Their importance will grow as businesses more deliberately integrate the sites into an overall clicks-and-mortar marketing strategy.[10]

Four marketing ideas from the enhanced-selling-process category appear in the quadrant where low frequency of purchase meets high perceived product differentiation. The ideas all relate to enriching a company's targeting in a context where customers' infrequent forays into the market must be captured and the benefits of distinctive products appreciated. As broadband access becomes the norm, the use of video will greatly increase the potential of customer input and benefit selling; the increasing availability of customer-activity information will support new ways of targeting customers.

The quadrant where high frequency of purchase meets high perceived product differentiation contains just one marketing idea—achievement selling, which focuses on reinforcing the customer's choice. Achievement selling aims to prevent a regular buyer of a distinctive product from taking the product's benefits for granted. It showcases a company's track record in meeting commitments. The track record then becomes the basis for repeat purchases.

At first glance, it may seem that the e-marketing-opportunity model is narrowly prescriptive, a mechanistic approach to a marketing strategy. Used as a recipe, the model will not work. Rather, it is a structure for facilitating a debate within a business's executive team. The team's first task is to agree on the business context—the quadrant that represents its product and market environment. If the team has difficulty agreeing, it needs to seek out the cause. Do team members have contrasting views on the level of perceived differentiation? Are they basing their thinking on different types of customers? What information will help resolve the different opinions to bring the team to a rich, shared picture of the e-marketing context?

There are a number of reasons why a business might quite correctly conclude that it is operating in more than one quadrant. It may have customers in both high- and low-purchase-frequency categories or customers who have contrasting views of the level of differentiation in the marketplace. More subtly, a single customer might be operating in more than one quadrant. For example, the typical customer of a popular music retailer might be a high-frequency purchaser of CDs, a medium-frequency purchaser of CDs recorded by a favorite artist, and a low-frequency purchaser of a particular recording.

Having decided in which quadrant or quadrants the business is operating, team members can debate the potential form and effectiveness of each of the relevant marketing ideas and can decide on priorities. The highest priority will be the cases in which it is clear that new technology can actualize the relevant idea in a way that is substantially superior to the idea's current incarnation. It is pointless to offer consumers, as one U.S. manufacturer does, the opportunity to buy chewing gum over the Internet. The manufacturer may have correctly ascertained that the typical customer is a high-frequency purchaser of a low-differentiation product; but the fastest source of chewing gum for that customer will surely be the nearest corner store. Web-based initiatives in the low-perceived-differentiation and low-frequency quadrant need particular attention: customers who are only occasional buyers may not find the Internet the most convenient vehicle for the refinement of choice unless they are regularly logged on for other purposes.

Even in information-oriented industry sectors, the appropriate e-marketing initiative may be an incremental enhancement within an integrated clicks-and-mortar marketing approach. The best solution to many customers' banking needs combines Internet access for account status, ATMs for cash withdrawals, and traditional branch facilities for financial-planning discussions.

THE E-SERVICE OPPORTUNITY

An analysis of a company's e-marketing opportunity identifies pragmatic and incremental steps forward, just as an analysis of its e-operations does. The longer-term future—and the more imaginative leaps—can be uncovered in the e-service opportunity.

The Shape of the E-Service Opportunity

E-services represent the ultimate aspiration of the Information Age, with their electronic orchestration of offerings that span the breadth and life span of a customer's needs within a chosen and defined market space. Although there is a gap between aspiration and achievement, a new wave of dot-com businesses and an increasing number of traditional incumbents are currently active in the e-service domain.

E-service starts with a full understanding of customers' needs across a given market space, a rich and expert picture of what happens to customers in the space, and what they are seeking to achieve. Synthesizing that macro understanding with data on the history and status of individual customers can allow companies to give customers advice on their specific needs. Baxter Renal has been cited as a good example of a company that redefined its business, going beyond the provision of the disposable bags required for kidney dialysis in the home to become a source of expertise in how patients can manage their lives around their treatment needs.[11]

E-service also requires authoritative knowledge of the products and services of all providers that might contribute in the target market space. Chemdex provides comprehensive knowledge within the biosciences arena; credible investment-advice providers do the same in their arena.

An e-service business can bring together in real time the first two components of the e-service domain (understanding of customer needs; knowledge of all relevant providers) to present customers with the best choices.

For example, software developed by Frictionless.com pre-evaluates options against customer-specified criteria. An e-business uses the software, then confirms that the option that meets the criteria best is indeed what the customer wants—and electronically negotiates the closure of the deal. Successful examples include Priceline.com, which allows suppliers (say, airlines) to make electronic offers to meet a customer-specified price (say,

$800 for a round-trip ticket from New York to Greece in August), and Mercata, which achieves lower prices by electronically aggregating a volume purchase on behalf of a group of individual customers (the more people who tell the site they want to buy a particular model of an appliance, for example, the lower everyone's price becomes).

The e-service business stands ready to make alterations if the need arises. Suppose a customer decides that a previously arranged vacation has to be canceled because of a family illness. After a single alert, the company will cancel all bookings and submit the customer's claim for the insurance it included in the vacation package. If another customer's building project experiences an unexpected problem, the e-service business is at hand to help troubleshoot and reschedule all future materials and services in accordance with the revised plan.

Visions of the perfect agent who knows your mind and acts in real time on your changing needs may sound too good to be true—and currently it is. But the e-service opportunity cannot be ignored or its identification deferred to some far-off date. Examining the scope of the opportunity can help in developing target capabilities and in setting priorities for e-operations and e-marketing strategies. CEO Jacques Nasser's service-based vision for Ford may take years to deliver, and the vision may change along the road, but it already has influenced the company's acquisition policy and its drive to make the whole work force more IT literate.[12]

Identifying the E-Service Opportunity

To identify the e-service opportunity, a company must first define the target market space. For an already established business, the obvious starting point is the brand image and values recognized by the existing customer base. An e-service initiative for Ford will have something to do with personal transportation; for guidebook publisher Lonely Planet, it will be about personal travel. Some businesses may have a wider choice. For example, the Virgin brand name evokes a style and approach to life more than a specific product or service. Virgin has the potential to establish market-space initiatives in a number of different fields, including entertainment, the media, and travel.

Next the company must decide whether the market space should be built around the customer's needs over time (for example, ongoing professional-development services) or around an event in the customer's life (for example, an everything-for-getting-married service or a corporate-road-show service). The company should choose an arena in which it is likely to have credibility with customers.

Because consideration of and insight into the customer context is the only route to selection and implementation of an e-service initiative, the appropriate framework for identifying the opportunity is the customer-service life cycle. Originally an IBM planning tool, it represents a simple intuitive structure for a discussion about the experience a customer undergoes at each of thirteen stages. Understanding the customer's psychological state at each stage is critical. Unless the customer is unhappy at some point in the customer-service life cycle, it is unlikely that the opportunity for an e-service business will emerge. But at any point that the existing cycle is defective, potential for an e-service business exists. (See Figure 2.5.)

Chemdex, for instance, enters at the distribution and availability stages because up-to-date market information is problematic in the fast-changing bioscience world. Having addressed the distribution and availability for the bioscience customer, Chemdex can extend its service into the later stages of the cycle. By contrast, Kodak, with its PhotoNet initiative, identified an aspect of performance—the ability of customers to share their images with friends and relatives—as the most susceptible to improvement. For John Deere, with its DeereTrax initiative, the target is the repair stage. DeereTrax monitors equipment usage, helping farmers do

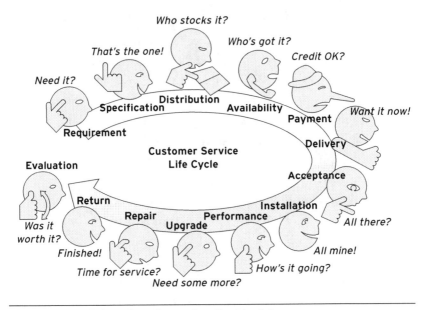

Figure 2.5. E-Service-Opportunity Model.

timely maintenance and avoid costly unscheduled downtime. Each company successfully targets a problematic stage in the customer-service life cycle and secures two vital benefits: the customer data that will assist in extending overall e-service and the resulting customer trust.

The final e-service issue is, Who needs it? The answer: all sectors. If another company (new or old) seizes an e-opportunity, it will own the customer relationship. Traditional providers will be reduced to commodity players. That is why it is so important for executives to spend time identifying what the opportunity might be. In the travel-information sector, for example, the emergence of e-service providers seems inevitable: the issue for a Lonely Planet is not whether its traditional product is replaced by on-line information from a service provider but when it will happen and what it will take to be successful.

DETERMINING THE SUSTAINABILITY OF E-OPPORTUNITY INITIATIVES

An analysis of e-opportunity is incomplete without a look at the potential for sustaining any competitive advantage gained by e-operations, e-marketing, and e-service initiatives. The diagnostic model points to three potential sources of sustainability. (See Figure 2.6.)[13]

The first and most obvious axis of sustainability, generic lead time, is a function of the technological and business changes required to implement a strategic initiative. It is tied to project analysis: How long will it take for technological and business changes to be replicated by competitors? Because applications of Web technology may be rolled out in a matter of weeks—or sourced from a specialist software supplier—companies often assume that lead time's contribution to sustainability is no longer significant. But that may not always be the case, particularly for e-operations initiatives. The

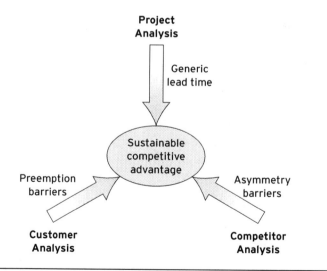

Figure 2.6. Sustainability Model.

upgrading of primary infrastructure may take years, not months, especially if a new generation of integrated ERP (enterprise resource planning) systems is required. And although supply-chain initiatives may have short technological lead times, they may well involve lengthy negotiations with numerous suppliers.

The second axis of sustainability, asymmetry barriers, involves competitor analysis. If a competitor copies the planned initiative, will that cancel out any competitive advantage? Or are there barriers that preserve the advantage? For example, asymmetry barriers protected Dell Computer from Compaq in the area of direct selling of customer-tailored PCs via the Internet. Compaq could not easily copy its archrival's success because it had not designed its products for mass customization, and its supply-chain structures, relationships, and processes were different from Dell's.

The third axis of sustainability involves customer analysis. Does the customer context allow for the creation of preemption barriers, or first-mover advantage? If there is a natural monopoly for the product or service, the answer is probably yes. Consider the electronic bookstore. If customers perceive that e-bookstores provide access to all books, they will buy consistently from the first place they enroll. They won't shop around. Their familiarity with navigating the Web site—and their knowledge that the e-bookstore has collected data on them that will smooth the book-buying process—makes replicating the relationship elsewhere seem daunting. Customers will stay with the first-mover company unless a competitor produces a substantially better offering that compensates for any switching costs. More commonly, the first mover retains the business unless the customer becomes seriously dissatisfied. Jeff Bezos' obsession with customer service demonstrates that Amazon.com understands the principle.

In the mid-1990s, the thinking was that sustainable competitive advantage was based almost entirely on asymmetry barriers, which favored asset-rich companies. When companies such as Amazon.com and eBay grew rapidly from effectively zero-asset bases, observers began to suggest that assets were liabilities and first-mover advantage was all. In fact, all three sources of sustainability—generic lead time, asymmetry barriers, and preemption barriers—are important. If Barnes & Noble is to lure loyal customers from Amazon.com, for example, it will need an integrated approach that capitalizes on its physical bookstores (its asymmetry) to offer on-line customers some advantages that Amazon cannot. What has changed in the analysis of sustainability is that some levers have become more available. Companies can increase barriers by protecting the intellectual property created in initiatives and by negotiating exclusivity with partner organizations (such as database owners and niche-product providers). Initiatives that organize customers into a community that adds value through mutual exchange can raise preemption barriers. Attention to the sources of sustainability— and a proactive approach to increasing them—remains a critical part of strategic development.

UNDERSTANDING THE DOMAINS OF E-OPPORTUNITY

For traditional bricks-and-mortar companies, components of e-operations and e-marketing are likely to represent immediate opportunities with real economic benefits. The e-service opportunity will usually take a longer time to realize, but charting an e-service strategy creates a strategic intent that will influence the evolution of the other two strategies.[14] The three domains are combined within an overall approach to a business strategy that exploits the new technology.

In an uncertain environment, learning from experience is critical. Few believe that we have penetrated even a fraction of the e-territory before us. The frameworks described here reveal the broad sweep of the territory, the kinds of opportunities available, and how choice of direction varies according to a company's starting point. More detailed maps that might enable the strategist to identify and select the precise route to a desired destination will take time to emerge. Meanwhile, businesses must select their course and, with compass in hand, stay as close as the new territory will allow to a bearing that leads to the other side of the jungle.

ADDITIONAL RESOURCES

With so much now being published on e-business, a time-efficient way of keeping track of developments is to read the authoritative and balanced special surveys published periodically by the *Economist*. Those dated June 26, 1999, and February 26, 2000, are still valuable.

Within the e-operations domain, insight into the role of infrastructure in competitive advantage can be found in Peter Weill and Marianne Broadbent's book *Leveraging the New Infrastructure: How Market Leaders Capitalize on Information Technology* (Boston: Harvard Business School Press, 1998).

E-marketing ideas can be stimulated by discussion of the scope for differentiation. Theodore Levitt's "Marketing Success Through Differentiation—of Anything" in the January-February 1980 issue of *Harvard Business Review* remains a classic. Another excellent discussion is contained in part two of Shiv Mathur and Alfred Kenyon's *Creating Value: Shaping Tomorrow's Business* (Oxford: Butterworth-Heinemann, 1997).

Some issues relevant to the e-service domain are discussed in Philip Evans and Thomas Wurster's *Harvard Business Review* article "Getting Real About Virtual Commerce," published in the November-December 1999 issue.

NOTES

1. K. Melymuka, "Ford's Driving Force," *Computerworld*, August 30, 1999, 48–50.

2. R. L. Nolan and K. Porter, "Cisco Systems Inc.," Harvard Business School case no. 3-98-127 (Boston: Harvard Business School Pub-

lishing Corp., 2000); and A.-M. Diamant-Berger and A. Ovans, "E-Procurement at Schlumberger," *Harvard Business Review,* May-June 2000, *78,* 21–22.

3. For an introduction to the language of parenting and a full set of parenting ideas, see A. Campbell, M. Goold, and M. Alexander, "Corporate Strategy: The Quest for Parenting Advantage," *Harvard Business Review,* March-April 1995, *73,* 120–142.

4. S. E. Prokesch, "Unleashing the Power of Learning: An Interview with British Petroleum's John Browne," *Harvard Business Review,* September-October 1997, *75,* 146–168.

5. J. Magretta, "The Power of Virtual Integration: An Interview with Dell Computer's Michael Dell," *Harvard Business Review,* March-April 1998, *76,* 72–84.

6. J. I. Cash and K. Ostrofsky, "Mrs. Fields Cookies," Harvard Business School case no. 1-89-056 (Boston: Harvard Business School Publishing Corp., 1989).

7. For the origin of the ideas on information's role, see M. E. Porter and V. E. Millar, "How Information Gives You Competitive Advantage," *Harvard Business Review,* July-August 1985, *63,* 149–160.

8. For a discussion of value-chain configuration concepts, see M. E. Porter, "Competition in Global Industries: A Conceptual Framework" in *Competitive Strategy in Global Industries,* M. E. Porter, ed. (Boston: Harvard Business School Press, 1986), pp. 15–60.

9. For more on the effect of the first construct and the relevance of the second, see J. M. de Figueiredo, "Finding Sustainable Profitability in Electronic Commerce," *Sloan Management Review,* Summer 2000, *41,* 41–51. (Reprinted beginning on p. 7 of this anthology.)

10. Only 2.7 percent of buyers of new cars in the United States in 1999, for example, used the Internet to conclude sales, even though 40 percent used it as part of the purchasing process. "Survey of E-Commerce," *Economist,* February 26, 2000, 6.

11. S. Vandermerwe, "How Increasing Value to Customers Improves Business Results," *Sloan Management Review,* Fall 2000, *42,* 27–37.

12. L. Copeland, "Ford Drives Employees to the Web to Help Connect With Online Customers," *Computerworld,* February 3, 2000.

13. B. Ives, P. R. Rane, and S. S. Sainani, "Customer Service Life Cycle," http://isds.bus.lsu.edu/cvoc/projects/cslc/html/; Vandermerwe,

"Increasing Value," 27–37; and D. Feeny and B. Ives, "In Search of Sustainability," *Journal of Management Information Systems*, Summer 1990, 7(1), 27–46.

14. For a definition of strategic intent, see G. Hamel and C. K. Prahalad, "Strategic Intent," *Harvard Business Review*, May-June 1989, 67, 63–76.

CHAPTER THREE

Profits and the Internet: Seven Misconceptions

SUBRAMANIAN RANGAN
RON ADNER

Most managers rightly see profitable growth as essential to their business. However, given the realities of competition and the irreducible uncertainty in business, there will always be a gulf between the pursuit of profitable growth and its achievement. When the Internet arrived, many believed the gulf would narrow. Unfortunately, the opposite has been true.

To be sure, the Internet is powerful. It is opening the way to new markets, customers, products, and modes of conducting business. But it also is prompting newcomers and veterans alike unwittingly to embrace some dangerous half-truths and to neglect serious tensions beneath seemingly sensible strategy choices. The consequences are visible in the long list of failed dot-coms. At established companies, the effects might be muted, but if the past is any indicator, they too are susceptible to the penalties of inadequate strategy scrutiny.

In assessing Internet-related business opportunities, companies must not let what is technologically feasible overshadow what is strategically desirable. To minimize any unintentional destruction of value, they must think through the full implications of the strategy choices they are making. In particular, they must be alert to seven widely held misconceptions.

THE "FIRST-MOVER ADVANTAGE" MISCONCEPTION

A landgrab mentality has pervaded the Internet, not just in start-ups such as Bluefly, ChateauOnline, and QXL.com, but also in established companies such as Microsoft, Telefonica, and Reuters. The logic is that one driver of success (if not the key driver) in Internet-related business is being first. That view has merit. Being first can give a company a frontier-pushing aura (as it did for Apple Computer); can generate free publicity and valuable brand recognition (Amazon.com and Yahoo! Inc.); can move companies down proprietary learning curves (Intel); and can provide a bigger opportunity to lock in unattached customers and achieve critical mass (America Online).[1]

Yet in Internet business, first-mover status is a precarious perch on which to rest strategy, and managers should not overrate the importance of early entry and the durability of the advantages it might bring. To see why, consider three strains of first-mover advantage.

The Limits of Preemption

The strategic strain of first-mover advantage rests on preemption—the premise that "the early bird gets the worm." It applies, for example, to airlines' choices of routes and oil refiners' capacity decisions. However, preemption works only when two conditions are satisfied.[2] First, the opportunity under consideration must be efficiently sized. The company must be big enough for the opportunity, and the opportunity must be big enough for just one company. (Think of the corner grocery store.) Second, the product or service must be simple enough that offerings are hard to differentiate, as is the case with gasoline, airline seats, and television-cable service. Otherwise, later entrants can induce buyers to switch by offering better products and service, as is the case in apparel retailing, restaurants, and software.

Those two conditions have important implications for Internet businesses. Most opportunities on the Internet are far from meeting the one-company-is-enough criterion. And even in exchanges and Web portals, where that criterion might hold, products and services are far from simple. In fact, there is tremendous scope for differentiation. Just ask QXL.com, the pan-European first mover in Internet auctions. Rival eBay is surpassing QXL even in its home market. Or ask Netscape, whose browsers were abruptly displaced (even on Macintosh computers) by Microsoft's Internet Explorer. Or PointCast: the first Internet company to deliver free news on-line, it is now a footnote in history.

The Importance of Being the Best

In the *traditional* strain, first-mover advantages are based on three sources: the scarcity of key inputs or distribution channels; sustained cost differentials between first entrants and subsequent entrants; and user-trial and user-switching costs.[3] None of those holds as much sway in Internet business as in traditional business. Consider Yahoo. In the Internet-portal business, neither the scarcity of inputs (information on Web sites), nor cost differentials (to build and maintain search directories), nor user-switching costs are significant issues. Yahoo! is not successful because of being a first mover, but because it is a *best mover.* If users come to favor Lycos or some other portal, Yahoo! will replay Apple's decline. That is true of other business-to-customer companies, including Amazon.com, TheStreet.com, and Travelocity. And, higher switching costs excepted, it is true of business-to-business companies such as FreeMarkets, Reuters, and SAP.

The Limits to Exploiting the New Rules

The New Economy strain of first-mover advantage relates to the concepts of critical mass and network externalities.[4] Critical-mass effects are present when a threshold proportion of actors (the critical mass) has adopted a particular product, technology, or market location, and the remaining actors tip to that choice. Network externalities are present when the benefits that accrue to an actor from adopting a particular product, technology, or market location increase with the number of others who make the same choice.

Critical mass and network externalities attract attention because they fuel user adoption and lock-in, and can trigger a winner-take-all dynamic. Lock-in might take the form of a coordination trap—it makes sense to switch only if everyone or nearly everyone else switches. It might also take the form of a system-compatibility trap: if users have made related investments in compatible complementary products and services, then switching on the focal item might entail expensive switching on related items as well.[5] In either case, the adopted standard prevails even if offers from other companies are objectively better.

This strain of first-mover-advantage theory is compelling to many managers, but they seem to be forgetting one thing. Although the new rules offer unprecedented opportunities, there is no guarantee that the greatest benefit will go to the one who most exploits them. For example, there is no guarantee that the benefits of user adoption and lock-in will go to the first mover. Consider that Microsoft overcame being a late mover in PC operating systems or that Matsushita beat Sony in VCR formats or that Cirrus prevailed over Citibank in ATM protocols.

There are several reasons that first movers may not win. First, even in the presence of critical mass and network externalities, the processes set in motion often take a long time to play out. If the market is insufficiently ordered, the first entrant may be too early.[6] Second, when individual companies try either to monopolize or expressly manipulate the standard, potential users (and other producers) likely will resist getting trapped. Finally, a standard might emerge, but not one that is proprietary to any single company. Witness the ubiquity of public standards such as keyboard layouts, cell phones, and the wireless Internet. In short, winner-take-all worlds tend to be accidental, not engineered. In that sense, new or not, the rules are not easily exploitable. It is time to stop grabbing the land and start cultivating it.

THE "REACH" MISCONCEPTION

A company's potential customers often are distributed in heterogeneous rather than homogeneous segments: for example, corporate and retail segments, affluent and economy-minded, professional and lay. And companies have long perceived that the more they can deploy existing activities and resources to pursue new customer segments and extend reach, the more they can grow their revenues and earnings.

With the Internet, the allure of heterogeneity, or reach, has grown even stronger. It is tempting both new and established companies to use their resources (including brand, bandwidth, capabilities, and content) to pursue unprecedented numbers and types of customers.[7] Reach is the reason that Reuters, a traditional business-to-business (B2B) player, contemplated a bold gambit to leverage a financial portal to offer retail customers the content and trading services that Reuters provides commercial institutions. It is the reason that WebMD wants to serve you and me *and* doctors *and* nurses *and* pharmacies *and* hospitals. And why Enron, another traditional B2B player, weighed a venture with Blockbuster that would have leveraged the cable bandwidth Enron sells to businesses so as to sell movies on demand to consumers.

Some ventures might indeed lead to new profitable growth, but reach is far from an unmixed blessing. The more reach a company attempts, the greater the risk it runs of undermining *fit*—the coherence with which a company's activities interconnect and reinforce one another. Fit is essential to a company's health and future success.[8] Digital Equipment Corp., for example, faltered when it sacrificed fit to reach by attempting to make PCs, workstations, minicomputers, and mainframes under one roof.

Greater reach might lead to growth, but it must be undertaken in a manner that preserves or reinforces fit. As eBay considers entering the B2B space or as Intel considers entering the B2C (business-to-customer) space, each must work out the implications of the reach-fit tension to ensure profitable growth.

A useful way to evaluate reach opportunities is along the core-context dimension.[9] (See Figure 3.1.) Core elements and core activities are key to customer value. More important, they drive other elements and activities in the business. Natural-language recognition and search algorithms are core for a site such as Ask Jeeves. A context activity for Ask Jeeves is the design of different interface menus to meet particular customer needs.

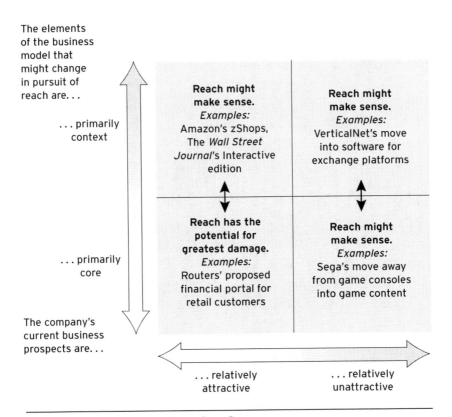

Figure 3.1. When Reach Makes Sense.

Companies in healthy businesses should be wary of reach opportunities that call for changes in core elements or activities. In contrast, changes required to accommodate reach might be fine if they affect only context elements or activities. However, interconnections within established activities may be extensive but not apparent, so companies will seldom find it easy to insulate core activities from changes in context. Moreover, changes in core activities, intentional or not, are hard to reverse.

Amazon.com's zShops (a network of Amazon-hosted Internet merchants) illustrate how reach can be balanced with fit. The zShop concept does not force Amazon to change its core activities; nor is it hard to reverse. Merck-Medco Managed Care and STMicroelectronics are other examples of companies that successfully balance reach with fit.

If the pursuit of reach means reconfiguring core activities that now cohere well—or making changes in context that will have serious repercussions on the core—beware. Even if the impact would be delayed, companies should resist the temptation. Of course, if the company's business prospects aren't that attractive, preserving fit is less of an issue.

THE "CUSTOMER SOLUTIONS" MISCONCEPTION

Another tempting growth strategy is to provide customer solutions. Here a company goes beyond providing a simple product or service and offers customers access to valuable *complements*—other products and services that they require to make better use of the core offering.

Companies generally offer customer solutions under one of two circumstances. (See Figure 3.2.) First, when a company has acquired a customer for one of its products or services, it might enhance its business by offering complementary products and services to the *same* customer. The customer gets greater convenience;

the company gets greater share of wallet. The extended service warranties that hardware manufacturers offer are a good example. Companies also offer a solution when the complements that customers need are too expensive or are unavailable in sufficient quantities. In that case, without a solution, the company would be unable to sell its core offering to a significant set of customers. Thus Accenture, for example, decided to complement its information-technology consulting services with strategy consulting for senior managers.

As in the reach strategy, however, there is an underlying tension to the customer-solutions strategy that many companies don't see. This time the tension is between providing a solution and maintaining focus. Focus is about specialization, doing one thing better than anyone else, and it goes to the heart of a company's business strategy. As Adam Smith noted two hundred years ago, specialization can drive both effectiveness and efficiency. When the market is large enough, it pays to specialize. If the market is competitive, it will hurt *not* to do so. That is why until recently Intel focused on hardware, why Microsoft focuses on software, and why Dell focuses on integration. Apple, on the other hand, tried to do all three. Its aim of providing customers with a convenient solution was noble, but it failed to see the penalty it would pay in both price and performance.

If companies decide to provide customer solutions internally, they must consider whether potential profits will sufficiently offset any accompanying loss of focus. Companies such as AOL Time Warner, Reuters, and Sony are implicitly or explicitly choosing convenience and solutions as their Internet business strategies. If they neglect the tension between providing solutions and maintaining focus, they will pay a price. The diseconomies of scope might be hidden, but they will eventually bring companies down. That point is as important today as it was before the Internet.

Intel, Charles Schwab, and Toyota Motor have enjoyed enviable successes. They have asked and answered the question: What business should we be in? Then they have worked to be among the best in their business. In a growing Internet-driven global economy,

Do customers now experience bottlenecks in getting complementary products or services?

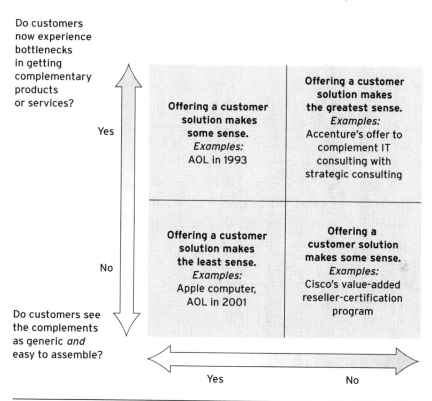

Figure 3.2. When Offering a Customer Solution Makes Sense.

specialization will become more widespread. Generalists that fail to confront the what-business-are-we-in question will find success all the more elusive.

THE "INTERNET SECTOR" MISCONCEPTION

Perhaps one reason companies don't ask hard questions about their business focus is that they view the Internet as an undifferentiated landscape. But although the B2B and B2C labels are useful shorthand, they do not help managers identify with the value propositions that ought to underlie their business. Knowing that you operate in, say, the B2B space gives you almost no clue about your company's raison d'être, customer value drivers, key internal competencies, or competitive landscape.

Before it can formulate and evaluate Internet-related strategy, a company must identify the specific Internet sector or sectors in which it is operating. (See Table 3.1.) Such identification is critical because three key aspects of competitive advantage are likely to differ across sectors: customer value drivers, performance drivers, and the metrics by which each is gauged.

For example, in the services sector, speed, convenience, and price might be key value drivers for customers. In the infrastructure sector, availability (twenty-four hours per day, seven days per week), scalability, and compatibility might top the list. Similarly, insourcing logistics and keeping a low proportion of fixed costs might be key performance drivers in the services sector, but in the infrastructure sector the performance drivers might be sufficient investment in product design, rigorous testing, and a modular approach to systems and operations. Also, in the services sector, performance and productivity metrics might include brand recall or maintenance cost and transaction value per registered customer. In the infrastructure sector, however, key metrics might include a customer-satisfaction and customer-retention index, annual billings per customer, and profits per employee.

Without developing and tracking sector-specific performance metrics, managers are likely to make poor decisions in allocating resources. That is why industries as varied as consulting, retailing, and publishing, to name a few, develop yardsticks suited to the specific nature of their markets and operations. In Internet-related businesses as well, developing sophisticated and sector-specific metrics—beyond Web-page hits and registered users—is essential to formulating and assessing strategy.

There may be more sectors than those we've identified. The exact sectors are not as important as realizing that focal offerings in Internet space vary and that customers will have different reasons for selecting them. Settling on a focal industry will help a company

Table 3.1. Six Broad Internet Sectors.

Sector	Broad Characterization of Focal Offers	Key Value Drivers	Companies That Target the Sector
Infrastructure	Access, communication, interpretation, digitization, interconnectedness, display, storage, retrieval, and processing	Availability, security, coverage, speed, scalability, mobility, and price	Akamai, AOL, BEA Systems, E Ink, Ericsson, Exodus, Global Crossing, Intel, Lucent, Microsoft, Nortel, Sun Microsystems, Telefonica, Tibco Software, and VeriSign
Applications	Organization, simplification, presentation, manipulation, analysis, tracking, matching, and reception and transmission of information	Functionality, reliability, efficiency, compatibility, upgradability, privacy, and price	Adobe, Ariba, Commerce One, Double-Click, Inktomi, Intuit, Marimba, Microsoft, Oracle, and SAP
Portals	Internet gateway, search and navigation, links to services and content, and broadcast medium (for advertising)	Exhaustiveness, speed, convenience, privacy, community experience, customizability, size and attractiveness of user base, and price	AOL, CEOExpress, Excite, iVillage, Star-Media Networks, TerraLycos, and Yahoo!
Content	Information (general and specific, current and archived), news, entertainment (including games), and databases	Accuracy, timeliness, completeness, appeal, interactivity, and price	AOL Time Warner, CNN, Bloomberg, EMI, Multex, Newscorp, Pearson, Reuters, and WebMD
Services	An act that satisfies a need or want	Quality of experience, efficiency, reliability, convenience, customization, privacy, and price	Amazon, bfinance, ChateauOnline, E*Trade, FreeMarkets, W.W. Grainger, Media Metrix, Merck-Medco, Merita-Nordbanken, Travelocity, and WebMD
Exchanges	A virtual trading place, and matching and creation of supply and demand	Transaction density, trust, transaction security, privacy, support services (such as insurance and delivery), and price	Bandex, ChemConnect, Covisint, eBay, Elemica, e-Steel, QXL, and Ventro

decide the depth and breadth of each product or service it wants to offer. It also will help when the company evaluates alternatives and changes to its scope. Failure to decide the company's core sector may keep it from being best—or invite it to conduct potentially dangerous experiments along the dimensions of reach and customer solutions.

THE MISCONCEPTION OF "BEST-OF-BREED-PARTNER LEVERAGE"

To resolve the tensions between reach and fit and between solutions and focus, managers are increasingly opting for a partner-leverage strategy—capitalizing on or creating a market opportunity by combining their resources and capabilities with those of other companies. There are many types of partnership arrangements: codevelopment and learning alliances such as those between Philips Electronics and Sony; partnerships to deliver existing products to existing customers more efficiently, such as Covisint (General Motors, Ford, and Daimler-Chrysler's on-line marketplace). The variant that is of interest here is *best-of-breed* partner leverage.[10]

In best-of-breed-partner leverage, a company identifies and works with one or more partner companies, each of which is called on to make a discrete and complementary contribution toward the pursuit of a target opportunity. Thus Palm Pilot partners with Nokia; and Cisco creates ties to Cap Gemini Ernst & Young and IBM. Best-of-breed partnerships may have different goals, such as to extend reach or enable a solution, but they share three characteristics that distinguish them from other partnerships. First, the partners' roles are stable and the relationship is expected to be long-term. Second, there is a significant degree of coordination and cospecialization among partners. Finally, no one partner has legal control over any of the others.

Best-of-breed-partner leverage can be a sensible approach, but even with the Internet, managers should not elevate it to the status of unambiguous virtue. True, the Internet makes it easier and cheaper to align activities across company boundaries, but it does not do much to align interests across those boundaries. Without aligned interests, joint value creation (even joint value appropriation) remains a strategic hope rather than a business reality.[11]

A more disciplined approach is to balance partner leverage against the less fashionable concept of control.[12] Control is what gives top management the right to exercise discretion over how resources will be allocated and which actions to pursue. Control is not that critical when things go well, but when they don't, as is inevitable at least some of the time, all sides will be clamoring for discretion over strategy. That is one of the main reasons alliances seldom succeed for long.

In deciding whether or not to rely on best-of-breed-partner leverage, there is no substitute for good judgment.[13] Good judgment, however, ought to be informed by the principles of prudence and process. The principle of prudence argues that partner leverage is worth considering only if the company needs access to an activity or business that otherwise would disrupt its fit or dilute its focus; and if relations with prospective partners are not going to be cumbersome. (See Figure 3.3.)

The principle of process says that when making decisions that will impact all the partners, companies must adhere to the elements of fair process—they must engage, exchange, and explain.[14] Intentions, actions, and volition play a key role in any endeavor, especially one that calls for various entities to cooperate. The track records of eBay, Intel, and Nokia, for example, show that it is possible for companies to balance partner leverage with control and use it to achieve profitable growth.[15]

THE "BORN GLOBAL" MISCONCEPTION

Seeing an end to border tyranny, many commentators and managers believe that Internet businesses can spread across the globe effortlessly. It's easy to see why they think that: bits and bytes travel at the

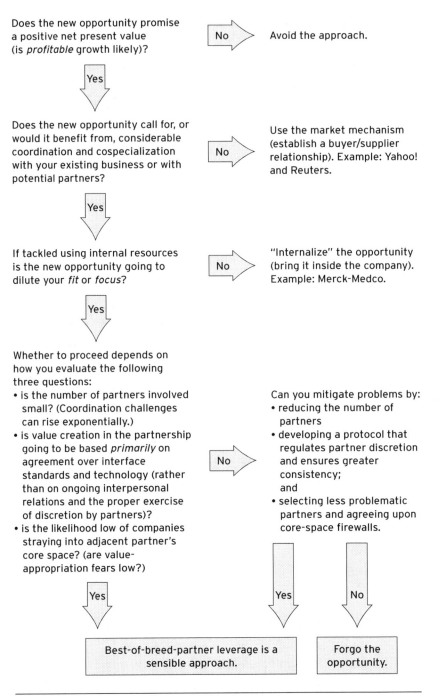

Figure 3.3. When Best-of-Breed-Partner Leverage Makes Sense.

speed of light and at very low cost; Web sites are accessible from anywhere the law and equipment permit.

Unfortunately, that born-global view, although appealing, is a dangerous half-truth. All successful global companies will go to the Internet, but not all Internet companies will be able to go global. To be successful abroad, they will have to learn what MTV, Wal-Mart, Honda, and others have discovered: you must first be successful at home, then move outward in a manner that anticipates and genuinely accommodates local differences.

To go global, Internet businesses must overcome at least three hurdles. First, potential customers must know that the company exists. There are so many sites: surveys by the Internet Software Consortium (http://www.isc.org) reported registered domain names in the tens of millions as of July 2000. Despite the emergence of search robots, a company typically must make a heavy investment in local marketing.

Second, users must trust the company enough to conduct business on its site. Trust increases with local presence. Local management and employees bring local relationships and contacts; local presence allows local media access and scrutiny and enables local legal recourse. All those factors contribute to trust. Contrary to the hyped model of servers in Boston, software in Bangalore, and customers in Berlin, dot-coms must establish local sites, country by country—as successful companies such as eBay, Schwab, and Yahoo! know well.

Finally, people must want to buy the offering. Unless you're an Intel, that means more than rolling out homegrown products and services. National borders embody discontinuities, which may include language, currency, income levels, consumer tastes, or differences in the regulatory and competitive landscape. The Internet doesn't eliminate them. Companies must adapt or fail. AOL is an also-ran in nearly all the foreign markets it has entered. Amazon, Priceline, and QXL.com also have discovered the myth of the born-global Internet business.

THE "TECHNOLOGY-IS-STRATEGY" MISCONCEPTION

The misconception that equates technology with strategy is perhaps the most deadly and persistent. Venture capitalist Vinod Khosla states that now "technology is a driver of business strategy" and that, within Old Economy companies, a visionary CIO will be "the key to a company's success."[16] Geoffrey Moore, another Silicon Valley guru, adds, "In this new age, IT is not *about* the business—it *is* the business."[17]

Technology has made immeasurable contributions to society and to the success of countless companies. Like electricity a hundred years ago, the electronic phenomenon we call "digiticity" is likely to have a profound influence on what, how, and for whom companies produce. Yet the fundamentals of economics and strategy have not changed and are not about to. Technology and strategy are strong complements, not substitutes. Companies that understand their technology better than their customers and their competition won't succeed in any economy, old or new. Would Lexus have penetrated the auto industry if Mercedes had thought more about customers than technology? Would AT&T have had to pull out of the credit card business if it had understood customer-credit scoring as well as it understood back-office operations? Then there are the billions that General Motors sank into technology during the 1980s and the costly debacles at Globalstar and Iridium Satellite.

The sooner companies stop confusing what is technologically feasible with what is strategically desirable, the sooner they will realize that a company can achieve and sustain profitable growth only to the extent that it delivers on two strategy fundamentals: product advantage and production advantage.[18]

Product Advantage

Product advantage is a company's ability to offer genuine and unusual customer value—in short, to be the best or among the best in class. Amazon, Adobe, Nortel, Nokia, Sony, and Schwab have demonstrated product advantage. Such advantage emerges from many sources (including serendipity), but the result always represents a valuable advance on genuine customer problems, needs, and aspirations. Thus, product advantages always correspond to *demand-side* insights, and companies should gauge product advantage against demand-side parameters, such as efficacy, excellence, variety, convenience, and speed.

Production Advantage
Product advantage alone is not sufficient for profitable growth, however. Customers—both corporate and retail—operate under budget constraints and perceive value not only in the performance of an offer but also in its price. That is why unit costs play an important role—and why a second strategic fundamental is production advantage.

A company has production advantage when it can extend its offering to customers at prices that the mainstream market deems affordable and that the company deems profitable. Nokia, Microsoft, and Intel have production advantage (as demonstrated by their high return on capital), but as yet, most newly launched Internet businesses, including Amazon, E*Trade, and Yahoo!, do not.

Like product advantage, production advantage can come from many sources. The common aim is to lower total unit costs without diluting product or service quality. Further, once a company achieves those lower costs, it must be able to sustain them. Thus production advantage corresponds to insights on the *supply side*. However, production advantage must be gauged not only against supply-side parameters (quality-adjusted productivity, throughput, learning-curve coefficients, turnaround times, and the like), but also against target-price parameters. The target price should reflect both customers' willingness to pay and the prices of rival offers.

When observers point to Cisco, Schwab, and Exodus Communications as technology leaders, they make an incomplete, if not incorrect, attribution for the success of these companies. Their success is first and foremost rooted in their insightful grasp of customers' needs, aspirations, and constraints. Working from that foundation, they used technology to deliver value in a creative, effective, and efficient way.

ASKING THE RIGHT QUESTIONS

The risk that attends a new and powerful technology like the Internet is that companies selecting growth opportunities let possibility overshadow profitability. The way forward will doubtless be paved with experimentation. But wise managers will shape the bounds and direction of their experiments with good judgment, asking questions about potential strategies rather than hastily embracing popular views. (See Table 3.2.) Because the relative dangers are not the same for Old and New Economy companies—and because the risk will not have the same relevance or severity for all companies at all times—each manager must carefully weigh the importance of each individual risk.

Options emerge from technology, choices from strategy. That is why we have emphasized that although technology and strategy are strong complements, they are not substitutes. To be members of the Profitable Economy, companies must attain both product advantage and production advantage. Although the landscape has changed, the path toward profitable growth has not.

Acknowledgments

We thank Lourdes Casanova, Ingemar Dierickx, Soumitra Dutta, Paolo Fulghieri, Javier Gimeno, Randal Heeb, Goncalo Pacheo de Almeida, Werner Reinartz, Jeff Reuer, Timothy Van Zandt, and the reviewers for their helpful comments. We especially thank Dominique Heau, and, for support of this work, eLab@INSEAD.

Table 3.2. Avoiding the Risks of Internet Misconceptions.

▼

The Risks	Questions Managers Should Ask
Overestimating first-mover advantage	• *Would we enter the business and procure attractive returns even if our likely rivals were already in the market under consideration?* A definitive yes or no are both good signals. *Yes* suggests that you have genuine product and production advantage. *No* suggests that timing is important. But the more you hesitate in answering the question, the more likely you are to be at risk of overestimating first-mover advantage.
Unintentionally diluting fit in the pursuit of reach	• *To what extent would the pursuit of the reach opportunity under consideration disrupt the core of our activity system in an existing business that is attractive to us and is expected to remain so?* The smaller the anticipated disruption or the less attractive the existing business, the safer it is to proceed with the reach opportunity.
Unintentionally sacrificing focus in the desire to offer "customer solutions"	• *First ask: Are we unable to tap into a potentially large and lucrative customer base because necessary complements to our products are too costly, unavailable, or difficult for the customer to assemble?* If any of those conditions hold, thinking about customer solutions makes sense. • *Now ask: To what extent will developing complements in-house call for expertise we don't have and dilute our focus in an attractive sector?* The lesser the extent to which both hold, the safer it is to develop a customer solution in-house.
Ignoring Internet-sector differences	• *To what extent have we tailored the ends, means, and metrics of our product and production advantage to the specific sector or sectors in which we operate?* The more you've tailored, the more likely you are to succeed.
Relying unguardedly on partner leverage	• *To what extent will our partners' interests diverge from our own, the quality of our offering be subject to our partners' discretion, and monitoring our partners entail prohibitive cost to us?* The lesser the extent to which each condition holds (or can be made to hold), the more sense it makes to rely on partner leverage.

(continued)

Table 3.2. Continued.
▼

The Risks	Questions Managers Should Ask
Going global prematurely	• *To what extent do we lead in our home market, understand the market discontinuities we will face abroad, and have competitive advantage over rivals abroad?*
	The more each condition holds, the safer it is to expand into the target foreign market. However, if your intent is to learn abroad, the second and third conditions can be relaxed.
Treating technology as strategy	• *First ask: To what extent are we doing something just because new technology means we can do it instead of doing what we should do?*
	The more that "should" dominates "can" in your thinking, the lower the risk that you are substituting technology for strategy. As a check, list the objections to what you are considering that are not technology related.
	• *Then ask: How grave are the listed objections?*
	The graver and more numerous the objections, the more reason to explore other alternatives.

ADDITIONAL RESOURCES

In recent years, many works have focused on the Internet and its impact on business strategy. Among them, a 2000 McGraw-Hill book, *Net Ready,* by Amir Hartman, John Sifonis, and John Kador, offers managers a big-picture view of the possibilities associated with the Internet. It makes the applications concrete by describing the practice at Cisco Systems, where Hartman and Sifonis are executives.

"Finding Sustainable Profitability in Electronic Commerce," by J. M. de Figueiredo, from the Summer 2000 issue of MIT *Sloan Management Review,* provides an insightful discussion on when and how companies can orient e-commerce strategies for competitive advantage. (Reprinted beginning on p. 7 of this anthology.)

Internet Business Models and Strategies, by Allan Afuah and Christopher Tucci, published this year by McGraw-Hill, attempts to link Internet technology, business models, the competitive landscape, and company performance.

A 2001 *Strategic Management Journal* article, "Value Creation in E-Business," by R. Amit and C. Zott, examines the sources of value creation in the business models of fifty-nine U.S. and European businesses. The article identifies the business model as a locus of innovation.

NOTES

1. For a review of several theoretical and empirical studies on this topic, see F. M. Scherer and D. Ross, *Industrial Market Structure and Economic Performance* (Boston: Houghton Mifflin, 1990), pp. 407, 586–589.

2. M. E. Porter, *Competitive Strategy* (New York: Free Press, 1980), pp. 336–338.

3. M. B. Lieberman and D. B. Montgomery, "First-Mover Advantages," *Strategic Management Journal,* September 1988, 9, 41–58; and I. Dierickx and K. Cool, "Asset Stock Accumulation and Sustainability of Competitive Advantage," *Management Science,* December 1989, 35, 1504–1511.

4. C. Shapiro and H. R. Varian, *Information Rules* (Boston: Harvard Business School Press, 1998), chapter 7. We have seen no consensus on the distinction between Old and New Economy companies. One way to contrast the two might be to categorize New Economy companies as those operating businesses in which standards tend to matter, product life cycles are relatively short, and network externalities generally hold.

5. G. Saloner, A. Shepard, and J. Podolny, *Strategic Management* (New York: John Wiley, 2001), chapter 9.

6. M. Cusumano, Y. Mylonadis, and R. Rosenbloom, "Strategic Maneuvering and Mass-Market Dynamics: The Triumph of VHS Over Beta," *Business History Review,* Spring 1992, 66, 51–94.

7. P. Evans and T. S. Wurster, "Getting Real About Virtual Commerce," *Harvard Business Review,* November-December 1999, 77, 85–94.

8. For a full discussion of the concept of fit, see M. E. Porter, "What Is Strategy?" *Harvard Business Review,* November-December 1996, 74, 61–78; and N. Siggelkow, "Change in the Presence of Fit: The Rise, the Fall, and the Renascence of Liz Claiborne," *Academy of Management Journal,* in press.

9. G. A. Moore, *Living on the Fault Line* (New York: HarperCollins, 2000), chapter 1.

10. For discussion of competitive leverage (using rivals' strengths to advantage), see M. Cusumano and D. Yoffie, *Competing on Internet Time* (New York: Free Press, 1998). For a discussion of internal leverage (leveraging core competencies), see G. Hamel and C. K. Prahalad, *Competing for the Future* (Boston: Harvard Business School Press, 1994).

11. For discussion on the importance of governance in Internet-related business, see N. Venkatraman, "Five Steps to a Dot-Com Strategy: How to Find Your Footing on the Web," *Sloan Management Review,* Spring 2000, *39,* 15–28. (Reprinted beginning on p. 83 of this anthology.)

12. O. E. Williamson, "Markets and Hierarchies" (New York: Free Press, 1975), chapter 2.

13. For a discussion of when and how alliance arrangements can play a role in organizing for innovation, see H. W. Chesbrough and D. J. Teece, "When Is Virtual Virtuous?" *Harvard Business Review,* January-February 1996, *74,* 65–73; and Y. Doz and G. Hamel, *Alliance Advantage* (Boston: Harvard Business School Press, 1998).

14. C. Kim and R. Mauborgne, "Fair Process: Managing in the Knowledge Economy," *Harvard Business Review,* July-August 1997, *75,* 65–75.

15. For a discussion of when and how companies might deal with this growing challenge, see A. Gawer and M. Cusumano, *Platform Leadership: How Market Leaders Drive Industry Innovation* (Boston: Harvard Business School Press, in press).

16. D. Champion and N. G. Carr, "Starting Up in High Gear: An Interview with Venture Capitalist Vinod Khosla," *Harvard Business Review,* July-August 2000, *78,* 99.

17. Moore, "Living on the Fault Line," 20.

18. For perspectives on how companies can create customer value and sustain competitive advantage, see C. Kim and R. Mauborgne, "Value Innovation," *Harvard Business Review,* January-February 1997, *75,* 103–112; and Porter, "What Is Strategy?"

CHAPTER FOUR

Five Steps to a Dot-Com Strategy: How to Find Your Footing on the Web

N. VENKATRAMAN

"The Internet changes everything." Although this might have been an overstatement just two years ago, it is clearly not so today. The impact of the Internet is obvious in business-to-consumer transactions: witness the proliferation of Web sites for facilitating sales and services across a broad range of offerings. But the real revolution is happening in business-to-business value chains as companies restructure their operations with trading partners.

The Internet also has had a profound impact on the valuation of individual companies and economic sectors. This can be seen not simply in the incredible market capitalization of companies whose business models are rooted in the Internet (for example, Amazon, eBay, Yahoo!, Priceline), but also of companies that provide the technical infrastructure for the Net economy (for example, Intel, Microsoft, AOL, IBM, Cisco). Such valuations—although highly volatile—are compelling established companies to seriously assess whether they will lose out to relative upstarts that are leveraging their lofty valuations into tangible capabilities through acquisition.

The Internet has also evolved beyond personal computers; soon it will be commonplace to access the Net through cellular telephones (Nokia, Ericsson), personal organizers (Palm Computing, Psion), videogame consoles (Sega's Dreamcast or Sony's PlayStation), as well as home appliances (Electrolux, Whirlpool), vending machines (Maytag), and automobiles (GM's OnStar and Microsoft's AutoPC). In short, the Internet has become more than a simple and effective way to exchange e-mail and documents; it is emerging as a critical backbone of commerce. And it is happening at a faster pace than many thought possible[1] and with which few feel comfortable.

But if you ask managers about the strategies for their Internet businesses, you get a bewildering array of responses. Some mention the functionality of the Web (you can get the details of our latest new product introductions); some highlight their choice of platform (we are driven on the Oracle platform or IBM's e-business infrastructure or Hewlett-Packard's latest suite of e-services). Some trumpet how they use the Web to enhance customer service (we provide enhanced customized service—such as specialized pricing and promotions or provide rapid response to customer inquiries), whereas others point to their success in integrating the physical and digital infrastructures to provide seamless service (our customers can interact with us in branches, by telephone, or over the Net without any differences in cost or service levels). Some mention their initial success in creating customer communities (we now have a regular and continuous dialogue with our customers and this has helped our marketing efforts considerably). These different observations simply underscore an important characteristic of the Net; its potential functionality is so broad and varied that we cannot and should not restrict our attention to a few narrow domains. Indeed, it is like the proverbial blind men describing the elephant: different managers see different facets of benefits but do not see the complete picture. Although most managers are cognizant of impending changes, the business landscape is fuzzy and fast-changing. We are navigating in uncharted waters.

How should companies develop effective strategies in such a situation? Four interrelated issues are useful in orchestrating conversations about the dot-com agenda. Effective strategizing for the dot-com business operation requires the management team to consider these issues together, not in isolation. Too often, companies focus on one dominant issue and let it be the driving force while paying scant attention to the other issues only to realize the ramifications and conflicts much later. The four issues and the fifth alignment challenge can be posed as questions:

1. What's your strategic vision for the dot-com operations?
2. How do you govern the dot-com operations?
3. How do you allocate key resources for the dot-com operations?
4. What's your operating infrastructure for the dot-com operations?
5. Is your management team aligned for the dot-com agenda?

Consistent answers to these five questions indicate an effective strategy for the dot-com business operations.

WHAT'S YOUR STRATEGIC VISION FOR THE DOT-COM OPERATIONS?

Even as recent as early 1998, most companies saw the Net as being only tangentially relevant to their business operations. Today, they realize the possibilities and opportunities but are daunted by the challenge of how to make the Internet and e-commerce an integral part of their business strategy rather than a stand-alone project. (See Figure 4.1.)

Articulating a strategic vision for dot-com business in precise terms is futile; the Net is evolving at such a dizzying pace that it's nearly impossible to work toward a specific end-state. It's more useful to approach the issue of strategic vision for dot-com operations as a continuous cycle involving building on current business

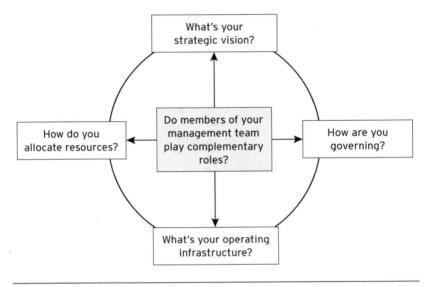

Figure 4.1. The Dot-Com Agenda as a Balancing Act.

models and creating future business models through selective experimentation. The aim is to balance refining the current business rules while creating new business rules for the dot-com agenda. (See Figure 4.2.)

Build on Your Current Business Models

For every corporation, the Net—at minimum—offers opportunities for reducing operating cost levels or enhancing services or both. Every company should identify ways to leverage the Net for restructuring the cost base. Even companies that don't find their business-to-customer interactions easily portable to the Net could find value in business-to-business transactions through restructured supply chains.

Cost Leadership. Strategy has always relied on cost differentials[2] and the Net does not negate this fundamental strategy axiom. Indeed, the Net exposes the inherent weaknesses of high-cost com-

Figure 4.2. The Dot-Com Operation as a Cyclical Reinvention.

petitors—whether they are big or small. Jack Welch, the legendary chairman of GE, has already sponsored a ninety-day, all-company initiative under the banner of "destroyourbusiness.com" for thinking about how to use the Web to eliminate bureaucracy. In every conceivable case, the cost of Web-based transactions is an order-of-magnitude lower than traditional ways and decreasing at a faster rate. The cost of an Internet-based banking transaction is about one-fiftieth of the cost of a human teller transaction. New breed stockbrokers like E*Trade and Ameritrade have inherently lower cost levels and are forcing traditional players, such as Merrill Lynch, Schwab, and Fidelity, to dramatically lower their price points. We will see more such cost-based competitive pressures in many other sectors of the economy.

The centrality of cost leadership in the dot-com arena can be best seen in the personal computer marketplace—where net-savvy customers look for the best value and the stock market ruthlessly punishes high-cost operators with lower capitalization. Dell has consolidated its market superiority by migrating its build-to-order model to the Web[3]—forcing companies like Compaq, NEC, Sony, and Toshiba to radically restructure their operations to avoid being left behind. Cost leadership is also relevant in other markets—automobiles (with the introduction of autobytel.com, Microsoft's carpoint.msn.com, and autoweb.com), electronic goods (gigabuys.com), toys (etoys.com), and others. The two major on-line travel agencies (Travelocity and Preview Travel) have recently merged to further consolidate their operations and reduce the cost of on-line bookings. Web-supported, low-cost airlines are springing up in Europe (easyjet.com). Companies not pursuing cost-based advantages through the Web will be left behind in the massive sea change under way.

Enhancing Services. The dot-com operations allow for enhanced services. We have come a long way since Federal Express Corp. (FedEx) introduced us to the possibilities of tracking packages over the Net. Today, customers expect logistics companies to make their inventory chain visible. Placing content on Web sites is a powerful differentiator: customers can now get critical information at their convenience. Indeed, customers expect timely updates (delivery schedules, product updates, account information), product enhancements (patches for software glitches), rapid resolution of problems not found in the FAQ list (through e-mail and remote-monitoring capabilities), as well as personalized interactions through customized navigation paths on company Web sites (see, for instance, Dell, GM, and Toyota).

American Airlines' new AAlert e-mail service tells specific customers when their chosen destinations or departures are featured in special deals. Other airlines are scrambling to provide similar service features. Cellular phone customers can modify, adapt, and upgrade ringing tones (nokia.com), and consumers can see breaking news footage at their own convenience (cnn.com, bbc.co.uk).[4] Companies will further enhance personalized service as more and more devices are connected to the Net.[5] Next-generation home appliances such as refrigerators, washing machines, and microwave ovens will be connected to the Net as homes become wired and smarter.[6]

Create New Business Models

The power of the Web lies in the creation of new business models. It has become fashionable to talk of "new business models" when discussing the Net—this phrase has emerged as a catchall way to highlight the impact of the dot-com operations. We do need to be more precise: new business models are those that "offer, on a sustained basis, an order-of-magnitude increase in value propositions to the customers compared to companies with traditional business models." In doing so, these new models disturb the status quo and create new rules of business. Traditional companies cannot easily match the value propositions offered by these new business models without substantially altering their margin structures. They also find it difficult to go beyond incrementally refining the current rules to create radically different rules. However, an important part of the strategic thinking for every company is to develop scenarios of new business models—even though they might challenge the status quo and cannibalize current revenue and margin streams.

Look at the music marketplace: the big four—Universal, BMG, Warner EMI, and Sony—now control about 80 percent of industry sales, and on-line distribution accounts for about 1 percent of sales, representing the sale of CDs by mail order. But the availability and increased acceptance of music players that use the mp3 format (mp3.com) are likely to create major disruptions in the economic landscape. As more Internet sites (Amazon recently entered the fray) support the downloading of music onto mp3-compatible devices (see, for example, the Rio player, at rio.com), every major record label needs to rethink its business models. Featuring more than twenty-five thousand performers affiliated with over a hundred independent labels, mp3.com enjoys a market capitalization of over $2 billion and has been legitimized by Sony's decision to make a version of its popular Walkman that will play music in the mp3 format. The major labels are already responding with their own aggressive plans, which include abandoning traditional music formats. It is a far cry from listening to vinyl records on turntables!

The music marketplace is not an exception. The retail financial services industry is changing with multiple players from historically disparate segments jockeying to create new business models. Priceline.com is revolutionizing travel and related services by letting customers specify their desired prices and serving as a mechanism for competing companies to bid for customer requirements. It started with airline tickets and has since expanded to cover hotel rooms, home financing, and new car purchases and leases.

Their model of "buyer-driven commerce" is supported by a string of patents and could prove to be a powerful new business model. Amazon is more than an electronic bookseller. New market mechanisms that incorporate auctions (see, for example, freemarkets.com) are beginning to challenge industrial companies. New electronic aggregators are also emerging in many areas such as steel (e-steel.com) to reduce inefficiency and redistribute value. Indeed, one is hard-pressed to think of markets that may be unaffected by the Net. We clearly have not reached a steady state, and it is unclear whether we ever will.

Experiment with Scenarios

So what should companies do? We need to abandon calendar-driven models of strategy perfected under predictable conditions of the Industrial Age. We should embrace the philosophy of experimentation, since the shape of the future business models is not obvious. The strategic challenge is to spearhead experiments[7] to assess probable future states and migrate operations to the desired state. Establishing the vision and rationale for these experiments—including the mandate to proactively cannibalize current business models—is a critical hallmark of leadership for the dot-com world.

Coordinated experimentation is required to develop the building blocks for success in the dot-com arena. Leading consumer-product companies are now assessing the strength of brand equity and brand pull in the Web world. Having established a credible brand franchise in the physical space, The Gap is now experimenting with gaponline.com. But will it translate well on the Web? Somewhat unconnected with Procter & Gamble's major brand names, the company has unleashed a new unit to create custom-designed cosmetics (reflect.com) along the lines of Dell's build-to-order approach. Nike—a brand leadership phenomenon of the late twentieth century—is trying to create consumer pull through custom-designed shoes (www.nike.com/id) and through its strategic alliance with fogdog.com—an on-line sports gear retailer. Unilever, Kraft Foods,

P&G, and other global consumer-products companies are also seeking to port their operations to the Net.

Experimentation is not limited to rethinking brand equity. Look at retailing—a market that has seen major disruptions caused by Internet versions of category killers. Current leaders in the traditional marketplace are experimenting with ways to defend their market positions while adapting their strategies for the Web (see, for instance, toysrus.com, walmart.com, nordstrom.com, and sears.com.) Even top-line niche players like Tiffany's and Harrods are experimenting to identify the best possible ways to migrate their operations to the dot-com world without diluting their brand image.

Publishing is much the same—likely to be significantly reshaped by the Net, even though dominant new business models with assured profitability have yet to emerge. Today we have the dot-com add-ons to paper-based publications (see, for example, fortune.com, businessweek.com, ft.com). Experiments to assess the likelihood of revenue generation from on-line publication (such as the *Wall Street Journal* interactive edition, wsj.com) are under way with no conclusive results; yet the publishing industry cannot afford to neglect the Net. These experiments require more than merely porting their print content to the Web; they involve rethinking the distribution of content as well as restructuring relationships to integrate content from multiple sources.

In television and broadcasting, NBC is leading the way beyond conventional broadcasting and has already created a portfolio of experiments. Witness msnbc.com, its partnership with Microsoft to combine cable and the Internet. It has also created nbc.launch.com to focus on music, and has recently combined all its activities under NBC Internet, to coordinate its Web experiments. CNN.com is partnering with WebMD to become a health-information portal for its customers (www.cnn.com/health). Indeed, all leading television networks are experimenting with different ways to incorporate the Web as part of their strategy.

Selective strategic experimentation is the sine qua non of strategy formation[8] for the dot-com world. However, a major danger is that these experiments could be seen as stand-alone tangential projects decoupled from the mainstream operations. It is important that they be seen as building blocks for migrating and transforming the corporation to the dot-com world. Strategic experiments—when properly conceived and executed—can reveal powerful new ways to succeed in the dot-com world, where history offers little guidance.

The bottom line. A business strategy that fails to recognize the Net is destined to fail. Past success is no guarantee of future success, and calendar-driven strategic planning is giving way to strategic experimentation and rapid adaptation. The challenge is to pursue experiments that not only augment current business models but also create new business models and rules of competition.

HOW TO GOVERN THE DOT-COM BUSINESS?

The challenge of how best to govern the dot-com operations is daunting. Managers must attract and retain key management talent; they are intrigued by the differential market valuation of dot-com operations and are struggling with the requirement to give adequate management time and attention to the dot-com strategy and operations. At the same time, they find that the dot-com operations differ from their traditional operations and find it difficult to reconcile them.

Two major categories of decision influence the governance mode: operational decisions (production, sourcing, logistics, marketing, and human resources) and financial decisions (investment logic, funding sources, and performance criteria). The governance of dot-com business is best seen as a trade-off between these two categories: how firms differentiate and integrate operational and financial decisions. The basic governance choices can be arrayed along the diagonal as a continuum from subsidiary (spin-off) at one end and seamless (transparent) at the other end. (See Figure 4.3.)

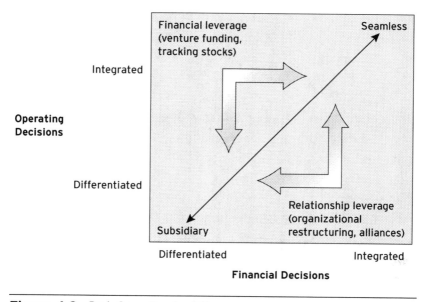

Figure 4.3. Dot-Com Trade-Offs.

Decoupling Your Dot-Com Operations and Finances

When faced with the fast-paced changes unleashed by the Net, managers may benefit from differentiating the operations and decoupling the financial arrangements. Take the case of nordstrom.com—the newly created subsidiary of Nordstrom formed to accelerate the growth of its Internet and catalog direct sales but with minority funding from Benchmark Capital. The new subsidiary— Nordstromshoes.com—is aimed at selling leading brands of shoes. The funding from the venture capital community allowed the subsidiary to invest in site development and to create the appropriate software as well as a distinct advertising campaign—without being handicapped by the requirements of using only internally generated resources. In a related vein, walmart.com is being contemplated as a separate company with funding from Accel Partners.[9]

This governance mode makes sense under the following conditions: (1) the company is willing to explore new business models apart from the constraints of current operations; (2) the subsidiary or spin-off can be created without being constrained by current technology and legacy operations; and (3) the company bestows the subsidiary with the freedom to form alliances, raise capital, and attract new talent.

Morphing Old Practices into New Ones

Now let us look at the other end of the continuum—where operational and financial decisions of the dot-com operations are intermingled with the traditional business domain. In some cases, differentiation of the dot-com operations may be inappropriate, because it could dilute the level of management attention needed to ensure success. The dot-com operations are seamlessly integrated as the traditional company morphs to become the dot-com company. Take a look at Encyclopedia Britannica (eb.com): it was an undisputed leader in its category, experimented with CD-ROM, and has finally evolved into a dot-com operation by making its content available free on the Net.

Cisco is a dot-com company whose operations cannot be segregated into dot-com and non-dot-com components. As CEO John Chambers observed: "In 1998, Cisco is the best example of a company using the Internet technology to gain a sustainable competitive advantage with over 70 percent of customer inquiries handled on-line and 64 percent of orders placed via the Web."[10] Cisco may be leading the pack, but it is by no means alone. Intel is a dot-com company with more than 40 percent of sales conducted through the Net. As Intel Chairman Andy Grove remarked: "In January 1998, the company had exactly zero customers on-line. Phones, faxes, and overnight parcel carriers served as the conduits for placing orders. By June 1999, over 560 companies in forty-six countries were using Intel's Web-based order-management system to place orders, track deliveries, post inquiries, and get product and pricing updates. Today, this system produces nearly $1 billion in sales *per month*."[11]

This *seamless* governance mode makes sense under the following conditions:

1. There is no meaningful way to separate digital and physical operations without creating confusion in the minds of customers.
2. Senior management is committed to embracing the opportunities and challenges of the Net to redefine the value proposition as well as aggressively react to competitive moves.
3. The entire organization can be mobilized to migrate to the dot-com world (as Egghead Software did when it abandoned its physical presence in the retail software market to migrate to the digital world with egghead.com).

Finding Your Place on the Governance Continuum

Different companies rightfully choose different governance models depending on their views of the centrality of the dot-com operations. Lloyds TSB, the United Kingdom's largest bank, has decided to keep its dot-com operations integrated—for the moment—but with a different brand identity. In contrast, Bank One, a leading U.S. retail bank, with its Wingspan bank and Halifax with its Greenfield.co.uk established their dot-com operations as separate subsidiaries. Governing in the dot-com world depends on a dynamic interplay between the two decisions on this continuum. It can be understood through two transition paths: one is to leverage financial instruments and the discipline of financial markets, whereas the other is to restructure relationships—both internally and with alliances and partnerships.

The *financial leverage transition path* allows companies to exploit two popular mechanisms: (1) issuing separate stock through an initial public offering (IPO) of the dot-com operations and (2) infusion of external venture capital funds. Dixon's in the United Kingdom floated 20 percent of its Freeserve Internet Service Provider (ISP) operations as a separate stock (ticker: FREE), which had, at its peak, a market capitalization of about $8 billion. Prudential, the U.K. life insurance company, is in the initial stages of floating its Internet-only banking operations. Playboy Entertainment plans to tap the financial market for its dot-com operations. Microsoft, the market capitalization leader, has spun off its Expedia Internet travel business as a separate company (ticker: EXPE). In the words of Brad Chase, senior vice president of Microsoft's consumer and commerce group, the IPO would allow the business "to use its resources to partner with other people, to buy other Web sites, and grow its vertical marketplace."[12] NBC Internet is a separate trading stock (ticker: NBCI) with a market capitalization of more than $4 billion. These initiatives reflect an important strategic consideration: the financial markets bring external discipline to governance that is critical under fast-changing conditions.[13]

An alternative to the use of tracking stocks is to pursue private placement through venture capitalists. Venture capitalists such as Kleiner Perkins and Benchmark Capital are aggressively working with traditional companies that are developing dot-com operations; their aim is to unleash hidden value in those assets that may not have been properly governed—and, hence, are inadequately valued. This is an interim position before taking the dot-com operations public. Indeed, the question of whether to infuse external venture capital to spearhead the dot-com operations is a key strategic issue facing every company today.

The relationship leverage transition path focuses on organizational arrangements to bring the governance issue into sharper focus. When General Motors created a separate division, e-GM, it signaled a major commitment to the Internet as a future business platform. This unit is responsible for coordinating all the dot-com initiatives, including its OnStar initiative, to establish the individual car, itself, as a portal. It is testing the shape and scope of this e-franchise and the role of retailers in the revamped value chain of the dot-com world. GM's Vauxhall division in the United Kingdom, a major initiative of e-GM, is perhaps the first automotive company to announce a set of six models for sale only on the Web.

To consolidate its Internet initiatives, Kraft Foods has created a separate organizational unit, which is one step short of a subsidiary, because Kraft does not radically separate the financial decisions. It provides an organizational context to question possible areas of cannibalization, as well as to coordinate multiple experiments taking place in the dot-com arena. Raising the organizational level of attention to the dot-com operations is an essential step in crafting a coherent strategy, because multiple conflicting decisions must be coordinated across traditional and dot-com spaces.

The transition to the dot-com world is not limited to internal restructuring, but also involves alliances and partnerships. Ford Motor Corporation is exploring the potential of the Internet in its marketing activities in partnership with Microsoft. Sotheby's is jump-starting its dot-com operations by forming an alliance with Amazon.com to expand its auctions business beyond its traditional high-end collectibles (see sothebys.amazon.com).

Clearly, these two transition paths are complementary ways to position along the governance continuum; this is not a static decision, since a mode of governance is only appropriate for a given context, and the context is fast-changing in the Internet world. Recognizing the complementary roles of both financial and organizational instruments in this dot-com world is key. We may see Disney spinning off its Buena Vista subsidiary, we may see the Ford-Microsoft relationship evolve into a separate business primed for IPO, and we may see walmart.com as a separate stock. Clearly, the governance of the dot-com operations for every corporation is a critical management issue that could either unleash or constrain the hidden value of core assets in this time of profound transformation.

The bottom line. More than understanding the potential challenges and opportunities posed by the Net, the biggest stumbling block for an effective strategy will be lack of adequate attention to the governance issue. In Internet time, mistimed and ill-prepared strategic moves can be costly. Pursue financial and relational leverage paths to continually fine-tune the governance position along the continuum between subsidiary (spin-off) and seamless (transparent) modes.

HOW DO YOU ALLOCATE RESOURCES FOR THE DOT-COM BUSINESS?

Closely related to governance is the allocation of resources: how best to assemble and deploy the key resources for succeeding in the dot-com world. One manager in a major corporation remarked that ". . . the dot-com operations is a war for talent; it is a war for three types of resources—human, technological, and financial." It is a war because traditional companies need these critical resources to migrate their operations to the Net, and new entrants seeking to establish their superiority in the new world also need them. The new Internet start-ups are attracting young talent away from established industries—witness the profile of recent graduating classes in top universities joining Silicon Valley start-ups, and look at the roster of corporate big names joining Internet start-ups. Start-ups enjoy an edge over traditional companies. They are leveraging their newly established wealth to acquire resources that the traditional companies find difficult to match.

Four different but interlinked approaches are required for assembling and deploying the required resources. (See Figure 4.4.)

Placing Strategic Bets

Here the company commits internal resources to differentiate its dot-com operations from those of competitors. These resources may be financial, technological, or human. Bank One has publicly indicated that its growth in traditional areas will be marginal and has redirected its resources to dominating the on-line world (bancone.com). Electrolux is betting that it can control the kitchen network in the era of networked kitchens. John Deere is pursuing precision farming so that operators who are using tractors connected to the network receive real-time guidance on services. Nike is betting on selling customized shoes through the Net, and Maytag wants to establish superiority in Net-enabled vending machines. The leaders in the traditional world, such as GE, NBC, CNN, Pearson, Wal-

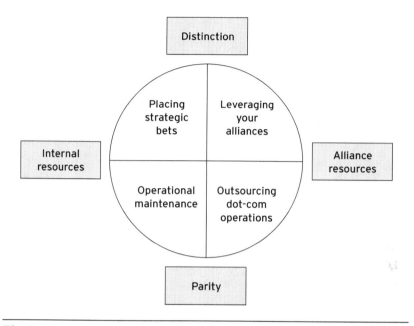

Figure 4.4. Interlinked Approaches to Deploy Dot-Com Resources.

Mart, SKF, Citicorp, and Kraft Foods, are making significant strategic bets in dot-com experiments.

From a human resource point of view, the real challenge is to stem the impending brain drain away from the traditional established companies toward the dot-com start-ups. A former Wal-Mart senior officer now runs Amazon.com's logistics. George Shaheen of Andersen Consulting now runs WebVan. Companies such as GE, IBM, and British Telecom have lost senior managers to Web start-ups. What are the key human resources required to run the dot-com operations, and what changes in incentives are required to make this happen? Articulating these strategic bets is absolutely critical.

Strategic bets should be placed on a set of probable opportunities instead of predictable ones. When investments in the dot-com world are viewed as real options, companies can potentially invest in a broader range of opportunities than otherwise.[14] Instead of fully funding a smaller set of relatively predictable projects, the aim should be to acquire a set of options with rights to acquire and leverage certain capabilities, should they prove successful.

Learning How to Leverage Your Alliances

Differentiated capabilities can be created through alliances and partnerships. The dot-com operations are by definition networked and call for assembling complementary strategic capabilities through relationships. Pearson, the United Kingdom's media giant, is forming a strategic relationship with AOL, and its importance is signaled by the fact that Pearson's CEO now sits on the AOL board. Yahoo!'s success is based on its portfolio of alliances. Microsoft is a master at exploring multiple avenues for acquiring resources—through mechanisms such as equity investments, cross-licensing, joint development, and ventures. More than ever before, it is the pattern of strategic alliances and relationships that indicates strategic strengths in the dot-com world. These alliances are not limited to the players in the physical world linking up with dot-com players. Even first-generation dot-com companies such as Amazon, Priceline, and eBay are steadily evolving and refining their alliance structures to redefine their business models. Amazon's equity investment in drugstore.com is another case in point. A new breed of firms like Viant (viant.com) actively collaborates to build digital businesses for companies such as American Express, BankBoston, Compaq, Radio Shack, and Kinko's.

These alliances will reflect more joint profit sharing rather than fee-for-service. For instance, Sony is working with EDS to create, design, and build the Metreon entertainment center Web site (metreon.com), one of Sony's dot-com initiatives, and EDS will receive a share of the revenues. We will see more alliances—with risk-reward sharing—for accessing and deploying resources in the dot-com world. Consulting companies that are building digital businesses will move away from fee-for-service toward equities and risk-reward sharing. This trend will continue at a faster pace.

The dot-com operations are network-centric. Hence, they call for strategic approaches that are not anchored on resources inside the firm but fundamentally involve resources acquired and leveraged in a network of relationships. They call for strategies to be seen as a "portfolio of capabilities that are acquired and deployed through a portfolio of relationships." This is a far cry from strategy seen as primarily resource deployments inside the firm. Positioning and navigating in a complex network of resources is a hallmark of differentiation for companies like Amazon, Yahoo!, AOL, and Microsoft.

Outsourcing Dot-Com Operations and Maintaining Operational Parity

These are areas of the dot-com operations in which activities like Web hosting, back-end processing, and order fulfillment can be conducted outside the firm. More than in the traditional world, dot-com operations (by virtue of their networked infrastructure) allow for complementary players to be easily linked. Companies increasingly find it easier to rely on standard services from established players like IBM, HP (Hewlett-Packard), Oracle, Microsoft, EDS, and AT&T so that they can build their operations on a robust and stable platform. Given the rate of change in technology and the impressive cost-performance shifts, it is more important to rely on best-in-class providers rather than create these operations inside.

Whether or not you outsource, your IT support operations must achieve competitive parity. Resources should be allocated on the basis of predictable models and supported by techniques such as activity-based costing. The aim is to ruthlessly achieve the lowest operating costs for the required level of functionality, as well as to evaluate possible risks and rewards of outsourcing.

The bottom line. Effective strategies for the dot-com world are based on the pattern and timing of resource deployment. The overall logic of resource allocation for the dot-com is different from the predictable models of the physical world. Assemble resources from multiple sources and manage them on a dynamic basis.

WHAT'S THE OPERATING INFRASTRUCTURE OF YOUR DOT-COM BUSINESS?

The next major requirement is to design the operating infrastructure. It is tempting to describe its technical characteristics by saying that we are wired or we are net-enabled or we are digitized. More important, we need to understand the characteristics of the infrastructure that provide value for customers—the features that draw customers to the dot-com world and encourage them to continue to use the Net as a primary way of using products and services.

The first wave of the Internet was about the number of computers connected to the Net—which ushered in the network economy.[15] The second wave is about relationships and business models that leverage the key characteristics of the network economy.[16] These business models straddle the traditional and dot-com spaces for delivering superior customer value propositions. Hence, the infrastructure could either support the strategy or fail. It is useful to look at the operating infrastructure as four building blocks that reflect an integrated physical-digital platform. (See Figure 4.5.)

Attaining Superior Functionality

Do customers find their on-line experience supported by the appropriate functionality? Better quality images, audio clips, and 3-D rendering have enhanced the power of the Web to be realistic. (See Web sites using the functionality offered by Real Networks—realnetworks.com—or Macromedia—macromedia.com.) Take, for instance, the sale of a Gulfstream corporate jet for about $23 million: Elite Aviation bought a jet from gulfstreampreowned.com after a virtual inspection using 360-degree interactive video technology from Interactive Pictures Corporation (ipix.com).

As technology evolves, we will see far greater functionality—especially as wireless applications protocols (WAPs) become commonplace and wireless devices like cellular telephones and personal digital assistants (PDAs) are connected to the Net. United Parcel Service tracking is now possible on a Palm VII. The music industry will

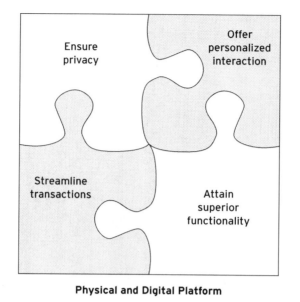

Physical and Digital Platform

Figure 4.5. Putting Together a Dot-Com Operating Infrastructure.

be reshaped by emusic.com, mp3.com, and others. Television will be altered when new initiatives such as replayTV, which records specified shows on a hard disk, are more widely adopted. Changing functionality will make dot-com operations appealing to a broad range of companies and customers.

Offering Personalized Interactions

Can we make each customer feel unique on the Net? The appeal of the Net lies in its personalization potential. Customers want to be connected to other customers (C2C interactions) and appreciate personal business-to-customer (B2C) linkages. We see this in popular sites such as My Yahoo!, My Schwab, and My Dell. The challenge is to encourage each visitor to establish a Web-based personal identity without invading privacy. Amazon.com shot into prominence early with its personalized recommendations. Now many consumer sites incorporate personalization of some kind.

Personalization will become increasingly important as more devices connect to the Net: think about automobiles and cellular phones connected to the Net (D2D interactions). Significant opportunities and challenges await those who design operating infrastructures that support virtual extensions of the customer.

Streamlining Transactions

The power of the infrastructure lies in its simplicity and efficiency. Increasingly, the winners will be differentiated by their ability to execute streamlined transactions: Amazon pioneered and patented one-click settings—an important differentiator in its bid to establish supremacy. A single, secure way for customers to sign in to multiple Internet sites using one member name and password, Microsoft Passport (passport.com) streamlines processes and delivers personalized value. SAP is creating many modules to port business processes to the Web (mySAP.com).

Consider FedEx, which gave customers immediate access to transactions and delivery status. Dell took it one step further and allowed its customers to see the status of their custom-built machine at every stage of the cycle. Now car manufacturers want to adopt similar functionality to streamline operations. Indeed, for B2B activities, streamlined transactions and cross-sharing of information become central as the firms strive for radical improvements in efficiency. The weaknesses in legacy operations will be exposed in this arena. For instance, data updates should be on a near-continuous basis—especially when selling time-sensitive perishables like airline or concert tickets. Similarly, Internet-only banks, such as wingspan.com, must substantiate their claims of making sixty-second mortgage decisions without increasing the banks' financial exposure. Product configurators for personal computers and cars, for example, must be linked to the production-planning system so that firms can accurately provide delivery dates and prices.

Streamlined operations require a reliable infrastructure. Commerce in the last century has been facilitated by the increased reliability of telephone and telecommunications (think about the reliability of telephones and ATMs) and logistics (FedEx, UPS, and rail carriers have contributed to modern supply chains). Reliability plays a key role in enhancing customer confidence: when sites like E*Trade and Schwab—which account for an increasing share of stock market trading—are off-line, they weaken not only their customers' confidence but also cast doubt on the dot-com movement.[17] As more devices connect to the Net and as more functionality is processed through the Net, reliability will emerge as a major catalyst for Net-based business and a key differentiator for individual companies. (See Table 4.1.)

Ensuring Privacy

Will my transactions be secure? Will my information be safeguarded? The idea behind "pragmatic privacy" is to convince customers that their privacy will be safeguarded and personal information used only for the purpose of delivering superior value to them.

Privacy emerges as a major inhibitor because customers still are not comfortable with electronic transactions. Credit-card companies have played an important role in offering the same level of protection on the Web as in the physical space, and the browser software companies (Microsoft, Netscape) have incorporated critical safety features into their latest software. Demonstrating the power of various encryption protocols in ways that customers understand will go a long way, but security is more about consumer perception than technical features or protocols per se. Companies like GE are embracing leading security encryption protocols—for example, the RSA Keon AdvancePublic Key Infrastructure software for digital certification (rsasecurity.com). Others are adopting VeriSign (verisign.com) or digital original certificates, such as *e*Original, which are created for various applications (eoriginal.com).

Privacy is closely related to security. Customers become concerned about privacy[18] on the Net, due in part to the proliferation of software cookies that help Web sites learn about visitors such as DoubleClick (doubleclick.com) and Firefly Passport (firefly.net). These companies have gone out of their way to make customers feel

Table 4.1. Thinking Like a Dot-Com: How a Consumer Products Company Can Develop Its Web Strategy. ▶

Operational Areas	Build on Current Strategies by . . .	Experiment with Potential Strategies by . . .	Adopt These Strategies Now
Business-to-Consumer (B2C) Operation	• Using the Web as an auxiliary channel to deliver products and services. • Creating consistency across the different channels.	• Migrating to Web-based customization. Examples: Dell Premier Pages or use of e-mail to offer special prices.	• Adapt customer-specified pricing models to change the rules. Example: priceline.com. • Aggressively shift to a build-to-order model.
Business-to-Business (B2B) Operation	• Using the Net to streamline supply, inventory, and procurement—thereby increasing working capital.	• Evaluating whether auctions or other new market mechanisms are appropriate. • Exploring cooperative agreements to reduce cost of inputs.	• Pursue joint development and new product creations through Web-based links with suppliers and business partners.
Consumer-to-Consumer (C2C) Operation	• Orchestrating customer communities to learn which product features are valued the most and collect customer complaints.	• Experimenting with customer communities to test new product ideas. • Including customers in product development.	• Co-opt customer communities to create and reposition brands. • Proactively leverage customer advocacy to enhance and market brands.

- ... But Keep in Mind the Implications and Challenges of Your Actions

- You must govern augmentation efforts using traditional organizational structures that straddle the physical and digital operating infrastructure.

- You must allocate financial, technological, and human resources internally.

- You must ensure that the IT infrastructure is consistent across physical and digital domains.

- Including customers in product development.

- You must manage experiments through a portfolio of alliances and relationships with business partners.

- You must plan on hiring additional managers to lead experiments.

- You must reward those managers whose experiments successfully refine and redefine the rules of competition.

- Consider spin-offs and subsidiaries if the dot-com business differs from traditional operations.

- Convince corporate leaders that cannibalizing current products may be necessary.

- Explore new avenues of financing for spin-offs and subsidiaries.

- Recognize the importance of new business models and the competitive value of creating new rules.

comfortable about their safeguards to privacy. But the real responsibility lies with the companies that use these software cookies. Sites
like GM OnStar (onstar.com) or GE (ge.com) explicitly state how
they plan to deal with privacy issues, and some audit firms are also
beginning to offer services as trusted third-party guarantors of how
companies safeguard customer data. Being forthright with customers
about privacy will go a long way in enhancing use of the Net.

The bottom line. Digital infrastructure should be designed and
deployed to enhance customer value propositions. Design the infrastructure so that dot-com operations make it easier for customers
to do business without sacrificing customer trust about reliability,
security, and privacy. Straddle physical and digital spaces with relevant linkages to partners and alliances to offer a seamless and effective way for conducting the business.

IS YOUR MANAGEMENT TEAM ALIGNED FOR THE DOT-COM AGENDA?

Who leads the corporation to the dot-com world? Is this an opportunity for the senior IT manager to earn the right to become a member of top management? Or is it the marketing manager who
articulates how the customer value propositions can be redefined?
What roles should the CEO and COO play? Articulating the roles
of key members of the management team is central in shaping the
strategy of the dot-com operations.

Many companies treat their dot-com operations as a project:
certain boards of directors feel relatively comfortable delegating
responsibility for carrying out the dot-com "project." Some see this
as an extension of technology-led business initiatives. The words of
a frustrated manager capture it best: "The board seems to think that
this is like implementing SAP—fund it, delegate it, and ensure that
we do not hear about it until it is implemented. This is far different
from SAP; we are not just trying to automate and integrate our busi-

ness processes in a standardized way; we are trying to create new value propositions for customers . . . and we can't manage it like another project—decoupled from serious discussions and fundamental choices and commitment from the board."

The dot-com operations require a pattern of leadership alignment that differs greatly from other business transformation activities. Even business reengineering efforts billed as major transformational projects pale in comparison to the tasks and challenges pertaining to the dot-com operations. This is because most reengineering projects—despite claims to the contrary—focus on rectifying weaknesses in the current business models. Very few companies have truly created or redefined their business for the wired, digital world. In contrast, the dot-com world is about value creation. It involves strategic challenges of business creation; important governance issues of organizational structure; and new avenues of financing, changes in operating infrastructure, external relationships, and patterns of resource deployments.

I can't emphasize enough the importance of senior management alignment in mobilizing the organization to recognize and respond to the dot-com world. Ask each key member of your management team to identify who plays the leadership and supporting roles for the four preceding questions. Such an exercise may help the managers recognize and accept that mobilizing the organization is a team issue and that everyone plays complementary roles. Without overly stereotyping management roles, such a table—only an illustrative approach shown here—can be helpful in orchestrating a constructive dialog within the management team. (See Table 4.2.)

If the management team is not in sync, it is easy for the dot-com agenda to be hijacked by one or two members reflecting a partisan, parochial perspective. Every company needs a champion to get started, but it needs more than one champion to succeed. It is encouraging to see many leading companies already embracing the dot-com world. But it is more than Web sites; more than promises to consumers. It is more than merely grafting the Web on as part of

Table 4.2. Complementary Management Roles of a Dot-Com Operation Might Look Like This.

Management Role	Strategic Rationale	Governance Logic	Resource Allocation	Operating Infrastructure
Chief executive officer	Leadership role	Leadership role	Supporting role	Supporting role
Chief operating officer	Supporting role	Supporting role	Leadership role	Leadership role
Chief information officer	Leadership role	Supporting role	Supporting role	Leadership role
Chief financial officer	Supporting role	Leadership role	Leadership role	Supporting role
Chief marketing officer	Leadership role	Supporting role	Supporting role	Leadership role
Chief human resource officer	Supporting role	Leadership role	Leadership role	Supporting role

business strategy; more than paying lip service to the projects that deal with electronic commerce. It is a serious challenge with profound opportunities and threats to the status quo.

SUCCEEDING IN THE DOT-COM WORLD

New companies with an Internet focus have grabbed the headlines. Employees and stockholders of these start-ups have reaped the benefits of new wealth. At the same time, stalwarts like Jack Welch of GE, Jack Smith of GM, and Harvey Golub of American Express have unleashed creative energies within their corporations to develop dot-com visions.[19] Some have recognized the value of the Net for B2B transactions, whereas others have focused on B2C transactions. And as new devices emerge and become part of the critical backbone for dot-com operations, every company will need to develop a strategy for the dot-com world. Ultimately, business strategy will be dot-com strategy.

Andy Grove wrote a book titled *Only the Paranoid Survive*.[20] He wrote it before the onslaught of the Net. But his thesis is apt for anyone thinking about dot-com business. We are in the midst of major shifts: traditional logic, so fundamental to the industrial revolution, is challenged every day by the possibilities of the dot-com world. Well-understood sources of value creation through tangible, physical assets are being replaced by newfound sources through digital assets and networks of relationships. Every market—from agriculture to automobiles to financial services, entertainment, and health care—is affected by interactive technology. New entrants are crafting powerful new business models and rewriting the rules of competition. Established companies urgently need to embrace the dot-com agenda; failing this, they will be left behind. They need to blend their traditional and dot-com operations while confronting the challenge of brain drain as their top talent jumps ship for other dot-com operations. The game is far from over, and we will see powerful transformations as companies embrace the Net and craft innovative strategies that successfully blend physical and digital infrastructures. It's up to managers to take the necessary actions to align their visions to the dot-com world.

While it is too early to declare the leading corporations of the Industrial Age to be the dinosaurs of the digital era, clearly they face daunting challenges.

NOTES

1. For example, see M. Cusumano and D. Yoffie, *Competing on Internet Time: Lessons from Netscape and Its Battle with Microsoft* (New York: Free Press, 1998).
2. M. Porter, *Competitive Strategy* (New York: Free Press, 1980).
3. M. Dell, *Direct from Dell* (New York: Harper Business, 1999).
4. Personalization and dynamic customization are important avenues for redefined customer interactions in the post-industrial world. See N. Venkatraman and J. C. Henderson, "Real Strategies for Virtual Organizing," *Sloan Management Review,* Fall 1998, *40,* 33–48. See

also D. Peppers and M. Rogers, *Enterprise One to One: Tools for Competing in the Interactive Age* (New York: Currency Doubleday, 1997).

5. The latest version of Palm Computing's Palm VII has infrared wireless capability to access the Net, and a variety of services and accessories will support this platform.

6. For a broad overview, see N. Negroponte, *Being Digital* (New York: Knopf, 1995). For up-to-date views, see nicholas.www.media.mit.edu/people/nicholas/. See also N. Gershenfeld, *When Things Start to Think* (New York: Henry Holt, 1999); and also see Gershenfeld's Web site www.media.mit.edu/ttt.

7. For an elaboration of this view, see G. Hamel and J. Sampler, "The E-Corporation," *Fortune*, December 7, 1998, pp. 80–92; and G. Hamel, "Bringing the Silicon Valley Inside," *Harvard Business Review*, September-October 1999, 77, 70–84.

8. For a good general discussion of the role of experimentation, see several articles in the fortieth anniversary issue of *Sloan Management Review*. In particular, see C. C. Markides, "A Dynamic View of Strategy," *Sloan Management Review*, Spring 1999, 40, 55–63; E. D. Beinhocker, "Robust Adaptive Strategies," *Sloan Management Review*, Spring 1999, 40, 95–106; and P. J. Williamson, "Strategy as Options on the Future," *Sloan Management Review*, Spring 1999, 40, 117–126.

9. Miguel Helft, "Wal-Mart Teams Up with Accel," *Industry Standard*, January 6, 2000, www.thestandard.com/article/display/0,1151,8649,00.html. See also www.accel.com/news.

10. J. T. Chambers, "The New Economy Is the Internet Economy," white paper (San Jose, California: Cisco Systems, 1998); and see http://www.cisco.com/warp/public/750/johnchambers/internet_economy/.

11. See www.intel.com for speeches by Andy Grove and other Intel senior managers.

12. Alex Lash, "A New Strategy for MSN. Again," *Industry Standard*, September 27, 1999, www.thestandard.com/article/display/0,1151,6571,00.html.

13. For a detailed discussion on the role of financial markets in disciplining decisions, see M. Amram and N. Kulatilaka, "Disciplined Decisions: Aligning Strategy with Financial Markets," *Harvard Business Review*, January-February 1999, 77, 95–104. See also M. Amram

and N. Kulatilaka, *Real Options: Managing Strategic Investments in an Uncertain World* (Boston: Harvard Business School Press, 1999).

14. Real options have emerged as a powerful approach for dealing with resource allocations under uncertainty. See N. Kulatilaka and N. Venkatraman, *Real Options in the Digital Economy* (Financial Times Mastering Management Series, September 1999); also see www.real-options.com; K. Leslie and M. Michaels, "The Real Power of Real Options," *McKinsey Quarterly*, 1997, *3*, 4–22; and www.mckinseyquarterly.com.

15. See, for example, Kevin Kelly's *Wired* magazine columns; and K. Kelly, *New Rules for New Economy* (New York: Viking Books, 1998). For discussions on the information economy, see C. Shapiro and H. Varian, *Information Rules* (Boston: Harvard Business School Press, 1999).

16. New business magazines, such as *Business 2.0* (www.business2.com), deal with the creation of business models for the new economy. See also *Wired* (www.wired.com); and *Fast Company* (www.fastcompany.com).

17. This is evident in the volatility of the stocks of those dot-com companies whose sites have experienced outages.

18. See, for example, A. Cavoukian and D. Tapscott, *Who Knows: Safeguarding Your Privacy in a Networked World* (New York: McGraw-Hill, 1997).

19. See, for example, E. Brown, "Big Business Meets the e-World," *Fortune*, November 8, 1999, *140*, 88–98. For articles dealing with how established companies are striving to respond to the dot-com agenda, also visit *Fortune* (www.fortune.com) and the *Economist* (www.economist.com).

20. A. S. Grove, *Only the Paranoid Survive: How to Exploit the Crisis Points That Challenge Every Company* (New York: Random, 1996).

CHAPTER FIVE

Pathways to E-Business Leadership: Getting from Bricks to Clicks

LESLIE P. WILLCOCKS
ROBERT PLANT

As established business-to-consumer (B2C) companies set out to take advantage of the Internet, many have found the task far more difficult and potentially destabilizing than they had anticipated. No mere business tool, the Internet goes to the heart of the corporation, challenging its existing business models and customer relationships.[1]

The challenges force traditional companies to address some fundamental questions, including, What do the Internet and its associated technologies mean for our business, our competitive strategy, and our information-systems strategy? Which former imperatives need to be considered if we are to build a sustainable Internet business? How do we leverage the speed, access, connectivity, and economy created by Web technologies to extend our business vision? And how do we organize in order to execute our business-Internet strategy?

The answers to those questions largely determine the success of a company's Internet initiative. To investigate how organizations can effectively deal with the challenges, we examined fifty-eight major B2C corporations from three continents and a wide range of industries. (See box, Research Methodology.) We found fifteen "leaders," twenty-five "laggards," and eighteen "medium-performing" organizations. Leaders shared generic characteristics that distinguished them from other companies. (See box, Characteristics of B2C E-Business Leaders.) However, they also followed distinctive routes. Although they may have started with strategy based upon the idea of technology leadership, they migrated through interim stages to a market strategy. Only then were they capable of yielding sustainable, consistent e-business profits. Leaders were the fastest and most focused at moving from an "e" that stands for electronic to an "e" that represents earnings.

MAPPING THE E-BUSINESS EVOLUTION

As we searched B2C e-business initiatives for common paths and practices, two things became clear. First, the move to the Internet was an evolutionary process for bricks-and-mortar companies; second, it involved planning and flexibility in the face of market and technology developments. To illustrate that evolution, we created a framework with four crucial strategic quadrants: technology, brand, service, and market. (See Figure 5.1, p. 120.)

In practice, laggard companies never made it past the technology quadrant. Because they had no business model governing their use of Web technology, they became mired in debates about whether Web technology was a silver bullet or a passing fad. Thus, profits and market share remained elusive. Leading and medium-performing organizations, on the other hand, quickly moved beyond their starting points. They migrated toward a market strategy by concentrating either on a brand strategy or service strategy. Few migrated directly to a market strategy.

▼

Research Methodology

The study was carried out in the United States, Europe, and Australia in 1999 and 2000. With more than 130 executives, we conducted interviews lasting forty-five minutes to two hours. We also collected internal and published support documents. We interviewed car manufacturers and retailers, technology suppliers, biotechnology companies, and financial-services companies (including credit-card, brokerage, insurance, and banking companies). We spoke with executives at airlines, information providers, pharmaceutical companies, energy utilities, and a range of retail and service operations, such as Coles Myer, Levi Strauss, Dixons, United Parcel Service, Alamo, Ryder, Lennar, and manufacturers such as Lockheed and RS Components. We examined a variety of sectors to identify generic and sector-specific practices characteristic of organizations that lead, lag, or perform otherwise in their use of Web technologies. The study went beyond business-to-consumer (B2C) and also looked at business-to-business (B2B) and development and sourcing practices. We decided to use "B2C" also to cover consumer-to-business (C2B) organizations, such as Priceline.com, and consumer-to-consumer (C2C) concerns such as eBay—though those companies were not in our sample.

Criteria for assessment of leadership included the degree to which a company's Web site applied across the customer-resource life cycle, the degree to which Web technologies enabled a company to achieve market growth and profitability disproportionate for its industry, the extent to which a company was able to attract and retain customers, the amount of spending on marketing and e-development and the expected returns, and the company's position in its sector and against competition. We gained some quantified measures in each case but more often relied on subjective judgments by respondents. The sample was opportunistic and deliberately spread across sectors and across what we prejudged as differently performing organizations, with a deliberate overrepresentation of companies we thought to be leaders.

▼

Characteristics Of B2C E-Business Leaders

B2C E-Business Leaders share the following attributes. They . . .

▼ Regard the Internet as a cornerstone of a network-centric business era. Leaders follow the advice of microprocessor pioneer Carver Mead, who said, "Listen to the technology. Find out what it is telling you." Charles Schwab, John Chambers of Cisco Systems, and Michael Dell of Dell Computer Corp. listened to Web technology in relation to their businesses and included it in their strategies as "first-order thinking."[1]

▼ Distinguish the contributions of information from those of technology. Enduring advantage comes not from technology itself but from how information is collected, stored, analyzed, and applied.

▼ Recognize that competition, opportunities, and customer expectations evolve rapidly. Working in Internet time requires that businesses operate nonstop (24 × 7 × 365); update their Web sites constantly; exploit Web technologies strategically; anticipate changes in customer and supplier expectations and needs; and prepare for changing competitor activity, the threat of new entrants, and new products or service-based differentiation.

▼ Learn quickly and have the capacity to shift focus. Leaders concentrate on building an integrated technology, information, and marketing platform.

[1] M. Earl and D. Feeny, "How to Be a CEO for the Information Age," *Sloan Management Review,* winter 2000, *41,* 11-23.

Interestingly, there emerged both more progressive and less progressive ways of operating within each quadrant. For example, by the end of last year, twenty-four of the study organizations had begun to operate on the edge of the market quadrant. But as market conditions became more competitive, their ability to own their market proved as elusive as profitability, let alone high margins. Many of our respondents talked of "being in the game for the long

▼ Follow a top-down or outside-in route to business innovation via the Web. In the top-down, business-led approach, the top team focuses on business plans and goals and the integration of Web technologies into business initiatives. Examples include Prudential, Coles Myer, Charles Schwab, Fidelity Investments, and Direct Line. With the outside-in approach, managers working at the periphery of the organization identify new applications for Web technologies—as they did with "skunk works" in earlier rounds of technology.[2] Areas within Motorola, Lufthansa, Cisco Systems, and Millipore have followed the outside-in approach.

▼ Inform their e-business processes with critical business thinking. Leaders ask themselves whether their company has the intellectual capital and capability to envision and execute a sustainable Internet strategy. In the direct-grocery business, Tesco Direct and ColesMyer.com seem like good long-term prospects because of their multichannel strategies built upon established brands and business strengths.

▼ See the Web as part of a larger strategic investment in e-business. E-business leaders, such as Ford, Motorola, Coles Myer, Tesco, Dell, Cisco, and Federal Express, have made substantial investments in intranet, extranet, and supply-chain applications.

---

[2] For a discussion of the incremental development of strategic systems through learning characterized by bricolage (making something from materials at hand) rather than top-down determined systems, see C. Ciborra, *Markets, Teams and Systems* (Cambridge: Cambridge University Press, 1993), pp. 170–183; and for a proposed multiple methodology for the development of a portfolio of strategic applications, see M. Earl, *Management Strategies for Information Technology* (London: Prentice Hall, 1989), pp. 67–94.

---

haul" and the need to "sort out channel conflicts," "the complexity of integrating Web sites with legacy systems and business processes," and the need "to include the whole management team and employees in the transformation process."

Particularly interesting has been the variety of practices relating to brands. One of the early misconceptions about the Internet was that brands would cease to matter, that existing brands could

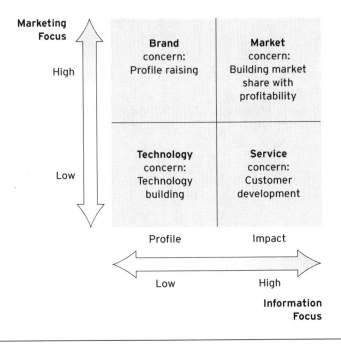

Figure 5.1. Business-to-Consumer E-Strategic Grid.

be challenged easily by start-ups. On the contrary, we found that in an e-world characterized by information overload, multiple products and services, and expanding search time and search costs, brand provides a valuable shorthand for safe, reliable quality and delivery. But although some companies recognized the value in brand building, often their efforts resulted in an expensive and ineffective use of resources—and failed to deliver.

THE TRANSIENCE OF TECHNOLOGY LEADERSHIP

In all sectors we found e-initiatives that focused primarily on the technology. Some eighteen companies, including Citicorp, BMW, Pratt & Whitney, W. R. Grace, and Genentech, began in the technology quadrant in the mid-1990s. Others followed in the period from 1997 to 2000. But, as many discovered, being first technology mover is not always a successful strategy even when applied to a viable business model. Information-systems success carries its own risks.[2] Moreover, in classic prime-mover examples such as the Sabre airline-reservation system, it's the intelligent management of information that explains success.[3] Sabre used technology to improve the process for making reservations, tracking customer preferences, accurately pricing products and services, and responding to patterns of behavior over time. In addition to using technology strategically, companies must deploy it in the appropriate organizational and managerial context. When technology is treated as an asset with a role in transforming the business, there is much greater likelihood of technology leadership and eventual business payoff.[4]

Lagging Practices

Technology laggards are companies that share the following characteristics:

▼ The IT department was made responsible for e-business developments
▼ Senior business managers underfunded and undervalued IT and e-business developments
▼ IT and Web-based technologies were treated as a cost center rather than a profit center
▼ The CIO was positioned as a specialist functional manager

Such companies typically remain stuck in the technology quadrant, where their projects are rationalized as "pilot" or "learning" vehicles. Laggard companies that try to move their initiatives to one of the other quadrants underachieve.

Leading Practices

What, then, characterized the technology leaders? Companies such as Lufthansa, Motorola, Citicorp, and Royal Caribbean Cruises made judicious moves into Web technologies with a view to harnessing them for leadership in business terms. In other words, the companies focused on matching appropriate technology to business strategy and customer requirements. Most also ensured that appropriate technology capability and capacity were internally in place or available through partnering. All were building technology platforms to support Internet, intranet, and extranet applications, with a view to reinforcing, improving, or changing the value propositions of their core business. In theoretical terms, technology leadership amounted to early adoption of Web technologies to achieve a competitive advantage. In practical terms that meant learning the technology in the context of developing an information or marketing strategy—and thus being able to shift focus fairly rapidly from the technology quadrant to one of the other quadrants.

A Case in Point: The U.S. Power Industry

Technology leaders are able to see the business opportunity that Internet technology presents, shift focus, and move into another quadrant. Consider the U.S. power industry. The Federal Energy Regulatory Commission (FERC) has ordered the industry to use OASIS (Open Access Same Time Information System), an advanced Internet technology that helps utilities buy and sell natural gas and pipeline capacity efficiently. Although FERC mandates that utilities work to reduce customers' power consumption, the two utilities we studied saw an opportunity there: they could use OASIS to create additional value for customers and thus increase and lock in market share. With the low-cost Internet technology boosting their ability to monitor power usage (even of individual appliances) and to advise people on how to save money, they could gain customers. Their strategic focus moved from technology to market; they used technology to add value. Their plan to get closer to customers through the Internet and create wider market coverage was already bearing fruit by late 2000.

As the utilities discovered, to position a business in the technology quadrant is strategic in that it is an investment in the future, but the business value lies in moving company focus to brand or service—and then to market.

BRAND AS STRATEGY

Many organizations we studied exemplify IBM CEO Lou Gerstner's assertion that "branding in a network world will dominate business thinking for a decade or more." But although branding on the Web can indeed fuel market growth, it can generate problems for companies that fail to deliver on the promises their brands represent. As the organizations studied translated their brands to the e-business context, they generally concentrated on one of four approaches: brand reinforcement, brand repositioning, brand creation, or brand followership, the first two proving more effective bridges to profitability than the latter.

Brand Reinforcement

One of the first routes out of the technology quadrant is to seek brand reinforcement via the Internet. Instead of treating the Internet as a new sales channel, established companies use it to reinforce customers' awareness of, and regard for, the brand. In 1998 BMW astutely moved from a technology strategy to one that bridged both the technology and brand quadrants. Rather than sell autos over the Internet, BMW aimed to make its site "drive and feel like a BMW"— and use it to steer potential new-car owners to a traditional dealer. That way, it preserved its traditional face-to-face interaction with customers and avoided conflict with its dealers.

Levi Strauss tells a different story, revealing that the power of existing brands alone offers no guarantee of Internet market success. When the company launched its on-line stores levi.com and dockers.com, it prohibited key retail partners from selling Levi Strauss merchandise over the Web. Retailers reacted by turning their attention to private brand offerings. Meanwhile, Levi Strauss proved inexperienced at selling on-line. Sales floundered against increasing on-line costs—estimated at between $10 million and $100 million—and by summer 2000, Levi's had closed its on-line operations.

Brand Repositioning

Several organizations surveyed used the Internet to effectively reposition their brands. Dow Jones, for example, responded to major on-line threats by extending its global vision and creating a new service bundle for the Internet. Meanwhile, the airline Lufthansa sought to reposition itself as a highly customer-focused travel agency and information provider through its on-line InfoFlyway service.

In the United Kingdom, supermarket chain Tesco moved from brand reinforcement to brand repositioning over two years. First, in 1998 it reinforced its brand by creating Tesco.com, a wholly owned Internet subsidiary that allows customers to order groceries on-line for delivery and uses existing retail outlets for supply. In 1999, although the on-line business had lost £11.2 million on £125 million in sales, it also had attracted 500,000 users and was anticipating a profit in two years. By the end of 2000, Tesco had invested £56 million in its on-line retail business, dedicated seven thousand staff members to it, and had almost all six hundred local stores on-line. At the same time, Tesco used the power of its existing brand and relationships with shoppers to reposition Tesco.com as a seller of services and goods other than food and to launch Tesco Personal Finance, an on-line joint banking venture with the Royal Bank of Scotland. Senior executives said they expected nonfood goods ultimately to comprise half of e-sales and both Internet businesses to move into the market quadrant and reach profitability in 2001.

Brand Creation

Brand creation has been most evident among Internet start-ups such as Pets.com and Buy.com. But Internet-only companies are not alone in launching expensive new Internet brands. Consider Prudential Assurance, a financial-services company that, in October 1998, launched Egg, an on-line bank that offers savings accounts, credit cards, loans, and a shopping mall. By mid-2000, the subsidiary had acquired 940,000 customers, including 250,000 credit-card customers. Moreover, it had taken £7.6 billion in deposits and lent £679 million—and was being floated as a separate entity on the stock market.

But although Egg quickly achieved brand recognition in the United Kingdom, the cost was high. Egg spent £75 million on advertising in its first year and expected a loss of £377 million before breaking even sometime in 2001. Egg succeeded in attracting customers, but it did so by offering a savings account that paid a high interest rate—a strategy described by rivals as "handing out £20 notes in exchange for £10 ones." A series of customer-service debacles further eroded its position: Web-site outages, long waits on the telephone, lack of integration between credit-card and savings-account systems, and delays in the launch of new cut-price unit trusts (managed portfolios of investments). Ultimately, the company expects to derive profits from cross-selling new products and services to its savings-account customers (thus moving to the market quadrant), but it is currently in the red.

Brand Followership

Brand followers copy early on-line movers in their approach to branding. For example, parts supplier RS Components looked to Dell Computer. Land Rover emulated other car manufacturers. Many on-line wine shops and bookstores modeled themselves after wine.com and Amazon.com (though Amazon has used its technology patents to slow brand followership through litigation). In rare instances, brand followers can succeed, but they need to reposition quickly. Otherwise, they merely reflect a reluctance to build on Internet opportunities.

What are the lessons? On the plus side, the Internet allows global branding and wider market reach. On the minus side, delivering on the brand (the "promise to the customer," as it has been called) can be expensive and difficult. As Levi Strauss and Egg show, a high-profile brand means little if it is not connected to knowing customers well and delivering the services they require.

THE SERVICE PAYOFF

Service leaders in our study developed an almost obsessive focus on customers and information. That focus tended to be a more effective transitional strategy than a focus on brand. (In fact, brand leaders that migrated to the market quadrant adopted elements of the service strategy because the migration forced them to focus on information for customer reasons). Service leaders quickly learned to take advantage of the Internet to gather data about customers and provide them with information on their own terms. The companies variously used that information in adaptive profiling, mass customization, and one-to-one marketing concepts.[5] They applied customer-resource life-cycle analysis and focused on customer retention. Moreover, integration of technology led to seamless service. As an Office Depot executive commented, "The integration of systems is key; customer support and service through this is something we put a lot of emphasis on." Companies that crossed into the market quadrant effectively turned such concepts into business practices.

Leading service-focused organizations developed service variations for specific contexts. Value-adding practices include the following:

▼ *Personalization.* Companies can offer on-line mass customization by tailoring a product's attributes or presentation to individual customers. For example, Dow Jones, the publisher of the *Wall Street Journal*, introduced the Interactive Edition, which allows subscribers to organize the newspaper according to the information they deem most relevant.

▼ *Tiered service levels.* Dell allows customers to select their own level of service according to categories: "all," "registered," "contracted," or "platinum" service.

▼ *Collecting information and enhancing the customer experience.* Alamo Rent A Car, Office Depot, RS Components, Dell, Cisco, United Parcel Service (UPS), and Federal Express (FedEx) first collect data about the customer-resource life cycle and then use the data to support customers' preferences and track purchases through to delivery and after-sales service.

▼ *Keeping it simple.* FedEx, Alamo, Direct Line, and Dell excel at making it easy for customers to do business with them and to do their jobs. For example, Dell developed customized firewall-protected intranet sites for more than two hundred of its largest global customers, permitting clients' purchasing staff to view and select all products that meet the configurations authorized by the client.

▼ *Responding to what customers do not like doing or do badly.* In the United Kingdom, Direct Line recognized that getting auto insurance is a chore for car owners, and so it offered one-stop insurance by telephone that saved customers time and money. The service netted Direct Line more than eight million customers. Direct Line now operates through a Web site integrated into its core insurance business, and it has expanded into other insurance areas, such as household and travel insurance. A Scandinavian company, MeritaNordbanken, discovered that customers hate paying bills and do it inefficiently, often incurring late fees. Therefore, in early 2000 it developed a now widely used Internet bill-payment application.

▼ *Providing a one-stop shop for service.* Pratt & Whitney and Nortel Networks have developed virtual call centers, allowing customers to make purchases and resolve questions and problems from a single Internet site. Lufthansa also moved its ticketing services online, saving customers the potential time and expense of using a travel agent or the phone.

▼ *Balancing customer self-service with support.* Off-loading some of the service tasks to customers may save money, but it may not enhance the customers' experience. Hard-goods supplier W. W. Grainger achieves a successful balance by delivering on-line catalogs customers can easily customize, scan, and order from. And as credit-card company American Express offers an ever greater array of on-line financial services, it engages in ongoing efforts to balance self-service with customer support.

▼ *Knowing the customer best.* Lufthansa identifies "superior knowledge of customers" as a competitive goal. Its InfoFlyway service demonstrates that focus by tracking customer tastes closely and offering home pages in more than thirty-five languages. The award-winning site also delivers individual e-mail and offers account access, monthly auctions, hotel links, travel guides, baggage tracing, and an on-line booking system for seven hundred airlines. The payoff: in 1998 the service had developed 400,000 registered users who had made 41,000 electronic bookings, producing £17.6 million in revenues.

IN SEARCH OF (PROFITABLE) MARKET GROWTH

Let us now bring together a mapping of the optimal paths leaders have been pursuing through the e-strategic grid. (See Figure 5.2.) What distinguishes the most successful companies is their ability to integrate marketing, customer service, and use of information and technology to deliver a profitable long-term market share or niche strategy. Behind that integration has been a "reengineering on steroids" stage—reorganizing and re-educating people, reconfiguring processes, and remodeling technology infrastructure. The integration of processes, technology, and skills gave the leading organizations the platform to convert their strategic intents into business value. In bricks-and-mortar companies we found integration capability a scarce and not easily replicable resource.

Businesses operating in the upper right of the market quadrant stood out in their ability to combine marketing, service, and infor-

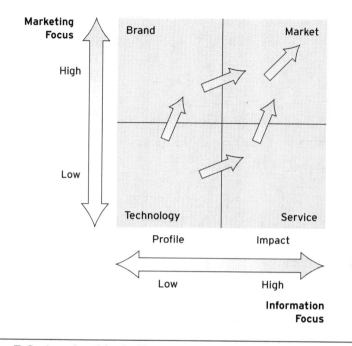

Figure 5.2. Leadership Paths on the E-Strategic Grid.

---

mation capabilities in order to achieve disproportionate Web-based B2C market growth and profitability. The most notable among them were Fidelity Investments, Cisco Systems, Charles Schwab, Office Depot, and Dell. By 2000, other companies had moved in varying degrees into the market quadrant, but generally their integration was less effective, as was the intensity and focus with which they deployed the relevant capabilities. Companies such as W. W. Grainger, MeritaNordbanken, Direct Line, Lufthansa, Alamo, Royal Caribbean Cruises, UPS, and FedEx were driving hard to gain market share, but only some were generating profits.

Lessons from Leading Practices

After experiencing an early but indifferent technology start, car-rental company Alamo quickly moved into the service quadrant. There it redeveloped its Internet offering to reflect customer prefer-ences and its recognition that the Internet plugged straight into the heart of its mission. Alamo managed the problem of channel conflict with travel agents by developing a special Web site tailored to their needs. And it realized that customers prefer to pay for their cars at the counter rather than on-line and therefore chose not to develop an on-line payment system.

UPS integrated Web technologies into its business model and greatly extended the power of the model and the number and speed of services offered. (See box, E-Leader Case Study: UPS in Distribution, pp. 132–133.) So did Office Depot. Like UPS, it had the advantage of prior robust, integrated technology infrastructure. It could easily have used the Internet merely as an information catalog, but instead Office Depot treated it as a means of transacting business. Similarly, Charles Schwab, another company founded on a strategy of technological innovation, spent five years transforming itself from a traditional broker to an on-line financial-services company that today is conducting more than 70 percent of its customer transactions on-line.

The companies making it deep into our market quadrant share certain characteristics: they integrate Web technologies into their core, use information gathered on-line to gain insight into the customer and to augment service, and focus intensively on customers and marketing. Moreover, they have identified ways of using Web technologies strategically and seek ways to sustain their advantage— through brand, size, and customer relationships as well as differentiation. They also made key decisions at the right time about how and when to structure their moves to e-business. (See box, Choosing a Bricks-and-Clicks Organizational Structure.)

The Importance of Differentiation

The practice of differentiation is key to B2C e-business success. In most sectors, commodity-based, price-sensitive competition on the Web will not be a sustainable business model. A business must enter the competitive arena with a customer offering (the inseparable bundle of product, service, information, and relationship) that is an

▼

Choosing a Bricks-and-Clicks Organizational Structure

The traditional companies in the market quadrant have found solutions to the dilemmas posed by issues of structure. Our findings suggest that integrating Internet initiatives into an existing business makes sense only if

- ▼ The brand extends naturally to the Internet
- ▼ Executives have the skills and experience needed to pursue the Internet channel, and the company can attract and retain the right people
- ▼ Executives are willing to judge and manage the initiative by different performance and reward criteria
- ▼ Distribution and information systems translate well to the Internet and provide a competitive superiority
- ▼ The integrated company remains attractive to potential alliance partners on such dimensions as brand strength and speed of action
- ▼ The cultures of the e-business and of the existing business gel in a mutually supportive way

Otherwise, our findings support and extend the suggestions of R. Gulati and J. Garino that forming a separate business unit can be a more viable alternative.[1] That is true when

- ▼ A different customer segment or product mix is being offered
- ▼ Pricing needs to be different to stay competitive
- ▼ Channel conflicts and threats to the current business model exist
- ▼ Outside capital is needed and is best raised by a stand-alone operation
- ▼ There are problems retaining or attracting the right talent;
- ▼ A key partner is reluctant to connect with the parent company
- ▼ The parent company's culture would undermine the e-business's effectiveness.

[1] R. Gulati and J. Garino, "Get the Right Mix of Bricks and Clicks," *Harvard Business Review*, May-June 2000, *78*, 107-114; for another perspective, see also K. Moore and K. Ruddle, "New Business Models: The Challenge of Transition," in *Moving to E-Business*, L. Willcocks and C. Sauer, eds. (London: Random House, 2000), pp. 99-123.

▼

E-Leader Case Study: UPS in Distribution

Global package deliverer United Parcel Service (UPS) increased its market share, leapfrogged competitors, and extended its business model by leveraging the Internet's networking, information, and interactive capabilities. Thus it exemplifies a company's migration from the technology strategy through the service strategy to the market strategy of the B2C e-strategic grid.

By focusing on building profitable market share, UPS is now able to deliver 12.4 million packages a day around the world and handle 55 percent of all e-commerce shipments, compared with rival FedEx's 10 percent. Facilitating those shipments are 2,500 distribution centers, more than 330,000 employees, and 500 airplanes. Smart use of Web technology also has enabled UPS to reinvent itself as an information-delivery company and problem solver. As such, it aims to help companies manage inventories, reshape distribution networks, and simplify accounting procedures. Says UPS President Jim Kelly: "UPS does business where the virtual and physical worlds meet, where 'tires and wires' converge."

That wasn't always so. UPS brought in Web technologies in the mid-1990s, but at that time FedEx, with its package-tracking system, led in its use of the Web for customer service. By 1998, however, UPS was catching up in building its technology infrastructure. (In 2000 UPS spent $1 billion on

alternative to or a close substitute for what rivals offer. The challenge over time is to continually differentiate the offering—and to make it less price-sensitive—in ways that remain attractive to the targeted market segment.

The support dimension of an offering represents those differentiating features that help customers choose, obtain, and then use the offering. All other differentiating features belong to what is called the merchandise dimension.[6] The support features of a car sold over the Web include availability of information, ease of purchase, the test-drive, promptness of delivery, and service arrangements. Companies can augment the support dimension through personalization information technology.) And it was developing the information capability for its customers down to the package level. From 1998 it introduced a series of service innovations on the Internet, including secure document exchange. It customized logistics to facilitate shipping units from different countries and have them arrive at the right place and time for assembly. In its Web-site design and Internet use, UPS seems to have applied four marketing principles across the company: listening to customers to determine their needs, creating a portfolio of services based on those needs, leveraging technology to forge tighter customer connections, and staying committed to international expansion.

By 2000, UPS had introduced an interactive facility that let customers order, pay for, and track document and package delivery on-line with precision. It offered a range of logistics services to businesses, including free on-line tools for adding Web-site functionality, reducing costs, and improving customer service. By 2000, UPS had built shipping links into more than 100,000 business Web sites. More than half of UPS business came from customers connected to the company electronically. In addition, customers using UPS OnLine Tools tended to increase their shipping volume by as much as 20 percent and to use UPS over several years.

(the personal attention paid to each customer's needs) and through expertise (the seller's superiority of brainpower, skill, or experience in delivering and implementing the offering). FedEx facilitates Internet tracking of parcels; Wine.com offers on-line access to wine information and the expertise of a sommelier.

Merchandise features include color, shape, size, performance characteristics, and in-car entertainment. Companies can further differentiate the merchandise component by augmenting content (what the offering does for the customer) or aura (what the offering says about the customer). Amazon.com makes available a wider range of books and products than do competitors; MeritaNordbanken provides wireless-application-protocol (WAP) phone access to a customer's account. Both companies' brands augment the aura of the offering. Leading organizations in our study strove to tap both sources of differentiation (particularly through leveraging information bases) to get closer to customers and lock them in.

What matters is achieving differentiation in a changing competitive context so that customers see the dynamic value proposition as superior to alternatives. Achieving such differentiation requires a knowledge of and relationship with customers and a speed and flexibility of anticipation and response that many organizations have found difficult to develop, let alone sustain. Moreover, differentiation has to be achieved in specific Internet environments where power often has moved decisively in favor of the customer.[7]

CONTEXT, TIMING, FOCUS, AND FLEXIBILITY

Statistical analysis of business-unit data elsewhere delivers strong evidence that information technology can have a significant, often positive, multifaceted effect on business productivity.[8] That effect comes not in isolation but as a result of interaction with other factors, such as organizational structure, percentage of knowledge workers, and relative competitive position. The context, timing, and focus of IT investment is emerging as all-important—a finding that our study and other studies on Web-technology investments demonstrate.[9]

But if a company is to exploit the Internet to achieve business goals, its journey through the e-business strategic grid has to be guided by both new management thinking and certain perennial principles and practices. If it all gels, real bricks-and-clicks strategy develops. However, the journey does not guarantee success. Strategy has to stay flexible because even leading companies find they cannot assume that their market position on the Internet will remain constant. It changes twenty-four hours a day, seven days a week, time zone to time zone, and market segment to market segment. Even more fundamental for the future—and disguised by the focus on competitive positioning issues—is putting in place the key human resource, IT, and organizational infrastructure to support the processes and behaviors designed to deliver on strategic intent. Increasingly, companies trying to crack B2C e-business will discover what the leading organizations already know—that e-infrastructure is a boardroom investment and ownership issue because it goes to the core of executing sustainable, anticipatory business performance.

ADDITIONAL RESOURCES

Recommended books are the 1999 *Information Rules: Strategic Guide to the Network Economy,* by Carl Shapiro and Hal Varian, and the 2000 *How Digital Is Your Business?* by Adrian Slywotzky and David Morrison, which presents case studies of Cemex, IBM, Schwab, General Electric, Cisco Systems, and Dell.

Michael Rappa runs a good Internet site on business models (http://ecommerce.csc.ncsu.edu/business_models.html).

Peter Weill and Mike Vitale's *E-Commerce Business Models,* published this year, is a well-researched analysis of eight foundational models.

For information on branding, see Michael Moon and Doug Millison's 2000 *Firebrands: Building Loyalty in the Internet Age.*

Readers also may find useful Chris Sauer and Leslie Willcocks' 2001 *Building the E-Business Infrastructure,* which provides a comprehensively researched review of infrastructure.

One of the best monthly magazines tracing developments is still *Business 2.0* (www.Business2.com).

NOTES

1. N. Venkatraman, "Five Steps to a Dot-Com Strategy: How to Find Your Footing on the Web," *Sloan Management Review,* Spring 2000,

41, 15–28 (reprinted beginning on p. 83 of this anthology); and D. Feeny, "Making Business Sense of the E-Opportunity," *Sloan Management Review,* Winter 2001, *42,* 41–50 (reprinted beginning on p. 35 of this anthology).

2. M. Vitale, "The Growing Risks of Information Systems Success," *Management Information Systems Quarterly,* December 1986, *10,* 327–336. The article points to systems that change the basis of competition to a company's disadvantage, lower entry barriers, bring litigation or regulation, increase customers' or suppliers' power to the detriment of the innovator, turn out to be indefensible and may even induce disadvantage, are badly timed, transfer power and are resisted by other market players, and may work in one market niche but not in another. That implies an overreliance on the technology and inadequate analysis of the competitive context to which it is applied.

3. T. Davenport, "Putting the I in IT," in *Mastering Information Management,* T. Davenport and D. Marchand, eds. (London: Financial Times Prentice Hall, 1999), pp. 1–6.

4. L. Willcocks, D. Feeny, and G. Islei, eds., *Managing IT as a Strategic Resource* (Maidenhead, England: McGraw-Hill, 1997).

5. B. J. Pine, *Mass Customization: The New Frontier in Business Competition* (Boston: Harvard Business School Press, 1993). Though written before the Internet took off as a business tool, the book is highly relevant to Internet applications.

6. S. Mathur and A. Kenyon, *Creating Value: Shaping Tomorrow's Business* (London: Butterworth-Heinemann, 1997); and A. M. Van Nievelt, "Benchmarking Organizational and IT Performance," in *Beyond the IT Productivity Paradox,* L. Willcocks and S. Lester, eds. (Chichester, England: Wiley, 1999), pp. 99–119.

7. See, for example, P. Seybold with R. Marshak, *Customer.com: How to Create a Profitable Business Strategy for the Internet and Beyond* (New York: Random House, 1998); and S. Vandermerwe, *Customer Capitalism* (London: Nicholas Brealey Publishing, 1998); and F. Newell, *Loyalty.com: Customer Relationship Management in the New Era of Marketing* (New York: McGraw-Hill, 2000).

8. See, for example, A. M. van Nievelt and L. Willcocks, *Benchmarking Organizational and IT Performance* (Oxford: Templeton College,

1998); and E. Brynjolffson and L. Hitt, "Paradox Lost? Firm-Level Evidence on the Returns to Information Systems Spending," in *Beyond the IT Productivity Paradox,* L. Willcocks and S. Lester, eds. (Chichester, England: Wiley, 1999), pp. 39–68.

9. R. Plant, *E-Commerce: Formulation of Strategy* (New York: Prentice Hall, 2000); and C. Sauer and L. Willcocks, *Building the E-Business Infrastructure* (London: Business Intelligence, 2001).

CHAPTER SIX

The Past and Future of Competitive Advantage

CLAYTON M. CHRISTENSEN

C ompetitive advantage is a concept that often inspires in strategists a form of idol worship—a desire to imitate the strategies that make the most successful companies successful. It is interesting, however, that strategists have viewed precisely opposite factors to be sources of competitive advantage at different points in the histories of a number of industries. For example, Henry Ford's emphasis on focus has been touted right next to General Motors' product-line breadth as the key to success. Today, the outsourcing flexibility inherent in the nonintegrated business models of Cisco Systems and Dell Computer is held up as a model for all to emulate, whereas a generation ago IBM's vertical integration was widely considered an unassailable source of competitive advantage. In the 1980s, power-tool maker Black & Decker aggressively consolidated its diffused international-manufacturing infrastructure into a few global-scale facilities so that it could counter the aggressive market-share gains that Makita had logged by serving the world market from a single plant in Japan. At that very time, Makita was moving aggressively toward manufacturing in smaller-scale local facilities around the world.

Indeed, strategists whose anecdotal understanding of competitive advantage runs only as deep as "If it's good for Cisco, it must be good for everybody" at best are likely to succeed in building yesterday's competitive advantages. If history is any guide, the practices and business models that constitute advantages for today's most successful companies confer those advantages only because of particular factors at work under particular conditions at this particular time.

Historically, several factors have conferred powerful advantages on the companies that possessed them—economies of scale and scope, integration and nonintegration, and process-based core competencies. What are the circumstances that cause each factor to be a competitive advantage? How and why do competitive actions erode the underpinnings of those advantages? Strategists need to peel away the veneer of what works, and understand more deeply why and under what conditions certain practices lead to advantage. In so doing, they might begin to predict successfully which of today's powerful competitive advantages are likely to erode and what might cause new sources of advantage to emerge in the future. (Many of the insights presented here are rooted in work on disruptive innovation presented in my 1997 book *The Innovator's Dilemma: When New Technologies Cause Great Firms to Fail.*)

ECONOMIES OF SCALE

In the 1960s and 1970s, concepts of competitive advantage often were predicated upon steep scale economics, and many tools of strategic analysis were built upon those economics (for example, growth-share matrices, experience curves, and industry-supply curves). Indeed, scale allowed successful companies such as General Motors and IBM to enjoy lower costs than their competitors. IBM, with 70 percent market share, earned 95 percent of the mainframe-computer industry's profits; General Motors, with 55 percent market share, earned 80 percent of the automobile industry's profits. Today steep scale economics explain the profits and dominant market shares of companies such as Intel, Boeing, and Microsoft.

Steep economies of scale exist when there are high fixed versus variable costs in the predominant business model. Large organizations can amortize the fixed costs over greater volumes, condemning small competitors to playing the game on an adversely sloped playing field.

However, Toyota taught the Western world that many fixed costs aren't ordained by nature but are artifacts of specific technological and managerial solutions to problems. By reducing in-process inventories, setup times for machinery, and the overhead costs inherent in an inventory-intensive batch-manufacturing process, Toyota flattened the scale economics of assembling a car. CAD (computer-aided-design) systems had a similar effect on reducing the fixed, up-front cost of designing a new model. As a result, there is now no relationship between an auto producer's market share and its profitability. Analogous innovations have flattened scale economics in steel, electric-power generation, and computers—and rendered transitory what were once thought to be sustainable advantages.

Strategists in industries that today see leading companies enjoying scale-based competitive advantage ought to ask themselves if the fundamental trade-offs that create today's high fixed costs might change—leveling the playing field in even more situations. Consider Intel. A barrier to potential competitors is the $700 million cost to design a new family of microprocessors and the $3 billion needed to build a new fabrication facility. However, disruptive technologies such as Tensilica's modular microprocessor architecture are flattening the scale economics of design. And small fabrication facilities, or minifabs, could reduce the fixed costs of production. Such technologies take root at the low end of the market first, but they are marching relentlessly up the performance spectrum.

In the pharmaceutical industry, megamergers have created $100 billion behemoths. The logic behind those mergers has been that the huge fixed costs and extraordinary uncertainty associated with clinical trials for new drugs confer ever greater advantages on ever larger companies. Historically, that has indeed been the case. But could something change the underpinnings of those high fixed costs?

Understanding of the human genome will flatten the scale economics in clinical trials. For example, we now understand that there are at least six distinctly different diseases that were once thought to be one disease—leukemia. Each of the six is associated with a specific, unique treatment protocol, and each can be precisely diagnosed through a characteristic pattern among about fifty genes. We now realize that in the past, most of the patients in a clinical trial for a new leukemia treatment didn't have the specific disease being studied. Compounds worked for some patients and not for others; and to determine clinical efficacy with satisfactory statistical results, large numbers of patients needed to be enrolled for long clinical trials. That created huge, front-end fixed costs and steepened the scale economics.

Now, however, a technician can draw a blood sample and compare the pattern in the patient's genes with a template and diagnose specifically which leukemia is present. In the future, 100 percent of the patients in a clinical trial will have the specific disease being studied, and smaller, faster trials will achieve clearer clinical outcomes. Scale will no longer confer superior profits upon larger companies; it will be an albatross. Today's merging companies are moving exactly in the wrong direction at exactly the wrong time because their strategists (and investment bankers) have not thought deeply about cause and effect in competitive advantage.

ECONOMIES OF SCOPE

A second source of competitive advantage, intertwined with scale economics, has been product-line breadth. For example, through the 1970s, Caterpillar's scope gave the company an unassailable advantage in construction equipment against smaller competitors such as Komatsu. Only Caterpillar was large enough to absorb the complexity-driven overhead costs of developing, manufacturing, and distributing a full product line. Caterpillar's dealers did not need to carry equipment from other manufacturers in order to offer customers whatever they needed. Caterpillar's huge installed base of equipment in the field meant its dealers, who were the largest dealers in each market, could afford to stock the parts necessary to offer twenty-four-hour delivery of any spare part to any Caterpillar owner. No competitor could match that—until the underpinnings of the trade-offs inherent in the advantages changed.

Caterpillar's economies of scope had pinned Komatsu into a niche position, until Toyota's methods for reducing fixed costs in design and assembly came to construction equipment. That allowed Komatsu to produce a broader range of products in its existing plants without a ballooning of changeover, scheduling, inventory, expediting costs, and quality costs that historically had plagued less focused factories. Furthermore, the advent of overnight air-delivery services meant that local dealers did not need to stock a complete inventory of spare parts in order to equal Caterpillar's service. Such factors leveled the playing field.

Retailing is an industry in which competitive advantages have waxed and waned. (See Figure 6.1.) In fact, four waves of disruptive technology have swept through the industry. In the first wave were downtown department stores such as Marshall Field's, which came to prominence in the early 1870s. The second wave consisted of mail-order catalogs such as Sears, Roebuck in the 1890s. In the early 1960s, the third disruptive wave broke, and discount department stores such as Kmart and Wal-Mart emerged. On-line retailing is the latest wave.

Two patterns have recurred in these waves. First, the disruptive retailers survived on much lower gross margins than the established retailers and earned acceptable returns by turning inventories faster. At the outset, because their salespeople had less product expertise than salespeople in the prior wave, the disruptive retailers

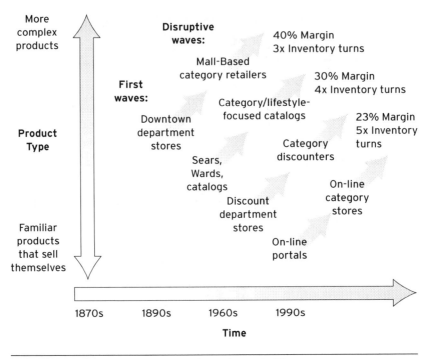

Figure 6.1. Historical Disruptions in Retailing.

could sell only simple products that were familiar in use, such as hardware, paint, and kitchen utensils. In each instance, the retailers subsequently migrated upmarket toward more complex, nonstandard products, such as clothing and home furnishings.

A second pattern was that in each instance, the dominant disrupters at the outset were broad-line department stores, or portals, whose scope conferred powerful competitive advantages. Marshall Field's, for example, was the portal of the 1870s. Before Marshall Field's, consumers didn't know where to go to get what they needed. But people walking through the new portal realized that what they wanted was probably in there somewhere. The Sears catalog served as a portal to rural Americans. Discount department stores also were portals, selling a little bit of everything. In each of the prior waves of disruption, however, the portals were preempted by retailers focusing on a product category or a lifestyle. Focused retailers had a similar financial model (measured by typical margins and inventory turns), but their focus simplified the shopping experience and enabled a deeper product line and better service. Hence, mall-based retailers such as Banana Republic and Williams-Sonoma have largely preempted department stores. Specialized catalogs such as L.L. Bean have preempted full-line catalogs. Focused discounters such as Circuit City, Toys "R" Us, Home Depot, and Staples are supplanting discount department stores. When customers learn where to go to get what they need, the portals' competitive advantage of scope becomes a disadvantage.

On-line retailing appears to be following the same pattern. Portal envy afflicts many venture capitalists and dot-com entrepreneurs because the most valuable real estate on the Internet has been claimed by America Online, Yahoo!, and Amazon.com. Nevertheless, history may prove the portals' current advantages transitory.

VERTICAL INTEGRATION AND NONINTEGRATION AS A COMPETITIVE ADVANTAGE

It was not that long ago that the ability to do everything internally at IBM, General Motors, Standard Oil, Alcoa, and AT&T was viewed as a powerful competitive advantage. Now the tables seem to have turned, and vertical integration seems to slow companies down. Cisco and other nonintegrated companies, which outsource much of their manufacturing and product development to partners or start-up companies they subsequently acquire, have the model that is the envy of today's corporate strategists. But what are the circumstances that confer advantage upon integrated and nonintegrated companies, and what could cause those circumstances to change?

Every product or service is produced in a chain of value-added activities. To be successful at outsourcing a piece of that chain to a supplier, a company must meet three conditions. First, it must be able to specify what attributes it needs. Second, the technology to measure those attributes must be reliably and conveniently accessible, so that both the company and the supplier can verify that what is being provided is what is needed. And third, if there is any variation in what the supplier delivers, the company needs to know what else in the system must be adjusted. The company needs to understand how the supplier's contribution will interact with other elements of the system so that the company can take what it procures and plug it into the value chain with predictable effect. If those three conditions are met, then it is possible to outsource a value-added activity.

Markets work when there is adequate information—and the three classes above constitute the information that is necessary and sufficient for markets to emerge between stages of value-added activity. But what about the innumerable situations in which market-enabling information does not exist—for example, when truly new technologies emerge? IBM's development of magnetoresistive (MR) disk-drive recording heads in the early 1990s is such an example. MR heads can increase a disk drive's data-storage capacity by a factor of ten—and yet achieving that increase is not an easy feat. A drive maker cannot simply outsource the heads and plug them into a product that was designed using conventional algorithms. The design of the disks, the actuator mechanisms, the error-correction software, and dozens of other aspects of the product need to be interactively modified as the MR heads are incorporated. MR technology is not yet understood well enough for engineers to specify to suppliers which attributes are most critical. Technology to measure those attributes is not well developed, and engineers can't predict accurately how variability in the properties of a head might affect the performance of the system. Nor do they understand how changes in product design might affect manufacturability or how subtle changes in manufacturing methods might affect product performance. Manufacturing therefore must be done in-house. When necessary and sufficient information doesn't exist at critical interfaces, integration is imperative.

In general, vertical integration is an advantage when a company is competing for the business of customers whose needs have not yet been satisfied by the functionality of available products. Integrated companies are able to design interactively each of the major subsystems of a product or service, efficiently extracting the most performance possible out of the available technology. (See Figure 6.2.)

When the prevailing functionality of products has overshot what customers can utilize, however, then the way companies compete must change. Making even better products no longer yields superior profits. Instead, innovations that enhance a company's abilities to bring products rapidly to market—and responsively and conveniently to customize offerings—become the mechanisms for achieving advantage. When the basis of competition evolves thus, then modular, industry-standard interfaces

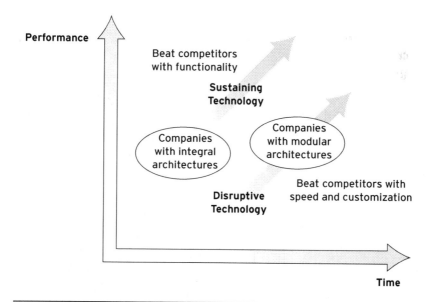

Figure 6.2. What Determines Competitive Advantage?

among the major subsystems of a product become defined, enabling nonintegrated, focused companies to emerge and provide specific pieces of value-added activity. Focused companies can operate on much lower overhead costs, and standard interfaces enable product designers and assemblers to mix and match components to tailor features and functions to the needs of specific customers. Hence, in tiers of a market in which customers are overserved by the functionality of available products, nonintegration is an advantage: a population of nonintegrated companies that interface through market mechanisms is faster and more flexible than an integrated company. (Supporting data appear in a Harvard Business School working paper the author and M. Verlinden wrote last year, "Disruption, Dis-Integration and the Dissipation of Differentiability.")

The opposite extremes of the computer industry illustrate the advantages of each structure. Machines that push the bleeding edge of performance, such as mission-critical servers, often combine nonstandard components designed and manufactured within integrated companies such as Hewlett-Packard. Machines not targeted at the frontiers of performance can be made more effectively in a nonintegrated model such as Dell's.

Cisco, which exploited the modular architecture of its routers to disrupt the telecommunications switching business from the low end, established in the minds of many the standard for a New Economy company. Cisco has efficiently outsourced much of its manufacturing to suppliers in its network and much of its new-product development to the start-ups it acquires. However, as Cisco has moved up into the most performance-demanding tiers of its markets—particularly optical networks—it is being forced to integrate, performing many more product-design and manufacturing activities internally than was necessary when it competed at greater distances from the bleeding edge. Cisco's competitors, such as Corning, JDS Uniphase, Nortel Networks, and Lucent Technologies, also are finding that they have to become more integrated—less outsourced—in order to compete.

Hence, if customer needs go beyond the current technology, vertical integration constitutes a competitive advantage. If the technology is well established, integration is an albatross. Today's strategists must strive to understand the circumstances in which a company and its business model compete and whether the model puts the company at a competitive advantage or disadvantage.

CORE COMPETENCE
AND COMPETITIVE ADVANTAGE

Some types of competitive advantage, such as those associated with the economics of scale and scope, are rooted in market positions. Others are rooted in business models; still others in the processes or competencies of organizations. Although the value of market positions and the relevance of business models can wax and wane, "tacit" competencies—internal processes—have been thought to be more enduring because they are harder to copy. Nevertheless, it turns out that competence residing in proprietary processes is also built upon temporary underpinnings.

DuPont, for example, enjoyed years of unparalleled capability to formulate new organic compounds. Its scientists did their work through collaborative trial and error. A scientist would mix and heat things in a beaker, draw a fiber out, and then consult with colleagues who had expertise in various dimensions of organic chemistry about what the material might do and how it could be improved. Over time, however, DuPont's strength, which had resided in the patterns of interaction and collaboration among its scientists, came to be embodied in quantum theory. Now that the science of how atoms combine in molecular structures to create materials with particular properties is well defined, success is open to all. Any company can specify the properties needed in a material and then use theory-based algorithms to determine which atoms need to bond with which atoms in which patterns.

Similarly, a company such as BMW might say that its competitive advantage resides in its internal processes for designing unique automobiles. Indeed, there has been a "BMW-ness" to its designs that other companies' processes have not successfully replicated. The process of designing a new automobile is fixed-cost intensive and historically has entailed extensive interaction and collaboration among large groups of engineers. However, in order to reduce costs and improve its ability to design safe automobiles, BMW recently has created a system that enables its engineers to use computer simulations to crash-test the cars they design—before physical models are built. The simulations enable BMW's engineers to observe the crashes carefully and to improve designs—a wonderful system. But a capability that formerly resided in the interaction among the company's engineers is now embodied in algorithms—which not only flatten the scale economics associated with product design, but could make BMW's core competence more broadly available. In general, scientific progress that results in deeper, more fundamental understanding transforms into explicit, codified, and replicable knowledge many things that once were accomplished only through proprietary problem-solving routines.

Every competitive advantage is predicated upon a particular set of conditions that exist at a particular point in time for particular reasons. Many of history's seemingly unassailable advantages have proved transitory because the underlying factors changed. The very existence of competitive advantage sets in motion creative innovations that, as competitors strive to level the playing field, cause the advantage to dissipate. That does not mean the search for competitive advantage is futile. Rather, it suggests that successful strategists need to cultivate a deep understanding of the processes of competition and progress and of the factors that undergird each advantage. Only thus will they be able to see when old advantages are poised to disappear and how new advantages can be built in their stead.

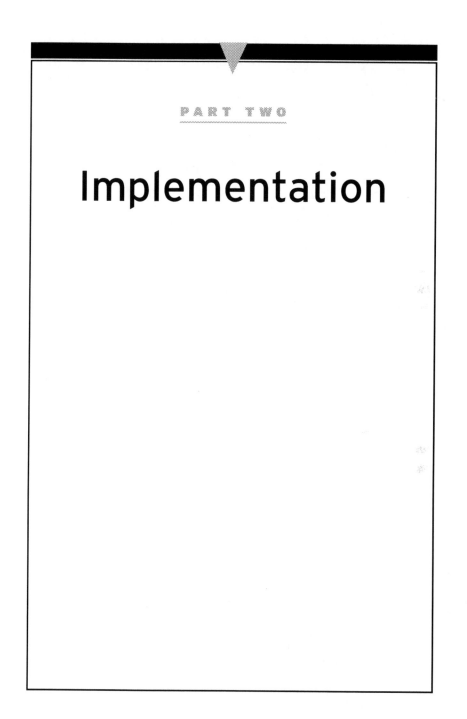

PART TWO

Implementation

CHAPTER SEVEN

Placing Trust at the Center of Your Internet Strategy

GLEN L. URBAN
FAREENA SULTAN
WILLIAM J. QUALLS

When consumers visit a retail Web site, how do they know that the information describing the products or services they want to buy is accurate and unbiased? When they order and pay for a product on-line, how do they know that their financial records will be protected, that the product will be delivered on time, or that they can return something that is damaged or fails to meet their expectations? The answer is they often don't know.

Consumers must make these and many other on-line research and purchasing decisions almost solely on the basis of trust. Yet most Web sites provide consumers with scanty information on which to base their trust. Some Web retailers are start-ups with little or no track record of fulfillment. Some may be on shaky financial footing and unable to meet their service and delivery guarantees. Some secretly collect data about each customer's Web activity and then sell this information to third-party marketing firms. Even well-regarded companies like AOL have suffered embarrassing security breaches, while auction sites such as eBay have been scrutinized for their failure to effectively police self-serving "customer reviews" posted by the sellers and their friends. It's no exaggeration to say that as consumers become more sophisticated about the Internet, Web-site trust is going to become a key differentiator that will determine the success or failure of many retail Web companies.

Trust has always been a key element in successful marketing.[1] In industrial marketing, the 20 percent of the sales force that sells 80 percent of the volume owes much of its success to building trust-based relationships with clients. To preserve trust and confidence in the relationship, a smart salesperson will even recommend a competitor's product if it better serves the customer's needs. In consumer marketing, brands such as Coca-Cola, Tide, and Disney act as trust marks, signaling consumers that they will get the quality they expect. For financial and insurance services, successful selling is heavily based on trust perceptions. Consider the recent Saint Paul Companies advertisements that show a girl on the Serengeti touching the horn of a rhinoceros. The ad copy reads: "Trust is not being afraid even if you are vulnerable."

In recent years, the Internet has established itself as a new medium for marketing consumer and industrial goods and services. However, most sites on the Internet today do not focus on building trust as part of an ongoing relationship with their customers. Many Web sites act merely as self-service catalogs: if you know what you're looking for, you can find and order the product or service. Such sites are commonly characterized by their crowded format, flashing banner ads, and off-price promotions. Pursuing the hard sell, these sites do not give customers much information or help in making buying decisions. Not surprisingly, they convert few of their visitors into purchasers, suffer low customer retention, and generate meager profits. Many companies have failed with such an approach to marketing on the Internet, primarily because they have failed to build trust.

For the Internet, trust-based marketing is the key to success. Companies can use the Internet to provide customers with a secure, private, and calming experience during which they converse with an on-site, trusted personal shopping advisor who is dedicated to helping them make the best decision. Trust-based Web sites provide customers with accurate, up-to-date, complete, and unbiased information, not only on their own products, but on all the competitive products available in the market. Their smooth, easy-to-use navigation makes searching, shopping, and comparing a pleasure. Moreover, they preserve and build trust through faultless fulfillment and satisfaction guarantees. It is not surprising that trust-based Web sites can enjoy higher rates of customer conversion and retention than sites that do not engender loyalty. Trusted Web sites actively promote deep customer loyalty, thus greatly enhancing the lifetime value of their customers. By mastering trust-based strategies, companies can build a positive relationship with their customers while increasing their market share and profits.

Leading-edge sites are just beginning to demonstrate some trust-building components. In this article, we will review the emerging trust cues that can be found on some Web sites and propose virtual advisors as a new element in building trust into the customer's shopping experience. Virtual-advisor software that mimics the behavior of a personal shopping assistant can become a powerful and cost-effective part of almost any company's Internet strategy. We have tested consumer reaction to such software at Truck Town, a Web site we designed to advise consumers on truck buying options. As you will see, most consumers who used the site trusted Truck Town's virtual advisors more than the dealer from whom they last bought a vehicle.

BUILDING TRUST AT EACH PHASE
OF THE ACCEPTANCE PROCESS

Before we consider the trust-building potential of virtual advisors, let's review some of the more established methods by which trust can be generated on the Web. (See box, The Keys to Building Web-Site Trust.) Trust is built in a three-stage, cumulative process that

▼

The Keys to Building Web-Site Trust

- ▼ Maximize cues that build trust on your Web site.
- ▼ Use virtual-advisor technology to gain customer confidence and belief.
- ▼ Provide unbiased and complete information.
- ▼ Include competitive products.
- ▼ Keep your promises.

establishes (1) trust in the Internet and the specific Web site, (2) trust in the information displayed, and (3) trust in delivery fulfillment and service. Trust in the information cannot be established until the Web site itself is trusted, and trust in fulfillment requires prior trust in the Web site and in the information it provides. Web trust cannot be established unless all three elements are well executed.

Web-site trust can be enhanced by ensuring consumer privacy.[2] Customers increasingly demand that their personal data be kept private. For this reason, Web sites should not employ cookies unless their use is specifically allowed by the individual customer. Internet businesses often use cookies to record a customer's activity on Web pages that display banner ads. In this way, the companies build customer profiles that can be sold to other marketing organizations. Some sites secretly collect even more granular information about their customers by using Web "bugs" to collect click-stream data on every step of their Web-site activity, even on pages that have no banner ads. Many privacy advocates and customers consider these powerful marketing tools to be an invasion of privacy and worry that they are being used to build personal dossiers on individual users. Companies that are serious about building trust do not employ such methods unless the customer explicitly approves their use.

Third-party seals of approval can provide an important cue to consumers that they can trust a particular site. For example, TRUSTe grants its seal to sites that adopt its standards for privacy and comply with its audits. Similarly, sites can build trust by assuring customers that their on-line payments are secure and can be executed only with proper authorization. VeriSign grants its seal of approval to sites that use its encryption and authentication services. An authoritative security policy with no embarrassing failures is a great trust builder. In the event security is breached or hackers disable the Web site, communicating with customers via toll-free telephone service can do much to preserve their confidence. Above all, Web sites that want to build trust must live by the privacy and security policies they endorse. The highly publicized attempt by bankrupt e-tailer ToySmart.com to sell its customer database to a subsidiary of the Walt Disney Co., its largest investor—or to auction if off to the highest bidder—is an example of how a company can be tempted to violate its own privacy policy. Failure to uphold privacy policies can affect not only the Web company itself, but its investors and business partners as well.

Building or transferring brand equity can also enhance Web-site trust. A brand name can provide an important trust cue connoting a Web site's credibility. Companies may be able to transfer brand equity from their existing bricks-and-mortar business to their Web site. For example, Barnes & Noble has attempted to capitalize on its reputation as a quality book seller by transferring its established brand and its attributes (selection, convenience, service, attractive prices) to the company's Web site. Web sites can also build new brands that generate confidence. Amazon.com has built a Web-trust brand by satisfying customers with the widest selection thorough information (reviews, ratings), low prices, rapid ordering and delivery, easy exchange, and quick credits.

Another way to establish Web-site trust is by creating customer communities that present user feedback to reduce the customer's perception of risk.[3] For example, eBay posts the number of positive and negative customer evaluations of each person or store that offers an item at auction and also allows bidders to contact past customers by e-mail. Although customer feedback is a potential trust builder, there are real limitations. Abuse by supposedly impartial reviewers can bias the input. An author's friends may write rave reviews on Amazon.com. Or more insidiously, a manufacturer may hire a firm to create favorable comments about its products and unfavorable comments about competitors' products. Consumer feedback is useful when the sites supplying such information couple effective policing policies[4] with a warning to their customers that such anonymous reviews may be unreliable. Other cues, such as best-site awards and celebrity endorsements, can be useful. Explicit pricing, return guarantees, telephone and e-mail support, and publication of the customer's legal rights help build confidence. Intuitive navigation that allows customers to control their Web experiences also builds trust.

After establishing trust in the site, the next task is to engender belief in the information. Information on the Web site must be complete and accurate. Sites that ask customers to make a purchase should provide all the information needed to make an informed decision: product specifications, prices, in-stock availability, delivery time and reliability (see BizRate.com for customer ratings of sites based on timely delivery), magazine reviews, customer recommendations (see Epinions.com for customer evaluations by self-designated experts), and return guarantees. All third-party information (for example, content from magazine articles and consumer feedback) should be free of bias. At minimum, the Web site should make its bias and information shortcomings explicit. For example, companies should warn customers if only their retail partners are providing the delivery and service ratings or if prices listed after completing a Web search are not arranged from lowest price to highest. Whenever possible, companies should allow customers to view information in the order they choose. Other powerful trust builders include posting reviews by credible sources, such as consumer-advocacy organization Consumer Reports, or audits of site information by reputable independent parties; frequently updating changes in products, prices, and availability; and allowing customers to personalize and specify the information displayed.

It is also important to provide customers with unbiased information about competing products, including those made by other manufacturers, thus enabling consumers to make fair comparisons.[5] Many Web intermediaries provide impartial information in virtually every product and service category. They pose a key challenge to incumbent companies unwilling to do the same. For example, Car-Point.com and CarsDirect.com supply information on all makes and models of autos. While it may seem radical for branded manufacturers like General Motors or Ford to supply fair comparisons, the Internet will inevitably force such companies to match the breadth of information offered by the new intermediaries—or "infomediaries." Companies resisting this trend will sacrifice their customers' trust.

The most important element of trust is fulfillment. Quite simply, trust is earned by meeting expectations. As small commitments are met, customer confidence grows in the belief that companies will also fulfill larger expectations. Critical functions include shipping the right product at the right time, effective installation, service, support, error-free billing, and credits on returned items. Automated tracking services and telephone-based customer fulfillment hotlines can maintain confidence when inevitable delivery problems occur. Trust is difficult to earn and easy to lose. Failing to meet customer expectations is the quickest way to destroy trust.

VIRTUAL ADVISORS AS EFFECTIVE TRUST BUILDERS

Web-site advisors are a powerful new way to build Web trust. Although a real-time human advisor might be cost-prohibitive, a virtual advisor enabled by software is able to mimic the behavior of a personal shopping consultant. A software program, not a live person, the virtual advisor is programmed to behave like an experienced human advisor. It asks questions, records responses, and proposes recommendations on the basis of the customer's responses.

In 1999, pickup trucks accounted for more than 15 percent of all consumer vehicles purchased in the United States. Each of the more than 90 product alternatives sold for more than $10,000. Clearly, consumers could benefit when making such complex and risky decisions. Imagine having the world's best expert on pickup trucks help you select the best truck. Such an expert would ask questions about your needs and preferences, provide you with full information on the variety of trucks available, and recommend vehicles that suit your needs. With this in mind, we designed a site called "Truck Town" to demonstrate how virtual advisors can create trust on the Internet. We used the analytical tools of utility theory to estimate customer preferences for each product alternative and Bayesian decision theory to revise these preferences as customers told the advisor more about their needs.[6]

Truck Town visitors can choose to be guided completely by the virtual advisor or may navigate the site independently. Truck Town's architecture allows the user to exercise considerable control over information acquisition, which is an important trust cue. Truck Town's welcome screen displays a map to help customers locate dealers, the bank, a newsstand, coffee shop, city hall, and customer-advice offices. An avatar in the form of a friendly, intelligent owl guides the customer to site features and answers questions about information sources. The owl explains that Truck Town helps customers make informed purchasing decisions and then refers customers to the town hall and the personal advisors for specific product information and recommendations. The second screen takes the customer to the town hall where Truck Town's mayor explains that all the information is accurate and up-to-date. He also answers queries about the satisfaction guarantee, return policy, and system audits.

In a national survey of consumers, respondents were asked whom they trusted most when buying automobiles: dealers, salespeople, mechanics, contractors, bankers, neighbors, or magazine editors.[7] Respondents said they would most trust an auto mechanic, a retired editor of an auto magazine, or a contractor who has purchased many trucks. On the basis of this ranking by consumers, Truck Town presents these three advisors, who are not modeled after specific individuals but are composites of the best practices of people serving in those roles.

The virtual auto mechanic in our example is named Craig, a middle-aged man dressed in a mechanic's uniform. (See "Meet the Auto Mechanic" in Figure 7.1.) After introducing himself, he answers queries about how he is paid, his strengths and weaknesses, and past customer comments. He then starts the conversation by asking the customer the size of the truck he or she prefers. (See "The Dialogue Begins" in Figure 7.1.) After conversation on the truck's intended use—for example, if it will be used to haul a trailer—Craig probes for other preferences, such as relative preferences for low price, performance, fuel efficiency, power, and style. Craig then creates a personalized showroom with four trucks that he thinks best fit the customer's needs. He bases his recommendations on how well the trucks match the customer's stated preferences and what similar customers have purchased.

The customer can then obtain complete information on the trucks' specifications (horsepower, towing capacity, load-carrying volume, fuel efficiency, bed length), configuration (selection of options), competitive comparisons with other truck specifications in a matrix table, and evaluations by other users. Customers can also obtain magazine articles and advertisements about all the trucks presented. Additional options are to "meet other people like me" or to be transported to the coffee shop in Truck Town where they can engage in a live chat session with other customers who have similar needs. The dialogue ends by scheduling a test drive or requesting a price and delivery quotation from an actual dealer.

Truck Town is an experimental Web site for truck and sport utility vehicle buyers that features a virtual auto mechanic.

Meet the Auto Mechanic

Research shows that auto mechanics are considered to be trusted sources of information by car buyers. Here, a virtual mechanic, Craig Lynch, begins to introduce himself. Lynch is a composite of best practices and knowledge—not an actual person.

The Dialogue Begins

After answering queries about himself, Craig—the virtual advisor—begins to ask the customer about his or her preferences.

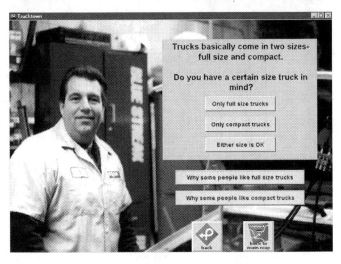

Figure 7.1. What Customers See on the Truck Town Web Site.

TRUCK TOWN'S TRUSTED ADVISORS

In June 1997, we conducted an empirical concept-and-usage study of the Truck Town prototype to assess the viability of a personal advisor. A sample of 280 Boston-area respondents who had bought a truck in the previous eighteen months evaluated Truck Town in terms of trust, quality of recommendations, and their willingness to use and pay for the service. Respondents spent an average of thirty minutes on the Truck Town site prior to answering the survey.

The results indicate that the virtual advisor developed during this research is able to generate trust in consumers. In answer to the question "Did you trust the advisor?" 82 percent of the respondents answered yes, 76 percent agreed that the information provided was trustworthy, and 88 percent agreed that the advisor recommended trucks that fit their needs. More important, 60 percent agreed that the advisor suggested alternatives they would not have considered otherwise. In terms of purchasing, 88 percent of respondents would consider buying a vehicle through Truck Town. On average, they would be willing to pay an additional $40 for this service.

In fact, 82 percent of respondents considered the Internet experience more trustworthy than an in-person dealer experience. Most respondents said Truck Town's information quantity (87 percent) and quality (83 percent) was better than that available from a dealer. Whereas approximately 80 percent would recommend Internet shopping on the basis of testing Truck Town, only 20 percent would recommend the dealer from whom they last purchased a vehicle.

These are encouraging results and suggest that the advisor-based Truck Town site successfully engendered acceptance of the advice and information provided. This is a key element in trust building. Assuming that trust correlates with sales, the Truck Town site demonstrates how establishing trust can enhance buying through this type of advisor-based system.

THE BUYER'S NEED
FOR INFORMATION OR ADVICE

An advisor is not necessary for all products. Trusted advisors provide great value if the purchase decision involves certain attributes such as high price (for example, trucks), complexity (for example, financial planning), learning (how to use digital cameras), rapid change (adapting to a new PC) or risk (health care). An advisor can help build trust and thus sales on the Internet for products having one or more of these attributes, though not necessarily all of them. For example, customers regularly pay more for branded pain relievers than for equivalent generic tablets, because they do not want to risk their health on unfamiliar products. A virtual pharmacist advisor for cough-and-cold problems could help customers make better decisions by supplying relevant information on medicines and their ingredients.

Not all people prefer to use an advisor. In our extended concept test, we compared the Truck Town advisor to an information-intensive site, Microsoft's Carpoint.com, which provides detailed information on all types of trucks. Approximately half of those who preferred the Internet to a dealer prefer the advisor-based site; the other half preferred the information-intensive site. A regression analysis indicated a significantly higher strength of preference for Truck Town among consumers who rated their knowledge of trucks lower, visited more dealers, were younger, and were more frequent users of the Internet.

These results suggest that advice is more valuable to those who are less knowledgeable and confident. Open-ended responses indicated that people who liked Truck Town valued its advisory capability, the personal quality of the advisor, and the easy-to-use and fun nature of the site. Those who disliked the site felt the town analogy was like a game, child-like, and unprofessional. Those who preferred CarPoint.com liked the depth of information, professionalism, direct access, and control. Criticisms of Carpoint.com focused on the selling intensity of the site and its sponsorship. Both sites gained trust, but one did it through an advisor and the other by providing information.

This research suggests that there are two different segments of buyers. One segment comprises those who have confidence and knowledge about what they want and therefore need an easy, direct information-search capability. The other segment comprises those who have less knowledge and want help or advice in making their choices. If one wanted to design a site to appeal to both segments, a direct-search format could be supplemented by a trusted-advisor button that provides a personal-shopping advisor. Alternatively, an advisor format could be adopted that becomes a direct-search site if the customer wants to access specific product data. It is important to match site navigation to the customer's cognitive decision process. It should be possible to fill the needs of both decision styles on the same site.

If you propose to use an advisor of some type, there are several technical approaches to choose from. They range from using intensive market-research questionnaires that obtain customer preferences to accessing toll-free telephone and e-mail connections with real people who answer questions. Of course, there are trade-offs in cost, analytic content, and trust. (See box, Which Advisor Strategy Is Right for You?) The importance you place on each of these factors will determine the best approach for you, but a virtual advisor may be an attractive alternative if the cost of human advisors is prohibitive.

SELECTING HIGH PRESSURE OR COMPLETE TRUST

Manufacturers and retailers must decide how much trust they should design into their Web sites. Strategies range from pressure selling to developing a full-trust relationship. (See Table 7.1, p. 168.)

▼

Which Advisor Strategy Is Right for You?

A business can use several approaches to implement advisory services, which differ on analytic content, cost, and trust generation. At one extreme, real people can serve as advisors via toll-free telephone numbers or e-mail. While effective in building trust, they can also be cost-prohibitive, since the company must pay for wages, facilities, and communications systems. Scrimping on any of these can lead to poor service and customer dissatisfaction.

At the other extreme are market-research methods that use elaborate questionnaires to generate the information needed to determine the product attributes that individual consumers value most. For example, Active Buyer's Guide (activeresearch.com) follows a six-step procedure, called conjoint analysis, which asks detailed questions about trade-offs in order to measure preferences for product attributes. Another method, collaborative filtering, directly measures customer product preferences to aggregate people into groups. If a customer is assigned to a group, it is assumed that he or she would like the products that group has purchased in the past.

Many sites on the Internet today are designed as high-pressure sales environments. A pressure-selling strategy tries to build business by promoting only the seller's products. Information is slanted to win sales; advertising employs flashing banners; messages are pushed along the digital network on the basis of the user's cookie and personal characteristics. Heavy promotion is used to move inventory or stimulate sales of high-margin items. Service is minimal. Results are measured in the short term.

In contrast, a full-trust relationship strategy advocates for the customer across all product alternatives, including competitors' offerings. Full and accurate information is presented; advertising is displayed only if the customer requests it; a calm, consultative atmosphere is maintained. Premium prices are justified on the basis of value added, "high touch" service guarantees user satisfaction

Both of these research methods are analytically strong and relatively inexpensive. However, one requires the customer to engage in lengthy self-appraisal, whereas the other assumes that the individual customer shares all the group's preferences.

A third approach—or middle way—is to use virtual advisors to enhance trust and support personal preferences by using reasonable analytic content (for example, Bayesian decision theory and attribute elimination). Such advisors may range from full personas (for example, Jill at CompUSA.com by Kana and Ida at etown.com by Ask Jeeves) to simple utility calculations that identify the most preferred brand (for example, software from Frictionless Commerce or from PersonaLogic, which rely on the customer's self-stated preferences to linearly weight the product attributes and arrive at an overall utility score). The cost of these types of system ranges from low to moderate. If trust is a criterion and resources are limited, we feel that virtual advisors represent the best approach to helping individual consumers make the correct decision on the basis of full information, learning, and shopping help.

over the product's life cycle, and benefits are measured by the customer's long-term loyalty to the franchise.

The third alternative, an intermediate trust-building strategy, can be implemented by offering honest information on some, but not all, products in the market. Manufacturers pursuing intermediate trust building would present an unbiased view of their own products, but would not provide information about competing products. However, their site would provide links to competitors' Web sites. Customers would be presented with advertisements, but they would be given an explicit option to remove them from their computer screens. The Web site would also offer value-based pricing and guaranteed service to ensure customer satisfaction. Intermediate trust building is a good step on the way to a complete trust relationship and may well be the most politically viable, near-term

Table 7.1. Choosing Between High Pressure and Complete Trust.

High-pressure Web sites employ transaction-oriented sales tactics: relationships with customers are short-term, and everything is predicated on closing the sale. On the other hand, trust-based sites are designed with the customer's needs in mind. They seek to build long-term, value-based relationships.

Trust Dimension	High-Pressure Selling	Trust Building	Trusting Relationship
Sales Approach	Get the business. Close the sale.	Honest matching to customer needs. Consultative sales.	Build relationships to become the advocate of the customer's interests.
Products	Offer manufacturer's products only. Sell highest margin products.	Manufacturer's products with links to competitors' Web sites.	All products available via links to competitors' sites.
Information	Slanted toward the manufacturer. Biased view of competing products.	Unbiased view of the manufacturer's complete range of products.	Unbiased view of all competing products and services. Credible advice.
Advertising	Flashing banners on a cluttered Web site. Hard selling, "buy now" approach.	Although ads are presented, the customer is given the option to omit them.	Ads are available on demand, but control is in the hands of the customer.
Price	Low prices, off-price promotions, deal-making orientation.	Honest, value-based offerings.	Offers value-added features and services at a premium price.
Service	Minimal service and support.	Guarantees to ensure customer satisfaction.	Ensure the customer receives all the benefits promised over the full life of the product.
Time Frame	Short-term view, transaction-oriented with high customer churn.	Intermediate time frame with focus on delivering extra value to the customer.	Long-term approach that wins and retains customers, increasing account penetration.

solution for executives who see great risk at either end of the trust-strategy spectrum.

Forces that move our strategic attention to the full-trust end of the strategy spectrum include competition from new infomediaries who give complete information on all brands, the desire to pre-empt other branded competitors, and the desire to better serve customers through innovation. However, conflict with existing non-Internet channels, traditional reliance on high-pressure sales and marketing, and the difficulty of changing old views in the organization all tend to direct our attention to the high-pressure end of the strategy spectrum.

Consider the dilemma of today's automakers as they try to choose between high-pressure selling and building customer trust. They want to respond to competition from new firms like CarsDirect.com, Autobytel.com, and more than twenty other Internet auto aggregators, but much of the existing dealer structure is resistant. Why be innovative with distribution channels if the existing forces can gain protection through franchise laws? Consumers can find competitive brand information on the Web, but many advertising and marketing executives cannot imagine providing fair and unbiased information about competitive brands on their own sites. What if their brand does not win in the comparison? Why should they undermine their own products? It would take an innovative and courageous executive to say: "If our brand is not the best, let's redesign it and make superior products." Indeed, a trust-based strategy creates powerful incentives to deliver the best products and services to earn customer loyalty. Of course, this is easier said than done, because the stakes are enormous. It can take several years and cost billions of dollars to design and build a new or improved automobile or truck. Nevertheless, if the auto companies do not meet their customers' desire for a trustworthy environment, they will delegate the marketing function to these new Internet aggregators and become suppliers to the new channel. Clearly, the automakers are impaled on the horns of a dilemma. Automakers—

and other companies in a similar position—must move now to adopt an intermediate trust strategy. They could even explore the benefits and risks of embracing Web trust by launching a pilot program around a particular product line or division—one they are confident would do well in competitive comparisons. The biggest risk is to do nothing and stick with pressure selling while the rest of the world evolves toward trust.

RESISTING, FOLLOWING, OR LEADING THE TRUST-BUILDING TREND

The trade-offs that automakers face today will soon confront most established firms in other industries. Trust-based marketing presents enormous opportunities for gain, but the threat it poses to existing interests—and to all inferior product lines—will be a major deterrent to innovation. It is tempting for an executive to avoid arousing conflict by waiting until it is obvious to everyone that the only choice is to use trust as a strategy. Unfortunately, by that time it may be too late to gain the momentum necessary to join the leaders in the world of trust.

Enduring customer relationships can generate enormous gains in both sales and profits. Loyal customers are less price-sensitive, and their loyalty reduces the threat of commoditization that is faced by many firms selling on the Internet.[8] Moreover, strong customer relationships open the door to cross-selling of services, an important avenue for business growth. For example, a trusted automaker could provide finance and insurance services for cars and perhaps extend into peripheral arenas such as property and casualty insurance. Trust on the Internet can leverage a firm's existing consultative selling skills. A bank that provides personal-financial advice to wealthy clients with more than $1 million dollars in investment assets could provide a virtual advisor to customers with $250,000 in assets. The result: large gains in profit at little increase in cost. Similarly, an advisor-based Internet presence could allow a firm to reach global segments that would otherwise be prohibitively expensive or impossible to reach through personal services.

Managers who consider moving toward an advisor-based system will undoubtedly worry that their decision will arouse negative reactions from existing channels and marketing power sources in their organizations.[9] They can overcome such resistance by converting channel members into allies in the trust-building process rather than adversaries that oppose change. Sharing the rewards of increased trust with the channel may help. For example, if trust widens the customer relationship, channel members may sell additional products in volumes that more than compensate for sales lost by competitive comparisons.

Companies that enjoy strong brand equity and high levels of customer loyalty may be able to follow a "wait and see" strategy. In this case, trust in the brand can substitute for site trust earned by providing competitive comparisons. However, if customers have less than perfect loyalty and need data on other products before making a purchase, brand equity may not be enough to compete successfully with intermediary sites that provide full information. For this reason, even companies with strong brands should begin exploring intermediate trust building.

Other factors conducive to a "wait and see" approach are the costs involved in implementing a full-trust information site and the initial desire to deliver basic functionality to an Internet site. Investing in trust building and competitive comparisons may also cause revenues to slump and short-term profits to plummet if the company's products are inferior to those of competitors. This prospect is not trivial given the stock market's propensity to examine quarterly results carefully. Profits would also be lost if the company were forced to invest heavily in redesigning its inferior products. Companies may also have to forgo revenue from the sale to other firms of customer demographic and preference information.

Ultimately, each executive must balance the potential risks and rewards to determine if a trust-based strategy is worth the considerable investment. Clearly, there is a big opportunity now. The pioneers in trust-based marketing on the Internet stand to gain significant long-term competitive advantage. But let there be no mistake: building a full-trust Web site entails big risks—noncompetitive products will not survive the process. Unfortunately, doing nothing has an even bigger downside. Those who wait too long to adopt trust building will be marginalized by existing firms that have learned how to earn consumers' trust as well as by entirely new competitors such as the infomediaries if they attack the auto industry with unbiased, honest advice.

TRUST AS THE CURRENCY OF THE WEB

A few years ago, a wise observer said: "The Internet changes everything." The same could now be said about Web trust. Fundamentally, we are experiencing an unparalleled growth in customer power. Today, customers can buy the best products with full information by using price-bots, such as DealTime.com, which displays all product prices available on the Internet. Consumers can form communities to exchange recommendations by means of sites like Deja.com, which provides consumer ratings on products. Industrial buyers can collaborate using Web sites such as VerticalNet.com. Consumers can also get peer input from vertical sites, such as iVillage.com, which provides specialized information for women. There are even signs of customers grouping together to get lower prices on Web sites like Mercata.com, which lowers prices as more customers agree to buy something. Similar exchanges are being formed in the business-to-business space to organize industrial buyers. Although to date these group-buying sites have failed to capitalize on Web trust in general, all the pieces exist to combine community, trust, and group-buying power to give customers dominance in the producer-customer relationship.

Indeed, the Internet puts such power in the hands of consumers that a new term is needed to describe the paradigm shift: we call it "consumer to business" (C2B) marketing. In C2B marketing, customers will demand the best products at the lowest prices. They will demand and receive trust-based relationships with preferred vendors. In the future, we fully expect that consumers will band together to design the products they want and then put out bids to trusted manufacturers that will be clamoring to supply them. Trust will be the key to survival in this C2B marketing future.

In our opinion, trust will soon become the currency of the Internet. One need only read the daily business press—replete with stories of security breakdowns, fulfillment debacles, and the misuse of customer information—to realize that trust, or the lack of it, has already become an issue requiring the attention of senior managers. Companies that want to do business in the Web world must learn to communicate and sell their products and services by providing trusted information, advice, and service. Consumers will enter into a trusting and enduring relationship with suppliers on the basis of the exchange of this information. They will give their loyalty if their expectations are fulfilled. Moreover, they will pay a premium price to the companies they trust. The companies that earn real profits in the rough-and-tumble world of Internet marketing will be trust generators selling products that deliver the best value in a complete, unbiased, competitive comparison.

Acknowledgments

The authors wish to thank the team of thirteen students who helped build Truck Town from 1996 to 1998. Special thanks go to Vince Barabba and General Motors for supporting this research and to Stefania Nappi and the staff of InSite Marketing Technology for their valuable comments and suggestions.

ADDITIONAL RESOURCES

A good introduction to issues of Internet marketing is the article by Joseph Alba and his colleagues on interactive home shopping in the July 1997 issue of the *Journal of Marketing*.

For a description of the fundamental theory of trust, see B. Barber's 1983 book *The Logic and Limits of Trust* (New Brunswick, New Jersey: Rutgers University Press).

Francis Fukuyama's book *Trust: The Social Virtues and Creation of Prosperity* (New York: Free Press) gives his view of the economics of trust in the global economy.

A collection of the most recent quantitative research on Internet marketing can be found in the winter 2000 issue of *Marketing Science.*

NOTES

1. P. M. Doney and J. P. Cannon, "An Examination of the Nature of Trust in Buyer-Seller Relationships," *Journal of Marketing,* April 1997, *61,* 35–52; S. Ganesan, "Determinants of Long-Term Orientation in Buyer-Seller Relationships," *Journal of Marketing,* April 1994, *58,* 1–19; C. Moorman, R. Deshpande, and G. Zaltman, "Factors Affecting Trust in Market Research Relationships," *Journal of Marketing,* January 1993, *15,* 81–101; Robert M. Morgan and Shelby D. Hunt, "The Commitment-Trust Theory of Relationship Marketing," *Journal of Marketing,* July 1994, *58,* 20–39; and R. E. Spekman, "Strategic Supplier Selection: Understanding Long-Term Buyer Relationships," *Business Horizons,* July-August 1988, *31,* 75–81.

2. D. Hoffman, T. Novak, and M. Peralta, "Building Consumer Trust in On-Line Environments: The Case for Information Privacy" (Project 2000) (Owen Graduate School of Management, Vanderbilt University, February 1998; http://www.2000.ogsm.vanderbilt.edu/); and T. P. Novak, D. L. Hoffman, and Y. Yung, "Measuring the Customer Experience in On-Line Environments: A Structural Modeling Approach," *Management Science,* Winter 2000, *19,* 22–42.

3. P. Kollock, "The Production of Trust in On-Line Markets," *Advances in Group Processes,* 1999, *16,* 99–123.

4. J. M. de Figueiredo, "Finding Sustainable Profitability in Electronic Commerce," *Sloan Management Review,* Summer 2000, *41,* 41–52. (Reprinted beginning on p. 7 of this anthology.)

5. G. L. Urban, J. R. Hauser, W. J. Qualls, B. D. Weinberg, J. D. Bohlmann, and R. A. Chicos, "Information Acceleration: Validation and Lessons from the Field," *Journal of Marketing Research,* February 1997, *34,* 143–153; and G. L. Urban, B. D. Weinberg, J. R. Hauser, "Premarket Forecasting of Really-New Products," *Journal of Marketing,* January 1996, *60,* 47–60.

6. For the technical-advisor algorithms and statistics for the concept of the virtual advisor described in this article, see G. L. Urban, F. Sultan, and W. Qualls, "Design and Evaluation of a Trust-Based Advisor on the Internet" (Cambridge, Massachusetts: MIT Sloan School of Management working paper, December 1999; http://ebusiness.mit.edu/ research/ papers/forum/).

7. G. L. Urban, F. Sultan, and W. Qualls, "Design and Evaluation of a Trust-Based Advisor on the Internet."

8. J. G. Lynch and D. Ariely, "Wine On Line: Search Costs Affect Competition on Price, Quality, and Distribution," *Management Science,* Winter 2000, *19,* 83–103; and G. Haubl and V. Trifts, "Consumer Decision Making in On-Line Shopping Environments: The Effects of Interactive Decision Aids," *Management Science,* Winter 2000, *19,* 4–21.

9. R. J. Lewicki, D. J. McAllister, and R. J. Bies, "Trust and Distrust: New Relationships and Realities," *Academy of Management Review,* July 1998, *23,* 438–458.

CHAPTER EIGHT

How Do They Know Their Customers So Well?

THOMAS H. DAVENPORT
JEANNE G. HARRIS
AJAY K. KOHLI

Internet portal Yahoo! records every click made by every visitor, accumulating some 400 billion bytes of data per day—the equivalent of 800,000 books.[1] Direct marketing giant Fingerhut has four million names of repeat customers and stores up to a thousand attributes on each one. Its data warehouse can hold 4.5 trillion bytes.

Can even a fraction of this data find its way into a thoughtful analysis of customer needs or more personalized, innovative services?

The answer is yes, but it may be a mere fraction. Companies are rushing to invest in technologies that enable them to track patterns in customer transactions. Yet when the transaction collection-and-tracking dust settles, most firms have a larger data warehouse but very few additional insights into their customers. In other words, they may know more about their customers, but they don't know the customers themselves or how to attract new ones.

Interviews with twenty-four standouts in customer-knowledge management, including Harley-Davidson, Procter & Gamble, and Wachovia Bank, reveal that a firm needs more than transaction data to gain such insight. Many of the executives interviewed say that their companies succeed because they consider the person behind the transaction by recording what customers do during sales and service interactions. By examining this "human" data, they can better understand and predict customers' behaviors, and they can rely less on technologies to collect, distribute, and use transaction-driven knowledge.

Not that the transaction data aren't important. Such data enable a firm to flash "Hello, Mary Jones" on the screen—along with a set of suggested products customized to her preferences—when Mary enters its Web site. But the smart firms realize they can't just collect data. The data have to translate into something meaningful about existing or potential customers. This requires first understanding which transaction-based approaches will provide the right data.

It may also mean mixing transaction and human data, a strategy that the customer-knowledge management leaders say gives them the best results. However, having a mix of approaches doesn't mean you have to integrate the data. Even the most successful firms seem unsure about how—or even whether—to integrate data types into a comprehensive customer database.

Clearly, questions and uncertainties abound. We have a long way to go in capturing a customer's psyche. But to compete for customer satisfaction, firms must work harder to collect, distribute, and use the right data.

WHAT THE EXPERTS DO

The really good customer-knowledge managers aren't afraid of the tough problems. We talked to executives in twenty-four firms known for their superior customer knowledge. (See box, The Companies We Studied.) All were attempting to combine transaction and human data. They were using a variety of tactics (depending largely on why they wanted the knowledge), but our interviews—and our

▼

The Companies We Studied

From marketing or IT sources, we learned of firms with successful initiatives that were centered on managing customer knowledge. Our goal was to better understand each company's initiative and to learn what factors had made them successful. We regarded the following twenty-four companies as particularly sophisticated or advanced in their approach to some aspect of customer-knowledge management or to the overall topic. We interviewed marketing or marketing-research executives in most of these companies.

Bank of Montreal	Harley-Davidson	Owens & Minor
Chase Manhattan Bank	Harrah's Resorts	Procter & Gamble
Clarica Life Insurance	Hewlett-Packard	RightPoint Software[2]
E-Lab[1]	J.D. Edwards & Company	Sabre Holdings
FedEx	Kraft General Foods	ShopLink.com
First Union	Marriott	3M
Frito-Lay	MasterCard	US WEST[3]
General Electric (Appliance Division)	Motorola	Wachovia Bank

[1] E-Lab has fully integrated its business with Sapient, an e-service consultancy.

[2] RightPoint was acquired by E.piphany, a maker of customer-relationship management software.

[3] US WEST merged with Qwest Communications International on June 30, 2000.

---

past work with other successful companies—revealed that for the most part the firms have seven common practices. (See box, What the Leaders Do.)

Focus on the Most Valued Customers

Customer-knowledge management initiatives take time and effort, so a firm has to know which customers are worth the cost. FedEx, US WEST,[2] and several banks categorize customers according to profitability: the customers who spend more get more services. In other cases, the customers requiring attention are obvious. In the

▼

What the Leaders Do

▼ Focus on valued customers. Figure out who is worth the effort and resources before you start.

▼ Define and prioritize objectives. Look at business strategies and customer-relationship goals and realign customer-knowledge management objectives accordingly.

▼ Aim for the optimal data mix. It's easier to use transaction data, but try adding some "human" data—information obtained when talking with customers. The exact mix depends on your objectives.

▼ Don't try to put all the data in one repository. It isn't practical yet for many reasons.

▼ Think creatively about human data. You'll need to be unconventional. Companies use many techniques for collecting this kind of knowledge: holding customer forums, monitoring customer service calls, having employees use the company's product so they know first-hand what customers are talking about.

▼ Look at the broader context. Many firms have switched from a product-centric to a customer-centric culture, which emphasizes the whole customer experience—from initial sales to maintenance and expansion. But don't focus too much on one customer type. You want to encourage customer-knowledge management solutions that can benefit the whole organization.

▼ Have a process and supporting tools. Manage your customer-knowledge initiative to get results. Know what you want to accomplish, create a plan, and get the right tools to achieve the desired results.

1980s, Procter & Gamble, which had been spending most of its effort on end-consumer research, shifted its focus to Wal-Mart and other large retailers because of their growing concentration and power. Likewise, Microsoft began to emphasize the needs of CIOs when senior executives visiting large companies saw that vastly more revenues would come from corporate, rather than individual, software purchases.

Prioritize Objectives

Initiatives are most successful when a firm first defines its customer-relationship objectives and prioritizes them according to business strategies. (See box, Meeting Customer-Knowledge Management Objectives.) The successful firms know which customers to focus on and what new behaviors the customers should exhibit. The aim of a FedEx customer-knowledge initiative, for example, was to increase the company's share of the small shipper market. However, picking up packages at small businesses is expensive. To serve the new customers cost-effectively, FedEx decided to encourage small shippers to bring their packages to FedEx drop-off points. The clarity of these objectives made it much easier to understand what knowledge to obtain and share about small shippers. FedEx succeeded in persuading these shippers to drop off their own packages and was able to increase its share of the small shipper markets.

Aim for the Optimal Knowledge Mix

Those we interviewed had long forsaken the notion of one all-encompassing solution for knowledge management. We were impressed with the breadth and creativity of techniques in Procter & Gamble, in particular. Long considered one of the world's best marketers, P&G uses data-driven approaches to gain consumer knowledge and human-centric approaches to understanding retailers.

▼

Meeting Customer-Knowledge Management Objectives

To ensure the success of any approach to customer-knowledge management, a company must understand clearly why it wants the knowledge in the first place. Our study revealed that several objectives were common to the leading companies, each one calling for a slightly different strategy.

▼ *Segment the customer base.* Look at past purchasing behavior. Using database-marketing techniques, pinpoint the customers who are most likely to buy particular products, respond to particular offers, or defect.

▼ *Prioritize customers.* Determine which customers need immediate response and which you can ignore or defer. American Century Investments classifies its customers into four categories according to the way they invest and thus knows which investors are most likely to respond to investment advice. FedEx and US WEST collect activity-based cost information to better understand the costs of serving different customer types. In fact, they have determined how profitable an individual customer is for them.[1]

▼ *Know what your customers want to know.* Do research on issues that will be useful knowledge for your customers. Frito-Lay participated in a study that compared a retailer's total return on investment for direct store-delivered brands (like Frito's) versus warehoused brands. Armed with knowledge about the customer's performance, the salespeople could make a stronger pitch for increased shelf space.

▼ *Understand your customer's Internet behaviors.* Send customized promotional messages and base offers on factors such as previous purchases. You can measure interest by monitoring the number of clicks on a link or by having a user register at a site in exchange for something of value. Advertising-server company DoubleClick has profiles on more than a million individuals that are detailed enough to deliver targeted messages. Most of the e-commerce companies we studied, however, had not begun to actively use customer-transaction data, although they plan to. As Terry Jones, president of Web-based

[1] P. C. Judge, "Do You Know Who Your Most Profitable Customers Are?" *BusinessWeek*, September 14, 1998.

travel agency Travelocity, put it, "In reality, most Internet sites know far less than magazines or credit-card companies."[2]

▼ *Engender customer loyalty.* Remember, it's far cheaper to retain an existing customer with good service than to lure a new one away from a competitor or find new ones. British Airways analyzed customer data to discover instances when an executive customer had flown one-way on BA but used another carrier for the return trip. It sent these valuable customers a special mailing, titled "Now We See You, Now We Don't" and offered them a special incentive to fly BA round trip.

▼ *Innovate existing products.* Observe how your customers use your products and services and apply that knowledge to continually improve them. Hewlett-Packard did not originally design its HP Laser Jet V to be portable, but eventually added handles because it observed that 30 percent of its customers habitually moved their printers. The company also designed the handles to be large enough to avoid breaking fingernails, since women often moved them.

▼ *Extend products or services.* ShopLink.com, an on-line retailer of groceries and household services, is beginning to analyze data about what customers generally buy on-line, so that it can extend its product array and possibly sell services to manufacturers. In markets crowded with offerings, a firm can stand out by providing value-adding, knowledge-based services. Travelocity.com offers customers who buy airplane tickets to ten large U.S. cities a "destination guide"– a magazine with useful information about their destinations.

▼ *Improve success in cross-selling.* Use customer knowledge to tap relationships in one part of the business and extend them to another. The world's largest banks are reinventing themselves into full-service companies, marketing a slew of financial services–from stock brokerage to insurance to mutual funds. Amazon.com steers its repeat book-buyers to other types of products according to interests they've shown in past purchases.

[2] "Travelocity's Knowledge-Driven Travel Services," *Knowledge Inc.,* August 1999, 2.

One of the more interesting methods is to build highly detailed mental maps that capture consumers' thinking about various products. The maps are based on extended discussions with typical consumers and on the input of P&G marketing people, who walk the floors with shoppers, noting what they say or don't say and what they do. With thorough mapping, the company can gain insight from just a few consumers. To evaluate products, P&G uses both mental maps and focus groups (an extension of mental maps that involves more consumers but with less detail). It also relies heavily on statistical data from point-of-sale transactions. Recently, it began to focus on managing explicit knowledge about key retailer chains as customers, and P&G encourages members of customer teams to capture and share important retailer insights with team members who serve the same retailer. In some cases, knowledge sharing is face to face. When teams are geographically dispersed, sharing occurs via knowledge repositories and discussion databases.

Because these different types of customer knowledge typically involve different types of customers, P&G doesn't attempt to integrate them. In the aggregate, however, P&G has compiled a huge amount of customer knowledge.

Avoid One Repository for All Data

Many companies advocate the integrated customer repository.[3] The idea is to put everything the organization knows about its customers in one physically or virtually integrated database. Using an integrated database, a salesperson in one location can learn everything about a customer; while talking on the telephone, a customer service representative can find out about a customer by accessing information with one click.

Yet on the basis of our contact with more than seventy firms and our interviews with leading customer-knowledge management firms, the fully integrated customer-knowledge environment seems to be more of an intriguing idea than a practical reality. Surprisingly, most firms aren't even striving to develop one—despite all the favorable press. Not only would the diverse forms of information be difficult to combine in one set of database records but the ongoing maintenance and structuring of such a complex repository would be almost overwhelming. And even if a firm succeeded in developing a fully integrated environment, it risks having a departing employee walk away with highly developed knowledge. Consequently, not many firms are ready to put what they know about customers in one easily accessible, computerized application.

Instead, customer data are fragmented across multiple systems and locations. One problem is that most firms have many customer types, each with a unique set of needs. How do you effectively integrate that diversity of knowledge or synthesize it into a consistent customer profile? Apparently no one has satisfactorily answered that question; even large firms are hesitating to combine hard (transaction-based) knowledge and soft knowledge into one customer database. Dell Computer, often praised as an exemplar of customer-relationship management, has not integrated the customer knowledge it receives on-line with what it gets from telephone call centers, for example.[4]

Clearly, firms need to pursue multiple types of customer information, and they need to become knowledgeable about multiple customer types. In the short run, they should try to integrate a given data type as much as possible—for example, put all transaction data on customers in one place. They should also ensure that each customer has a unique identifier so that everyone can easily locate all data and knowledge about the same customer. But for now, the best approach seems to be a mix of approaches, each in a separate database.

Think Creatively About Human Knowledge

Aside from the lack of integrated data, the most striking result of our interviews was the desire to use human knowledge. In fact, this is the primary factor that separates the leaders from the laggards. One Hewlett-Packard (HP) executive noted that the company strives "to delight our customers by providing them with what they value and may not even know they find important." This isn't an easy objective. Managing human knowledge presents the thorniest of management issues—explaining, in part, the current predilection for solutions based solely on transaction data. (See box, Making the Most of Transaction Data.) Yet we saw many creative solutions to managing both explicit (documented and accessible) and tacit (understood but undocumented and inaccessible) knowledge. (See box, Managing Data from Customer Encounters, pp. 190–194.)

Explicit Knowledge. Nordstrom's Personal Touch program is a good example of creative thinking in managing explicit human knowledge. The company knows that a person can extrapolate from past choices to current styles much more reliably than a computer, so it uses Personal Touch shoppers—fashion consultants seeking long-term customer relationships. The company trains the personal shoppers in color use, current fashions, and the matching of products to a customer's appearance, taste, and lifestyle. The personal shoppers record customer likes, dislikes, lifestyle, and apparel needs, ascertained through telephone contacts or face-to-face conversations. Then they apply their fashion expertise to sell the customers entire ensembles, not just individual items. The personal shoppers can also access a customer's purchasing history to gain insight into a customer's tastes or to suggest items that might complement a prior purchase. They can annotate a customer's records, noting, for example, to check later when alterations will be completed.

McKay Envelopes maintains detailed information about buyers' likes and dislikes. Fidelity Investments requires salespeople to record in a database knowledge about customers acquired during sales calls. This is particularly useful when a customer account is reassigned for some reason.

In Some Cases, Important Customer Knowledge Must Remain Largely Tacit. Both Harley-Davidson and the Jeep division of DaimlerChrysler "understand" that they must know their customers well before they can introduce product improvements that befit the brand. Both companies hire marketing professors (with strong backgrounds in the social sciences) to observe and interpret customer behavior at rallies and to discuss this behavior with managers and marketing professionals. This is an attempt to capture subtle observations and impressions in order to convert them into explicit knowledge.[5] This ethnographic approach, while capturing the essence of customer attitudes, is not easy to convert into traditional, qualitative terms.

To keep managers in touch, the companies have extensive programs in which executives fraternize with customers at rallies and owner group meetings. Harley executives regularly ride their bikes cross-country to join their customers. They not only learn from the customers they meet, but they experience firsthand how it feels to ride their product over long distances. Harley's intense and long-term focus on tacit customer knowledge seems to be successful; the company is in the enviable position of selling all the motorcycles it can make, with a long backlog of orders. It has one of the highest levels of customer loyalty of any business.

In General Electric's appliance division, customer-service personnel often gain tremendous amounts of tacit knowledge by observing how customers use (and sometimes abuse) the company's products. To convey that tacit knowledge to the right people, GE service reps systematically record comments from customers during service calls and give the comments to product developers for analysis. Thus, both engineers and researchers get a feel for the customer's voice and moods. Both also listen to incoming customer calls at regular intervals.

▼

Making the Most of Transaction Data

Although transaction data are relatively easier to manage than data from human interactions, it's still not simple. The biggest issue is how to collect only the data you need and not waste time and effort on useless information. Most firms gather too much customer data and then find it difficult to access the data that truly supports customer-relationship objectives.

▼ *Build relationships.* Clinique.com interviews customers about their natural hair color and their tendency to sunburn, among other attributes, so Clinique consultants can recommend the right products and periodically e-mail special offers to them. About a half million users have registered to date. Amazon.com uses pattern-matching software to recommend additional selections that are based on what other buyers of the same item also bought. The gimmicky, but still ingratiating, personalized greeting ("Hello, Mary Jones") that returning patrons see on Amazon's opening Web page is more recognition than most customers receive at their local superstore.

Financial services companies are among the greatest innovators in using transaction data to build relationships. First Union, one of the largest U.S.-based banks, recently implemented a new data warehouse. Although its size is impressive (27 terabytes), its primary value is in marketing initiatives. First Union combines this data with analysis, not only to enhance its direct marketing but also to improve product cross-selling, deepen its understanding of its customers, react more quickly to customer needs, and increase customer loyalty. The bank also analyzes customer characteristics to identify unprofitable customers, hoping to transform them into desirable customers. Finally, by analyzing both transaction and demographic customer data, First Union relationship managers are able to react in real time to consumer "events" (for example, a major savings withdrawal or deposit or the purchase of a house). It expects these capabilities together will contribute $100 million annually in revenues.

▼ *Deliver promotional offers.* Successful firms use past-purchase or other personalized data to target and deliver promotional offers. An example is the familiar "cents-off coupons" on the back of grocery-store receipts: buy peanut butter and you get a coupon for jelly. It's also a technique that direct-mail advertisers have used for years. American Express designed four different covers for its merchandise catalog; each household received the one that best reflected its past purchases. Internet-based businesses have optimized this capability by using click-stream analysis to deliver highly targeted banner advertising "on the fly." In such cases, the move from customer data to customer-service action is purely automated.

▼ *Engender loyalty.* Marriott builds customer loyalty by providing a consistent level of guest recognition and service across all their brands. For example, a guest's computer record alerts Ritz-Carlton desk clerks to any special interests or needs expressed at the time of making a reservation or during past stays at other Marriott properties. Having personalized information within the first few minutes of a guest's arrival can create a positive and lasting impression of the hotel's level of service. Similarly, call center software is now widely available to help businesses build a single view of a customer's experience across sales, marketing, and service by using data from a variety of sources. Examples include eFrontOffice from San Jose-based Clarify, now owned by Nortel Networks, and Vantive from PeopleSoft.

▼

Managing Data from Customer Encounters

There's a popular joke that goes roughly like this: a person noticed an obviously inebriated gentleman looking for something near a lamppost. When the observer asked what he was looking for, the drunk said, "My keys."

"So you think you dropped them here?" the observer asked.

"No, I dropped them farther down the street, but the light is much better here," the drunk replied.

When it comes to collecting data from face-to-face customer meetings, most firms are like the inebriated gentleman: they would rather look for the information from obvious and easy places, such as transaction data, than review sales and service reports that might offer considerably deeper insights into the customer.

After all, customers are people, not simply stacks of transactions. So any serious effort to manage customer knowledge must go beyond transaction-data analysis. Ironically, in a period of considerable enthusiasm for knowledge management, the forms of customer knowledge that are most human in nature are *least* likely to be captured and shared: customer comments, a salesperson's interpretation of who's really in charge, a synthesis of a customer's new organizational structure, or Mr. Jones' casual remarks to the sales clerk. Even among our leading firms, capturing and codifying this sort of human knowledge is a rare activity. Instead, companies prefer the area under the lamppost, where transaction data are deposited cleanly and effortlessly into the data warehouse.

It's true that human forms of knowledge are messy to deal with. Yet some firms have not been afraid to tackle the thorny problems of generating, distributing, and using human data—problems for which technology approaches are relatively useless.

Generation and collection. Most customer-knowledge management leaders recognize that it takes time to generate and collect human knowledge and that it creates extra work for those who interact with customers. Chase Manhattan, for example, wanted to increase market penetration and improve customer profitability among middle-market (midsized business) customers. To give these customers individualized attention, Chase compiles as much knowledge as possible about each one in an easy-to-access repository. Managers believe a major reason for the initiative's success is that they don't interfere with account executives when they collect information. Instead, the system gathers existing information from other sources and asks account executives only for corrections and input it can't get elsewhere. To date, the focus is on under-standing the middle-market customer's entire relationship with the bank (transaction-based knowledge). But after that is mastered, the focus can shift to capturing explicit human knowledge about middle-market customers. This might include specific details about the owners of the business, comments they make to account executives, and key issues within the customers' businesses.

One strategy successful firms use in generating and collecting human data is to solicit internal champions—typically those who would most benefit—to help pilot the effort. A customer team at Procter & Gamble was convinced that a special product-packaging initiative with its customer could yield rich dividends. It identified a brand manager who greatly needed a sales boost and was willing to try anything that could help. The brand manager allo-cated resources to the initiative, and it was successful. After one pilot suc-ceeds, other parts of the organization often join in later.

Many firms regarded the champions as critical and created incentives for them. Some reward the champions by considering their knowledge-generation efforts as part of their overall performance evaluation and com-pensation. Others reassure them that they would be the prime benefactors of more customer knowledge. For example, marketing executives from a major personal computer manufacturer combine the input salespeople pro-vide with data from other sources to direct the salespeople to potentially lucrative selling opportunities in their own territories.

The real challenge in knowledge generation is getting customers *to cooper-ate*. The smart managers do their homework *before* asking customers what they want. A P&G manager noted: "Rather than asking a trade customer what the company's needs are, I'll conduct research with shoppers, deter-mine what would be valuable to the trade customer, and then engage the company in a dialogue about the shopper research. This adds value for the customer and builds credibility and trust."

(continued)

▼

Managing Data from Customer Encounters (cont.)

Indeed, this approach is at the heart of a popular book about selling techniques.[1] The authors argue that knowledge-based selling to customers differs greatly from—and is far superior to—the traditional "cold call" approach, during which the sales representative has no inkling of the customer's needs or propensity to purchase.

3M's Telecom Systems Division holds a cafeteria fair at customer sites to see how that site is using 3M products and to expose customers to products they may not be using. 3M finds the insights useful in approaching other sites and customers and in helping customers learn about the range of its products and services. It also helps 3M understand how different sites (regions, countries) of the same business customer vary in their levels of satisfaction with the same product.

Distribution. Customer knowledge must reach all the necessary parts of an organization to be useful. Traditional knowledge-management approaches, such as an electronic knowledge repository, are helpful, because they are designed to support distribution. Modern technologies—the Web, e-mail, and Lotus Notes, as well as more specialized sales and service systems—make it easy to distribute explicit human interaction-based customer knowledge to everyone who needs it.

But distribution involves more than just how to send knowledge. There is also the question of what kind and how much to send. Several firms try to limit the information and knowledge to those who interact with customers. One firm uses software technologies that filter the knowledge according to a user's predefined categories of importance. The filters select relevant content and distribute the appropriate parts to the appropriate people. Another firm defines what types of information and queries are appropriate for a particular communication method (e-mail, voice mail). Once it establishes a norm for each communication type, it holds formal training sessions to educate employees on communication protocols and norms.

---

[1] J. Werth and N. E. Ruben, *High-Probability Selling* (Dresher, Pa.: Abba, 1992).

Using people to transfer knowledge is also critical. The solution can be as straightforward as colocating team members that serve the same customer so they can exchange knowledge face to face. The P&G team for Wal-Mart has dozens of members, all based in the same office. Colocation not only speeds distribution but also makes it hard for individuals to withhold important customer information or play similar power games.

In some firms, managers truly don't know what customer information they should seek from each other or who in their organization might be interested in what. Pepsi addresses this with its Pepsi Learning Forum, where senior managers present interesting insights about customer-related issues that might not get adequate attention in the daily rush. Topics might include subtle changes in consumer lifestyles and surprising attitudes toward salty snacks.

Using it. Perhaps the most important part of managing human interaction-based knowledge is using it to do something differently. Here, technology is of little value because what drives use is almost exclusively organizational and managerial. For example, if customer knowledge indicates the need for a substantial product redesign, the obstacles to using that knowledge—actually implementing the new design—are denial, procrastination, and a failure to listen. Technology can't resolve these.

Unfortunately, there is no general best practice here. Making customer data widely available to customers and internally is a good idea, but the proper course of action depends on too many unpredictable factors. Customers often say that they want one thing when they really want another, or they are simply confused. A manager must decide when to take a particular item of customer knowledge seriously and when to discount it or look for more corroboration. In many cases, products, services, and business models initially received negative feedback, but the company went on to have great success.

One success story is Owens & Minor, a distributor of health care supplies. The company analyzes transaction data to point out how customers can

(continued)

▼

Managing Data from Customer Encounters (cont.)

save money by changing purchasing patterns or vendors. The company secured at least one major long-term contract by showing a hospital chain how it could save over $100 million by changing its purchasing patterns. It has since started offering customers direct access to their own purchasing data over the Web.

Although there is no best practice, there are common pitfalls in using human data. One is to ignore negative customer feedback. According to a recent study of several technology-oriented industries,[2] a common response to negative customer feedback is claiming that the customer isn't "mainstream." But in several cases, these customers were actually on the market's cutting edge. When the customer turned to a new technology, the original firm lost significant market share.

Another pitfall is to focus on one or two needed changes and ignore the need for broader change. IBM, for example, had a highly systematic approach to registering, prioritizing, and monitoring needed changes in its mainframe systems in response to feedback from its well-organized user groups. However, the system was not at all helpful in dealing with customers' preferences for an entirely new generation of personal computers.

[2] C. Christiansen, *The Innovator's Dilemma* (Boston: Harvard Business School Press, 1997).

Look at the Broader Context

Most of the leading firms recognize that customer-knowledge initiatives do not exist in a vacuum. Rather, their success depends on the organization's roles and responsibilities, the workplace culture, and the organizational structure.

Establish New Roles. Many of the companies created new roles or functions to help manage customer knowledge. Nordstrom established its Personal Touch shoppers. Hewlett-Packard appointed a "customer data czar" at the corporate level to establish common customer name-and-address information to be shared by disparate business units. (It's difficult to compile substantial knowledge about a customer unless you're sure that everyone is referring to the same person!) Clarica, a large Canadian insurance company, created a customer knowledge center to develop strategies for how to manage the firm's many sources of customer knowledge. P&G is experimenting with dedicated librarians who synthesize customer data from different sources and periodically alert P&G personnel of potentially useful information.

Move Toward the Customer-Centric. Many of the leading firms have made the difficult switch to a more customer-centric culture[6]—something we believe contributes significantly to the success of their customer-knowledge management approaches.

Hewlett-Packard only recently made the switch—in this case, from an organizational culture built on product types, such as "midsize laser printers," to a culture centered on the "full customer experience," including customer support, buying, upgrading, selling, servicing, purchasing supplies, and maintenance.

HP development engineers now think more broadly about their products. For example, surveys suggested that customers would be more satisfied if the "Low Toner" message were to indicate how many pages could be printed before the toner supply ran out. This design change, which will appear in HP's future products, required adding sensors to predict how long the toner would last. Development engineers now better understand the need for such features; they see that even though a change isn't needed for technical excellence, it can contribute to market leadership.

Carefully Restructure. Most leading firms have realigned their organizations around customer segments, away from product groups. Microsoft (whose managers were not interviewed in this study) is a notable example of reorganization to become more customer-focused. Nearly 50 percent of executives interviewed in another recent survey (sponsored by Accenture) said that their company would organize around customer type by 2002, as compared with only 18 percent today.[7]

But in reorganizing, a firm should not focus its approach on only one customer type. If it does, it won't be able to develop valuable generalized solutions that the entire organization can use. One manager of a bank's customer-knowledge program said that his group had developed an effective approach to managing knowledge about his customer type, but groups with different customers were reluctant to adopt it. "Everyone thinks their customers are different," he noted.

Establish a Process and Tools

The need for a process and tools may seem obvious, but many firms seem to stop working after selecting a management strategy—in an attempt to avoid the planning that is critical to implementing it. The leading firms work hard to deliberately manage customer knowledge, using a defined process and creating tools as needed. Marketers at Kraft General Foods developed such a process and tool for managing customer data and translating it into knowledge. Using the "Three-Step Category Builder," they build an overview of a product category, analyze it and identify opportunities for new customers, and form a plan for handling that category. These steps help them work with retailers to build share in product categories. Automated templates and frameworks make it easy to do the analysis and collect the right kind of data. Sales representatives can quickly and efficiently obtain, analyze, and apply customer knowledge. A Kraft executive believes that "we have done so well [because] we focus on what is truly critical."

Kraft's carefully defined process for collecting, interpreting, and communicating customer category knowledge has paid off. By focusing on the data elements that drive sales, sales representatives get superior results using less than 20 percent of the data that competitors need for similar analyses. Stores that use the knowledge have a marginal sales growth of 3 to 4 percent relative to stores that don't employ it.

WHERE TO START

Obviously, not all firms have the resources to do everything the leaders do, but they can learn from them. (See box, Gathering and Sharing Data from Customer Encounters.) For a firm struggling with customer-knowledge management, a few lessons may serve as a good starting point:

▼

Gathering and Sharing Data from Customer Encounters

Nearly any approach to managing this kind of data is reasonable, but here are some general rules:

▼ Give every customer a unique identifier. It's hard to collect and share knowledge about a customer if you aren't sure everyone is talking about the same person.

▼ Find an internal champion. It takes time and work to collect this kind of data. Determine who will benefit from the results and involve this person or group in piloting the effort.

▼ Do your homework. You will have to spend more time talking to customers, so before starting this effort familiarize yourself with what your target customers value.

▼ Don't overwhelm everyone with useless knowledge. Manage only what people find useful by using filtering technologies to limit what you request and send.

▼ Start simply. Try to find employees who are located in the same office and serve the same customer. Daily face-to-face encounters facilitate the sharing of valuable information about common customers.

▼ Use transaction data wisely. Continue investing in collection and tracking technology, but look at business objectives to ensure you know what type of data your company needs.

▼ Try being more human-centric. Every company has some direct interaction with its customers or channel partners. Take advantage of those encounters. Although most firms don't capture and codify this kind of knowledge, managers can learn how to do so by looking at the way they manage other kinds of knowledge, such as product knowledge, competitive intelligence, or best practices. Start by focusing on particular customer types and objectives for better customer relationships.

▼ Don't worry about integrating data, but do look at data in a broader context. How do data satisfy your customer-knowledge management objectives?

Above all, don't be tempted by the easy path. Because there is not one best practice, successful firms are trying a variety of approaches. In any event, keep in mind that customers are more than transactions. The companies who know this and act accordingly will reap a continual harvest of new and returning customers.

ADDITIONAL RESOURCES

M. A. Berry and G. Linoff present twenty case studies about applying data mining to customer-relationship problems in the book *Mastering Data Mining: The Art and Science of Customer Relationship Management,* published in 1999 by John Wiley.

J. Curry and A. Curry provide the basic techniques for customer segmentation, direct marketing, and customer-oriented organization, along with an update on Internet applications of customer-relationship management in *The Customer Marketing Method: How to Implement and Profit from Customer Relationship Management,* published in 2000 by Free Press.

Defying the Limits: Reaching New Heights in Customer Relationship Management (San Francisco: Montgomery Research, 2000) is a collection of articles by academics, consultants, and practitioners on leading practices in customer-relationship management.

A. M. Hughes' book, *Strategic Database Marketing* (Probus, 1994), is a classic introductory text on database marketing.

J. H. Gilmore and B. J. Pine edited a compilation of *Harvard Business Review* articles on customer relationships in a book published in 2000, titled *Markets of One: Creating Customer-Unique Value Through Mass Customization.*

A book by A. Payne and his colleagues, entitled *Relationship Marketing for Competitive Advantage: Winning and Keeping Customers* (Butterworth-Heinemann, 1998), is a useful collection of articles on customer relationship marketing from academics and consultants.

D. Peppers and M. Rogers provide concrete approaches and tactics from the founders of the "one to one" school of marketing in *The One to One Manager: Real-World Lessons in Customer Relationship Management* (Doubleday, 1999).

In *Customer Connections: New Strategies for Growth* (Harvard Business School Press, 1997), R. E. Wayland and P. M. Cole give an overview of how to develop customer insights that includes a chapter on customer-knowledge management.

The following Web sites are relevant to this discussion:

www.crmproject.com contains the text of *Defying the Limits* (the book mentioned above) and a collection of articles on leading-edge practices in customer-relationship management.

www.customerinsight.org presents research from the University of Texas Business School's Center for Customer Insights.

www.cio.com/forums/crm/ is a collection of *CIO* magazine articles and other resources on customer-relationship management.

NOTES

1. H. Green, "The Information Gold Mine," *Business Week Online,* July 26, 1999.
2. US WEST Inc. merged with Qwest Communications International Inc. on June 30, 2000.

3. For example, see Rashi Glazer, "Winning in Smart Markets," *Sloan Management Review,* Summer 1999, *40,* 59–69.

4. C. Hildebrand, "One to a Customer," *CIO Enterprise,* October 15, 1999, 62.

5. This work is described in J. W. Schouten and J. H. McAlexander, "Subcultures of Consumption: An Ethnography of the New Bikers," *Journal of Consumer Research,* June 1995, *22,* 43–66.

6. A. Kohli and B. Jaworski, "Market Orientation: The Construct, Research Propositions, and Managerial Implications," *Journal of Marketing,* April 1990, *54,* 1–18.

7. Economist Intelligence Unit, "Managing Customer Relationships: Lessons from the Leaders," 1998; www.eiu.com/.

CHAPTER NINE

Building Stronger Brands Through On-Line Communities

GIL McWILLIAM

The popularity of communities on the Internet has captured the attention of marketing professionals. Indeed, the word *community* seems poised to overtake *relationship* as the new marketing buzzword. So-called community brands like the Geocities Web site ("home" of more than three million community members "living" in forty-one "neighborhoods") provide communication media for hundreds of thousands of individuals who share common interests. As consumer-goods companies create on-line communities on the World Wide Web for their brands, they are building new relationships with their customers and enabling consumers to communicate with each other. Many famous brands host on-line communities through bulletin boards, forums, and chat rooms, such as CNN (http://community.cnn.com), Disney (http://family.go.com/boards), the Shell International Petroleum forums (www.shell.com), Pentax (www.pentax.com; see the discussion group in the U.S. section), and the Bosch tools forum on (www.boschtools.com). Heineken (www.heineken.com) allows individuals to establish their own virtual bars, where, as bartender, they can chat with other visitors or meet their friends; similarly, Nescafé has a café (http://connect.nescafe.com).

In fact, the number of companies hosting consumer-to-consumer communication is escalating. Forum One, a West Coast U.S. consulting firm that specializes in monitoring consumer community sites, currently catalogues more than three hundred thousand on-line topic-based discussion boards (up from ninety-six thousand in September 1997). Some 85 percent of these are operated by commercial organizations (that is, they do not have .edu, .gov, or .org as the final suffix in their Web addresses), although many are small businesses and on-line retailers.[1]

The desire to create on-line communities based on brands raises many questions concerning commercial corporate objectives and their implementation, as well as issues about consumers' willingness to participate. "Is there some power to be had in claiming a word like 'community'?"[2] If there is, and if companies can harness it, will their creation of on-line communities necessarily reinforce their brands? The problem is that no one can guarantee the outcome, but the potential for success is there.

To extend the brand relationships established with their loyal customers into communities of brand consumers, strategists need to examine the long-established user communities in order to learn what makes them thrive. Strategists must also address the many issues surrounding brand-based on-line communities and incorporate the leadership and communication skill sets necessary to manage such communities.

FROM BRAND RELATIONSHIP TO BRAND-BASED ON-LINE COMMUNITY

Successful relationship marketing is difficult in the world of consumer services[3] and grocery products, where only 20 to 30 percent of a buyer's purchases in a category come from one brand.[4] Fewer than 11 percent of the people who buy cereal, cheese, gasoline, take-home beer, and paper towels are 100 percent committed to a single brand in a category.[5] Many more consider themselves to have a favorite brand that they buy most often from a portfolio of acceptable brands. If brand relationships are to be cultivated and managed over time, then the challenge for consumer brand owners is to devise a way to communicate that

▼ Customizes messages as it identifies the individual by name
▼ Rewards the individual for his or her continued support and interest
▼ Recognizes the passage of time and a strengthening of the relationship

If mass-market consumer brand organizations are to unlock the potential of the Web to help them form genuine relationships with their customers—relationships that are reinforcing, competitively distinctive, and long-lasting—they need to look seriously at how relationships have formed up until now on the Internet. Brand managers need to understand the bases for dialogue that can lead to strong relationships, which in turn provide the foundations for on-line brand communities.

Traditional User Groups

Communities of users, known as user groups, have a long history in the business-to-business world. Although user groups are more often associated with science and technology, they exist in many business sectors, including banking, insurance, real estate, and health care. The groups provide a useful forum for users to share experiences, solve problems, meet peers at conferences and events, and explore other companies and career opportunities, as well as keep current with technology and industry gossip. User groups are formed either spontaneously by buyers or at the initiation of the vendor. Spontaneously formed groups tend to have their origins in a group of local enthusiasts, such as the many user groups formed around the Macintosh computer.

Spontaneous groups are not restricted to the computer industry or the business-to-business arena. Car-marque enthusiasts run automobile clubs and organize annual shows where members display their proud possessions, trade spare parts and advice, and take part in competitions. Spontaneously formed clubs, however, can endanger a brand's reputation, as Harley Davidson discovered when the Hell's Angels attained notoriety for their outlaw-like behavior. Harley's response, arguably late, was to create the more respectable and law-abiding Harley Owner's Groups (HOGs).

The alternative to the spontaneously emerging user group is the one created and funded by a vendor to bring together its customers. For vendors, user groups offer many attractive links with key buyers and users. Vendors can contact them about new product design and product enhancements, and users often test new products. They also act as opinion leaders, providing insights into future trends and new application areas. And also important, they act as advocates for the vendor within the company.

Opportunities of On-Line Communities

In the traditional brand relationship, communication flows between the vendor and the consumer. Brand-based on-line communities have demonstrated the potential benefits of dialogue flowing between consumers via two utilities: real-time "chat" taking place in "chat rooms" and asynchronous discussions that play out over days, weeks, and even months in discussion forums or bulletin boards. America Online's real-time messaging may be considered a third consumer-to-consumer communication facility. All types may exist simultaneously on a brand's community site.

Chat rooms find favor when guest experts or well-known personalities are available to answer participants' questions. The spontaneity and unexpected turns of chat-room discussions appeal to many participants and visitors. In comparison, the threaded-discussion format prevalent on discussion boards is easier to read, since replies to specific questions are brought together under the original question.

The protracted nature of discussion forums allows for more thoughtful responses and greater editorial intervention.

The popularity of interactive communication gives the brand Web site an abundance of "free" content from the consumer community. Consumers benefit from their ability to recognize in each other "people like me" and to form genuine relationships with like-minded people. Both the content and possibility of forming relationships with other buyers and with the brand's managers act as a magnet, drawing consumers back to the site on a frequent and regular basis. This enables further commercial opportunities for the brand owners and legitimizes the investment in Web site development and maintenance. In this respect, connecting the brand site and the social aptitude of community participants potentially creates a new marketing tool.

By making sure that consumers can interact freely with each other and build a friendly on-line community, marketers can follow consumers' perceptions about and feelings toward the brand in real time. The value lies precisely in the volume of communication and interaction generated between consumers. The more communication and interaction, the stronger the community, and the better the feedback. Interactive on-line media will enable marketers to sense market forces with unprecedented accuracy and efficiency, thereby overcoming the limitations of today's one-way research methods.[6] Not only is such "naturalistic" research speedier but it gives rise to more brand creativity.[7] With the Web community as the brand's neural system, brand owners are able to respond to nuances in conversations that hint at unarticulated needs. The brand's buyers begin to set the research agenda.

New technologies are enabling the task of turning electronic discussions into useful managerial information. Tools like Artificial Life's STAn, a smart text analyzer, are designed to help companies retrieve and analyze information from on-line discussions by using fuzzy logic technology, neural networking, and straightforward statistical analyses (www.artificial-life.com).

Given the newness and size of the effort involved in managing a community Web site, it is tempting to outsource it to third parties, as many brand sites have done. The dangers of so doing, however, lie in the lost learning about the brand's consumers and the lost benefits of immediacy and rapid response. Perhaps more dangerous for the longer term, outsourcing these tasks compromises the corporation's ability to develop a new set of skills that may ultimately become as important and integral to the marketing job as are the skills involved in marketing research or strategic planning. Developing a brand-based on-line community may turn out to be a more critical task than launching a new brand variant.

WHY SUCCESSFUL ON-LINE COMMUNITIES THRIVE

Established communities on the Internet provide the potential brand community developer several measurements for success. These sites thrive because they offer their participants the following:

▼ A forum for exchange of common interests
▼ A sense of place with codes of behavior
▼ The development of congenial and stimulating dialogues leading to relationships based on trust
▼ Encouragement for active participation by more than an exclusive few

They Provide a Forum for Exchange of Common Interests

The Elsevier Science Group recently acquired BioMedNet, a virtual community of biologists and the medical community. The site features specialist discussion groups, a regular forum on a topical issue, a research database called Medline, a job exchange, and a daily newsletter, the *HMS Beagle*. The site is a research resource for the scientific community and a meeting place for specialists.

The company profits by selling advertising space on its new virtual bookshop, called Galapagos, through which it also earns sales commissions. In addition, it earns revenue through the sale of e-mail lists to advertisers. The site receives approximately three thousand registrations each week, and new members are asked if they want to receive promotions by e-mail (about 60 percent say yes). The sales and marketing director is reported as saying, "As long as the promotions are well targeted and appropriate, then people don't mind."[8]

Other types of business have also tapped into the natural gregariousness of their target audiences. In mid-1997, U.K.–based Reed Personnel Services funded its Red Mole (www.redmole.co.uk) site to attract college students to its graduate recruitment pages with a mass of serious and not-so-serious information. There, students can access a university guide in which they may rank institutions according to faculty, curricula, accommodations, and the nature of the students themselves. Red Mole students send each other more than 1,200 on-line "moleograms" a week, choosing from a selection of eighty e-cards. They can also research essay questions by posting queries on a message board or by taking out an annual subscription ($15) to the Knowledge Exchange, which posts graded essays on a wide variety of topics. They can join a discussion group called the Nonsense Exchange or compare prices of beer in various bars across the country. At the Working Mole section, run by the Reed Graduates Division, current students can look for part-time and vacation employment, and graduating students can search listings for full-time employment with Reed's corporate clients. With a steady stream of just under 1,500 students a month linking directly from Red Mole to the Reed Graduates or Reed On-line, Working Mole generates some 11,000 page impressions per month.

These communities have a distinctive focus. The audiences may be geographically dispersed and dislocated in time, but they share common interests that are perhaps difficult to serve profitably through other media.

The notion of sharing common interests also binds together the diverse and large communities in Geocities, Tripod, FortuneCity, or any of the community-brand Web sites. For example, more than three million individuals or families have spent time carefully crafting their own Geocities Web sites and, in turn, have shaped their own communities. Through their sites, people provide information about their lives, their families, their jobs, and their values. Moreover, they want to get in touch with other people who share similar interests—be it house renovation, rose gardens, macramé, or Mozart.

They Instill a Sense of Place with Codes of Behavior

Although occurring in virtual space, group members may well act as if the community is meeting in a physical public place with shared rules, values, and codes of behavior.[9] The use of the real estate analogy for creating on-line communities, such as that pursued successfully by Geocities, clearly allows people not only to understand what is on offer but also to grasp the community's norms and what is expected of them. The technology may be alien to some, but the concept has all the pull of comfortable familiarity.

Geocities sells its virtual real estate on this basis, offering more than forty "neighborhoods." Members who are science fiction and fantasy buffs might choose to "live" in Area51; golfers could choose Augusta; those who like art, poetry, prose, and the "Bohemian spirit" could pick SoHo; and those who prize "hometown, family values" could choose Heartland.

Although on-line relationships are established between individual members rather than between Geocities and its members, Geocities has to create and maintain the appropriate atmosphere. It does so by encouraging people to become community leaders of virtual "townships" and "suburbs." FortuneCity.com, which boasts a "population" of 3.1 million in its twenty themed districts, has district ministers who are "citizens of FortuneCity who offer themselves to be of service to the community."

This may be fantasyland, but it obviously works! Tens of millions of people have joined a variety of Web communities (Parent Soup, Women's Wire, Third Age, and Garden.com, among others). Their reasons for joining are both professional and social. According to a Business Week/Harris Poll in 1997, 42 percent of those involved in an on-line community said it was related to their profession, while 35 percent said their community was a social group, and 18 percent said they joined because of a hobby.[10]

They Promote Dialogues and Relationships

The threaded, asynchronous conversations that take place via many bulletin boards and newsgroups can be seen to replicate some features of face-to-face conversation, including immediacy, intimacy, and continuity. A study of an on-line group dedicated to discussing television soap operas[11] shows that conversation flows casually and colloquially, just as it might in face-to-face contact. Through these discussions, people exchange information and viewpoints. Because they are not meeting face-to-face, however, trust has to be earned over time. The group determines people's worth based on their ability to contribute and maintain conversations and relationships, on the interest generated in their contributions, and, ultimately, on the perceived validity of their insights. Status hierarchies can and do evolve over time.

They Encourage Active Participation by Everyone

Active participation is necessary to hold together an on-line community. It is generally believed that many, sometimes thousands of people, only read the messages posted on a bulletin board or a newsgroup, while relatively few people keep the dialogues and conversations active. Only those Web sites that allow for public consumer-to-consumer interaction are true on-line communities.

Internet commentator Esther Dyson[12] is clear that virtual communities involve participation and reciprocation. In stating that a community "is a shared asset, created by the investment of its members," she precludes Web site visitors from community definition. She contends that visitors, often referred to as *lurkers,* since they observe but do not participate in any discussion, are like tourists who pass through: they look and perhaps admire, but they do not contribute to the lifeblood of the community. Active participation as an investment also denotes reciprocation (since not to be replied to or verbally recognized in the virtual world is the equivalent of being ignored as a nonperson). In this sense, on-line communities evolve as participants gradually recognize and get to know one another, develop ideas about who is credible and responsive, and over time begin to develop a sense of shared values and responsibilities.

If response is a requirement for existence in a virtual community, the fact that not everyone is accepted into an on-line community has powerful implications for a consumer brand community. Frequently, norms of on-line behavior have a minimum requirement of contributors to be "on topic." In addition, they suggest that "many may speak, but few are heard." In other words, people may post a message, but there might not be any response.

Other evidence states that many bulletin-board communities comprise but a "small coterie of habitués." These findings suggest that some members may form into cliques within the greater community. The downside is that these individuals may also act as gatekeepers, deciding who is accepted into the community and who is ignored—in other words, which participants are allowed to exist.

Not all user groups are formed with altruistic notions. Some groups are born from opposition. For example, Team MacSuck was an on-line, anti-Macintosh computer group whose primary reason for existence was to prove "to MacLovers that the anti-Mac community is not a minority."[13] This was not so much a community of personal computer users as it was a loose community of some 1,200 Mac haters, brought together "in the belief that Macintosh computers are worthless and the people who use them are snobs!"[14]

MANAGEMENT ISSUES FOR BRAND-BASED ON-LINE COMMUNITIES

The now well-established virtual communities offer many useful lessons for those who wish to accrue benefits to a brand through an on-line community. They also hint at the difficulties inherent in creating and managing brand-based Web communities. Consumer product companies must address the issues of brand focus, community control, authenticity and ethics, community size and composition, and ultimately the objectives, management, and skills involved in running these community sites.

How Do You Attract Members to Your On-Line Community?

Any brand can want to develop an on-line community, but can every brand do it? Are all customers committed to a brand and desirous of having a brand relationship? Some brand products, like household cleaners, do not allow for much customer involvement. Other brands enjoy a natural focus by virtue of their high-involvement product offerings. Bosch, a manufacturer of power tools, hosts a forum for tradespeople and do-it-yourself enthusiasts to swap information and suggestions, including prices, which brand of power tool to buy, and how to fix cracks between walls and ceilings (see the tools forum on www.boschtools.com). The U.S. section of the Pentax site has a very active community of photography enthusiasts from around the world who exchange advice on buying special lenses, determining the best magazine to buy, fixing troublesome features, photographing butterflies, and so forth (www.pentax.com/discussion.html).

Other large consumer companies have built popular communities around associated interests. On its family.com site, Disney operates one of the liveliest bulletin boards targeted at mothers. Its discussion topics deal with parenting, marriage, health, food, education, holidays, and many other issues. Canada's Molson beer attracts ice-hockey enthusiasts to its site with information about the sport and message boards so fans can exchange views and gossip about their teams and ice-hockey heroes (www.molson.com). CNN hosts many discussion boards and chat sites, generated in part from viewers of its news broadcasts and in part from its regular audience that seeks out CNN when traveling. Not surprisingly, CNN has an active community of business travelers who share tips about packing, rate worldwide restaurants, and debate the hand-luggage policies of various airlines (community.cnn.com). The key is finding a related issue that captures people's attention. People must care about the issue, have opinions about it, and be enthusiastic enough to share their views.

Advantages may well accrue to the first movers in these cases. After all, there are only so many parenting or hobby-related sites that any one consumer will belong to. Johnson & Johnson is about to launch Mothers' Circle, a discussion group for mothers to exchange ideas, suggestions, and advice on its Your Baby site (www.yourbaby.com). Johnson & Johnson will be in competition for the attention of mothers with the many well-established, fully developed, and similarly focused communities to be found, such as iParenting.com (which has more than two hundred active discussion boards), parents.com, parentsoup.com, or parenttime.com. Pets Unleashed, which attracts pet owners to the Heinz pet foods site (www.heinzpet.com), is soon to launch an Owners' Corner, where pet owners can contact each other. Meanwhile, its rival Purina has partnered up with the busy and well-established Pet Place at the iVillage community site (www.ivillage.com/pets).

Running a successful Web site filled with games, movie clips, and creative graphics is not the same thing as running a brand community. The site must offer members not only entertainment but also a sense of involvement and even ownership. Communities require a truly bottom-up view of brand building, whereby the customers create the content, and are, in a sense, responsible for it. This view contrasts markedly with many brand strategists' traditional top-down view of business, where products and services are created by organizations and sold to customers.

How Many Members Do You Want, and How Active Should They Be?

Additional questions concern the size and composition of the brand-based community. Web community commentators have noted that the larger the community, the more likely it is to lose an essential intimacy. Good communities have "fractal depth"[15]—that is, they are capable of being segmented into subcommunities centered on specific topics of interest (user groups refer to these as special interest groups). The "higher-order issue," which will be the key attraction of the brand community site, must be capable of hosting many related interests and strong enough to give coherence and overall added value to each specific interest group.

We have already noted that thousands of people lurk, while only tens or hundreds participate. So how do we define this community? Do we include the silent visitors? How do we treat the shy habitués, as distinct from tourists? How representative of the entire community will be the few enthusiasts who keep the community alive? What are the brand community objectives? To attract more visitors? To have more active participants? These issues are of particular importance when hundreds of millions of consumers are buying the brand items, but only hundreds participate in a brand-based on-line community.

Should There Be Links to Other Sites?

Should the brand create content exclusively about itself? Or should the site contain links to other brand community sites? Related but noncompetitive sites would be harmless, such as a travel agency offering links to country sites or city sites. Indeed, links could be made to competitors' sites, depending on how general was the point of interest. A brand could establish a community around a sport and add links if the community expressed an interest in accessing a particular sporting event, like the international motorbike Grand Prix or the Tour de France for cycling. Although the ability to access competitors' sites—and therefore competitors' products—could be interesting to the community, is it in the brand's interest to provide access to competitors?

How Much Control Should the Brand Owner Exert over Content?

The origins of the Internet are noncommercial and, in a sense, democratic. The Internet developed as a user-controlled medium, and the success of community brands like Geocities suggests that users are still in control. In the consumer brand-based on-line community, it is likely the consumer will want to control the relationship. When building communities, marketers will have to treat their target market accordingly. To provide the best experience, brand sites will have to make consumers feel more like community members or partners and encourage them to initiate multilateral relationships.

By overly controlling the discussion or dialogue within communities, brand sites face the risks of losing the interest of their members and losing the rich creativity inherent in their audience. Decisions about how much control a brand host should exercise over its on-line community will reflect, or may ultimately influence, the brand's personality. For example, should the host adopt a strict controlling demeanor, or should it tolerate a less regulated yet potentially rebellious outlook?

The balance between freedom of speech and editorial or community control is apparent in on-line communities where the participants generate the content. eBay, the popular on-line auction house, which styles itself first and foremost as a community and second as a venue for on-line commercial transaction, is witness to the pains and pleasures of membership self-policing. Its individual buyers and sellers judge the decency of their transaction partners on public feedback forums. So important are these judgments that reputations may hold as much value as the goods that are traded. An article in the *Washington Post* details how one member was expelled from the community ("vaporized") for what the company considered her overly aggressive pursuit of dishonest participants.[16] The article also mentions that another collector misplaced an item to be sold because he was in the midst of a family crisis. Although the collector explained his situation, the buyer gave him a negative rating. The collector still feels bad about the feedback.

eBay executives are aware that a system of community policing does have its limits. They are now cracking down on "feedback abuse," whereby some participants have tried to inflate their reputations with positive feedback sent by friends, while others have been known to "feedback bomb" their adversaries with negative messages.

If consumer-goods brand owners are to use their on-line communities as a "reality check" on the success (or otherwise) of their activities, they will have to develop a tolerance for the excesses and opinions of their participants. Finding the line to draw will not be easy. For example, should they tolerate the appearance of negative comments about the brand host or comparisons with competitors' products on their sites?

Monsanto, the food and biotechnology company, retains a strong element of control over its discussion forums on its U.K. Web site (monsanto.co.uk). The firm provides specific questions for discussion, and comments submitted by anonymous contributors are not accepted. Shell International Petroleum, on the other hand, apart from eliminating obscenities, takes a completely uncensored approach to its on-line discussions. Its U.S. forum (www.shell.com) takes a bold step and allows highly critical comments from both individuals and lobbying groups. This is a very active site; it attracts comments from Shell employees as well as Shell customers.

America Online (AOL) has also experienced the difficulties of moderating on-line discussions in its many bulletin boards. The widely reported moratorium on its Irish heritage discussion for a seventeen-day cooling-off period brought forth accusations of it behaving like the "thought police." AOL prefers its communities to monitor themselves and trains its volunteer monitors to be "agnostic about the specific content and to look more at things like tone." The company admits that there is a delicate balance between maintaining a sense of community without violating the principles of free speech.[17] Given AOL's business and way of generating revenues, its investment in community training and policing is easy to justify. It is, however, a "brave new world" for those hitherto charged with marketing brands of diapers or disposable razors.

The policy on control is a tricky one to gauge. If the on-line brand community were to develop a sense of injustice and pit itself against the "management," then the brand owners would have an ugly situation on their hands. Not to allow negative comments, however, might create a sterile environment that would drive away participation and only encourage the emergence of "unofficial sites."

The appropriate response to unofficial and hate sites is a vexing issue. As already noted, hate sites do attract visitors, although it is rare for whole communities to coalesce around them. More often they are peopled with curious visitors who then move on. Wal-Mart, Toys "R" Us, Nike, United Airlines, and many others have been victim to hate sites set up by disgruntled employees or customers.[18]

Litigation appears to be a final resort but is rarely pursued, since international legislation makes this an extremely complex route. Prevention seems to be the better way. Some companies have bought the relevant Web addresses (URLs) that include "sucks.com" suffixes and "Ihate" prefixes. Perhaps the most effective approach is to neutralize the hate comments with user-initiated counterarguments, as Macintosh users did on the Team MacSucks site, or to allow well-argued criticisms to be voiced and counterargued by community members, as Shell does.

How Does Anonymity Affect Your On-Line Community Site?

It is widely understood among marketers (but possibly not among the general public) that some brands use moderators at their sites whose actual role and relationship to the corporation is deliberately hidden from the other participants; that is, they pose as ordinary consumers. The ethics of such a practice are, of course, open to debate.

One of the key contradictions of the medium is that for all its potential as a means of communication for social networking, socializing via the Internet can be anonymous. People can and do hide their real personalities and invent new ones for themselves.[19] Impression management scholars might argue that whether on the Web or not, we are always deliberately hiding some things and revealing others about ourselves and are thus always presenting multiple personae to cope with the variety of roles we play in everyday life. However, there is something about the facelessness of the interaction that may both attract some, while simultaneously repelling others, among a brand's consumers.

Brand owners may want to exercise some level of control, for example, to prevent the formation of a clique that is hostile to newcomers. The facelessness of participation certainly facilitates interventions in a community, allowing it to seem as if messages were sent by legitimate members of the brand community (that is, regular consumers rather than the brand employee). Clearly, there are issues of both brand-community authenticity as well as ethics to be considered here.

In one sense, these issues are being faced by brands that have pseudo-personalities (that is, named people) fronting hotlines or inquiry desks. Nor are these issues too dissimilar to the perception that many "letters to the editors" are invented by the publication in question. We might equally question the practice of placing brand products in motion pictures or in real life; witness Daewoo's practice of giving cars to college students.[20] Brand owners may see their anonymous intervention in bulletin boards and community sites as no more illegitimate than providing journalists with opportunities to experience their products or with stories to write up into articles.

However, given that the brand will ultimately be judged on the quality of the experience it offers through its community, these issues cannot be sidestepped by the brand's owners. Decisions and policies need to be made at the highest organizational levels. If the brand lives by the quality and integrity of the ingredients in its product or service offering, it must have equally high standards in its interactions with its virtual community members.

NEW SKILLS NEEDED TO MANAGE ON-LINE COMMUNITIES

Exercising the delicate balance between controlling and letting go will require a new set of skills within the brand organization. The community must not be overly proscribed in what it says or does, yet it should cohere with the brand values as they are intended. Brand-community management brings together three skill sets that exist separately in the nondigital world but are rarely sought after by traditional marketing management. These are the skills associated with community leadership and development, with supervision of volunteer managers, and with editorial expertise. In the electronic world of community brand management, these skills must coalesce either within the same person or at least within the community brand-management team. (See Table 9.1.)

Community Leadership and Development

Community leaders must have the necessary skills to create a purposeful and attractive community vision, attract and shepherd new members, stimulate member involvement and participation, and nurture the community spirit and keep it refreshed and relevant to members' needs over time. These skills are more readily associated with people who spend their time working in more traditional communities—for example, in leaders of religious groups, community help groups, parent-teacher organizations, and the user groups discussed earlier.

Using the model of the religious community provides insight into the practices that accompany these skills. For centuries, religious

Table 9.1. Skills for Managing On-Line Communities.

Leading and Growing the Community	Managing Volunteers	Creating and Editing Appropriate Content
• Creating, communicating, and coordinating the vision, purpose, and nature of the community, both internally and externally.	• Recognizing the talents that volunteers must have to succeed in stimulating participation.	• Understanding the interplay between serious and entertaining content, freedom of speech, and the brand community values.
• Understanding the prime motivations for community participation.	• Recognizing the determinants of trust and credibility within the community.	• Sensing membership concerns.
• Ensuring a pleasant and engaging experience from first contact to lasting relationship, while meeting corporate and community security and information needs.	• Understanding volunteer motivations and limits to volunteer capacities.	• Balancing opinion leadership and stimulating healthy debate among the membership.
• Managing the balance between attracting new members and maintaining community intimacy.	• Establishing a reward system, mentoring, and training for volunteers.	• Identifying topics of interest, managing guest-expert appearances, soliciting third-party input.
• Using political, diplomatic, and decision-making skills.	• Managing the key volunteer activities.	• Creating and managing the archive, and tracking community development for members and brand management.
	• Managing the relationships among professional managers, volunteers, and community members.	

leaders have acknowledged the importance of marking the passage of time and observing the cyclical rhythm of nature. Commentators involved with on-line communities have observed how equally important it is to mark such events in virtual communities.[21] Again, as with religious communities, special celebratory events are interspersed with frequent and regular communion, so that routines of participation are established. Similarly, an established calendar of events enables community participants to schedule their participation ahead of time. For example, Disney's Family.com site marks the passage of seasons by encouraging mothers to exchange ideas about keeping the children amused during vacations, costumes for Halloween parties, or new dishes or recipes to prepare for Thanksgiving. Parenthoodweb (www.parenthoodweb.com) organizes clubs for expectant mothers based on the month in which their baby is due.

Managing Volunteers

Volunteers serve at many community Web sites, providing a means of

▼ Keeping community management close to its roots (that is, the membership base)

▼ Keeping the costs of managing thousands of individualized and personalized relationships within sensible limits

▼ Recognizing and rewarding the desires and abilities of many deeply committed community members to increase their involvement with the community and the brand

Volunteers function as chat-room hosts and discussion moderators and as editors (often referred to as "sysops") for specific bulletin boards, where they delete unsuitable material or repetitive questions and answers. By 1997, some forty thousand sysops were on-line in the United States.[22] AOL enlists the help of more than ten thousand volunteers to patrol its bulletin boards and employs approximately a hundred subscribers (known as the Community Action Team) to determine when comments are unacceptable.[23]

Motivating, rewarding, and leading volunteers presents a set of challenges familiar to professionals who manage user groups, charities, or local community groups. The key to trouble-free operation lies in managing the tensions that inevitably arise when paid, full-time professionals interact with unpaid, part-time volunteers. The potential for conflict lies in unclear goals, feelings of exploitation, and an inability to detect when either group is treading on the other's toes (intentionally or not). Appropriate objectives, structures, training, open channels of communication, frequent contact, systems for arbitration, and early detection of overloads are essential for the smooth operation of the volunteer-professional interface. Volunteers' perceptions of overload are usually manifested in cries of exploitation. In a lawsuit filed against AOL, two volunteers allege that the company should have compensated them for their work (currently, AOL rewards volunteers with a free account).[24]

Tools are available to help volunteers handle everyday tasks. For example, Artificial Life has created smart "bots" (short for robot, an intelligent software tool that "lives" and interacts in a humanlike manner with the user). These bots respond to naturally phrased questioning and can be customized to adopt a distinctive personality.[25] Bots can be used to take over routine meeting and greeting activities or answer FAQs (frequently asked questions). "Chatterbots" specialize in small talk and can develop a memory and recognition system to enhance interchange with potentially thousands of returning visitors.

Editorial Expertise

Community members interact primarily through their own text-based content. Just as in the nondigital world, content generates content. To attract people into the Web site and then entice people to participate, the community editor-in-chief will have to develop new sources of content. To keep the audience's interest, the editor must be able to create or acquire articles from internal or external resources, choose appropriate reference material, compile directories, and archive material on the Web site.

The editorial task is also one of ensuring that the brand personality is portrayed consistently and communicated correctly through the site design. Recent data from an extensive program at Stanford University show that all interaction with computers is rich in its ability to convey personality, because users essentially treat computers as social actors.[26] Moreover, users anthropomorphize the machines and perceive personalities through the content and form of the messages built into software programs—even through simple error messages.[27] While we treat many technologies and all media in this way, the Internet allows for interaction with the personalities expressed. Computer-derived personalities will be deduced, interactively or otherwise, whether they are intended or not.

These three skill sets—leadership, managing volunteers, and editorial skills—will help the volunteer and professional managers as they undertake their new activities and responsibilities in the brand-based on-line community.

In addition to these skills, constant communication between the membership and its volunteer leaders, and between the volunteer managers and the professional managers, is necessary to make these communities work. Brand-community managers must also communicate with the professionals concerned with all other aspects of the brand—that is, those in traditional media communication, sales, operations, and new business development. (See Table 9.2.)

ULTIMATE SKILL: LINKING COMMUNITY STRATEGY TO THE TOTAL BRAND STRATEGY

Ultimately, a company's brand-based Web community strategy must be part of its total brand strategy. The various communication vehicles used by brand managers are widely acknowledged to work better when they are in harmony, either by providing the same core message to different audiences or different expressions of the same

Table 9.2. Managing the Brand-Based On-Line Community.

▼

Developing and maintaining an on-line community depends on professional and volunteer managers communicating with each other, while volunteer managers interact with members.

Responsibilities and Activities

Total Brand Strategy	On-line Community Strategy and Management
Professional Managers	
• Set broad competitive goals for the brand	• Set broad goals for the community and implement development
• Plan how to develop the brand	• Attract visitors to the Web site
• Devise advertising and marketing communications approach	• Oversee calendar and special events
• Establish overall sales strategy	• Train and supervise volunteer managers
	• Administer archiving of content
	• Monitor evolving areas of interest
	• Set editorial guidelines
	• Ensure site coherence
Volunteer Managers	
	• Welcome new members
	• Encourage participation
	• Identify interesting new topics
	• Nurture shared values
	• Arbitrate minor infractions
Community Members	
	• Mutual interaction and relationship building generates content and stimulates repeated visits

message. The integration strategy determines how the various aspects of the brand can be made to cohere and benefit the total brand. The integration skills required of brand-community managers are not new to brand management but are perhaps some of the most important.

Companies capable of multifunctional communication and integration will achieve the maximum early benefit from a brand community. However, keep in mind that once given a voice, the brand community will act as the living manifestation of the brand's personality and relationship with consumers. The obligations inherent in a brand relationship, now vocalized by the on-line community participants, will have to be fulfilled.

NOTES

1. See www.forumone.com.
2. N. Watson, "Why We Argue About Virtual Community: A Case Study of the Phish.Net Fan Community," in *Virtual Culture*, S. Jones, ed. (Thousand Oaks, California: Sage, 1997), pp. 102–132.
3. For examples of consumer cynicism about relationship attempts on behalf of consumer services companies, see S. Fournier, S. Dobscha, and D. G. Mick, "Preventing the Premature Death of Relationship Marketing," *Harvard Business Review,* January-February 1998, 76, 43–51.
4. See research based on the Market Research Corporation of America quoted in G. Hallberg, *All Consumers Are Not Created Equal* (New York: John Wiley, 1995). For similar European studies, see M. Uncles, K. Hammond, A.S.C. Ehrenberg, and R. E. Davies, "A Replication Study of Two Brand Loyalty Measures," *European Journal of Operational Research*, 1994, 76, 375–384.
5. A.S.C. Ehrenberg and M. Uncles, "Understanding Dirichlet-Type Markets" (London, South Bank University, and Sydney, University of New South Wales, working paper, 1999).
6. S. Munger, "Leveraging New Technology to Build Brand Loyalty," *Direct Marketing*, December 1996, 59, 58–60.
7. T. Duncan and S. Moriarty, *Driving Brand Value: Using Integrated Marketing to Manage Profitable Stakeholder Relationships* (New York: McGraw Hill, 1997).
8. R. Hurst, *Net Profit*, May 1998, p. 11.

9. For an extensive discussion of on-line codes of behavior, see M. McLaughlin, K. Osborne, and C. Smith, "Standards of Conduct on Usenet," in *Cybersociety*, S. Jones, ed. (Thousand Oaks, California: Sage, 1995), pp. 90–111.

10. "Internet Communities," *Business Week*, May 5, 1997, p. 64.

11. C. L. Harrington and D. D. Bielby, "Where Did You Hear That? Technology and the Social Organization of Gossip," *Sociological Quarterly*, 1995, *36*(3), 607–628.

12. E. Dyson, *Release 2.1: A Design for Living in the Digital Age* (New York: Broadway Books, 1998).

13. A. Muniz, Jr. and T. C. O'Guinn, "Brand Community," unpublished manuscript, August 1999 (contact oguinn@mail.duke.edu).

14. Quote from the Team MacSuck Yahoo listing, February 1999.

15. J. Hagel and A. G. Armstrong, *Net Gain: Expanding Markets Through Virtual Communities* (Boston: Harvard Business School Press, 1997).

16. M. Leibovich, "eBay, Cyburbia's New Subdivision, Stokes a Boom with an Emphasis on Community," *Washington Post*, January 31, 1999, sect. A, p. 1.

17. A. Harmon, "Worries About Big Brother at America Online," *New York Times*, January 31, 1999, p. 1.

18. "A Site for Sore Heads," *BusinessWeek*, April 12, 1999, p. 86.

19. For a discussion on people adopting multiple personae in Web communities, see R. C. MacKinnon, "Searching for the Leviathan in Usenet," in *Cybersociety*, S. Jones, ed. (Thousand Oaks, California: Sage, 1995), pp. 112–137.

20. L. Armstrong, "Daewoo: Big Car on Campus?" *Business Week*, August 31, 1998, p. 32.

21. See, for example, the advice given by E. Dyson *Release 2.1*, 1998; and K. Shelton and T. McNeeley, *Virtual Communities Companion* (Scottsdale, Arizona: Coriolos Group, 1997).

22. J. Hagel and A. G. Armstrong, *Net Gain: Expanding Markets Through Virtual Communities* (Boston: Harvard Business School Press, 1997).

23. A. Harmon, "Worries About Big Brother at America Online," 1999.

24. "Former Volunteers Sue AOL, Seeking Back Pay for Work," *New York Times*, May 26, 1999, p. 10.

25. For an example, see the bots on www.artificial life.com.

26. B. Reeves and C. Nass, *The Media Equation* (Stanford, California: CSLI Publications, Center for the Study of Language and Information, 1996).

27. B. Reeves and C. Nass, *The Media Equation*, 1996.

CHAPTER TEN

Four Smart Ways to Run On-Line Communities

RUTH L. WILLIAMS
JOSEPH COTHREL

Of the many ideas that have entered the business world by way of the Internet, few have proved more potent than "on-line community." America Online owes its success to the creation of community. Amazon.com has become a retail powerhouse thanks largely to the relationships it established with and among its customers. Despite the obvious power of community and the fact that virtual communities are not new, executives in most industries have barely begun to grapple with this new form of interaction, much less understand how it can be used to enhance their business. But before long, the ability to create and manage virtual communities will become a distinguishing feature of nearly every successful business.

Community interactions occur wherever people are connected over computer networks—whether these people are buying, selling, collaborating, or merely seeking diversion. On-line communities—which we define as groups of people who engage in many-to-many interactions on-line—form wherever people with common interests are able to interact. These interactions can have a big impact on business strategy and operations. And they pose unforeseen threats as well as opportunities. For example, customer communities eliminate the information gaps that companies traditionally relied upon to maintain profit margins. The Web makes it easy for customers to find alternative suppliers or to create purchasing consortiums to drive prices lower. Independent distributors create communities to gain clout over the companies whose goods they offer to the public. For example, they can compare notes to see whether scarce items are being fairly allocated by manufacturers. Employees form communities to discuss grievances about their managers. But along with such threats come remarkable opportunities. Employee communities can propagate needed change far more effectively than top-down mandates. Community efforts can vastly improve the coordination of channel partners and provide an unparalleled source of customer feedback. By developing new value-adding communities, or better managing those that already exist, companies can greatly enhance their prospects for success in the age of e-business.

This article explores how four organizations—Kaiser Permanente; About.com, Inc.; Sun Microsystems, Inc.; and Ford Motor Co.—have created on-line communities to support their business strategies. Together, these "four ways" suggest the many forms of on-line community used in businesses today and how to make them work.[1]

To gain an understanding of how these changes were coming about and what could be done to manage and promote them, we conducted a study of fifteen on-line communities representing a comprehensive range of platforms and member composition.[2] We examined four on-line communities. Each offers lessons that apply to almost any community effort. Moreover, we identified twelve fundamental lessons that provide a broader understanding of how on-line communities can be established and maintained.

KAISER PERMANENTE: COMMUNITY EXTENDS CUSTOMER RELATIONSHIPS

At the time of this study, Kaiser Permanente was the largest not-for-profit health maintenance organization (HMO) in the United States, serving eight million members in eleven states and the District of Columbia. Unlike other managed care institutions, which merely affiliate with doctors, Kaiser employed 15,000 physicians as well as a hundred thousand technical, administrative, and other health care professionals.

In the early 1990s, Kaiser began to explore the use of emerging technology to improve member services and promote preventive health care. In 1997, the HMO launched Kaiser Permanente Online, a free, members-only Web site combining services such as on-line appointments and access to nursing staff, as well as information such as a health encyclopedia and moderator-led discussion groups.

Create a Critical Mass of Functionality

Kaiser Permanente Online was originally intended to extend some of Kaiser's existing services to the on-line environment, making them more readily available and convenient for members. But behind this lay a far more ambitious goal: to help members take charge of their own health care decisions.

"Assembling 'a critical mass of functionality' was key to Kaiser Permanente Online's early success," says Tim Kieschnik, Kaiser's director of strategic development. Features like on-line appointment booking would attract users, provide a useful service, and help pave the way for more complex and valuable kinds of interactions.

Kaiser created an on-line environment in which information and services are meaningfully integrated. Discussions are often linked to content elsewhere on the site or even elsewhere on the Web. Members who encounter a new topic in a discussion group and want more details can send a message to an "advice nurse" or make a doctor appointment with the click of a mouse. This seamless weaving of discussion groups and other on-line offerings parallels the organization's overall effort to provide coordinated and integrated customer care.

Collect and Use Feedback from Members

Kaiser Permanente Online is a perpetual work in progress. Member feedback drives changes to its look, feel, and functionality. Monitoring customer attitudes is a core competence at Kaiser. The organization gathers feedback directly by asking members to rate the site on a range of attributes and offer suggestions for improvement, and indirectly by collecting data on how members use the site, including which pages are most popular, which services they use most frequently, and which discussion groups attract the most members. Kaiser has even created a discussion group devoted entirely to the Web site, thereby providing members an easy way to suggest new features and voice complaints.

Kaiser hopes its virtual community will improve customer satisfaction. The company believes it can improve members' perceptions of the HMO by drawing them into its virtual community. User surveys during the pilot phase revealed that one-third of respondents think Kaiser has achieved this goal. Kaiser believes that its ability to demonstrate the link between member satisfaction and virtual community services will create a solid business case for its continued investment in health care.

But Kaiser also wants to use community to improve patient outcomes. One measure of improved outcomes is "self-efficacy"—an individual's confidence that he or she can effectively function at the level desired. Self-efficacy plays a critical role in an individual's ability to recover from an illness or to deal effectively with chronic conditions. Kaiser is conducting a longitudinal study to assess the impact of discussion groups on self-efficacy, delving into such issues as health functioning, illness intrusiveness (that is, how much the illness impedes normal life activities), emotional distress, and knowledge about the disease and condition. Kaiser is also attempting to determine whether self-efficacy improves more for active than passive participants in its virtual community.

Harness the Power of a Personal Connection

Kaiser's on-line discussion groups present the HMO's "human side" to its members. A careful approach to on-line moderation has been the key to their success. Each discussion group is assigned a moderator from among the ranks of Kaiser's health care providers—doctors, pharmacists, nurses, and educators. In certain groups, Kaiser is even experimenting with "peer moderators"—members who facilitate discussion on a voluntary basis. One such instance is the HIV discussion group, which has been challenging yet successful. With its history of activism, the HIV community has often been at odds with the medical establishment, and Kaiser was no exception. The discussion groups enabled Kaiser to reach out to its HIV-positive patients in new ways. Kaiser used a peer moderator to engender trust, encourage participation, and plant the seeds of community. Many of those involved in developing and launching Kaiser Permanente Online have backgrounds in health education; they developed strong moderation skills by facilitating face-to-face learning and support groups. These skills have transferred well to the on-line environment. Other moderators—especially physicians—are more accustomed to dispensing advice than facilitating conversation. Offering on-line medical advice to an anonymous audience creates a legal quagmire that Kaiser is eager to avoid. The organization has therefore been very careful to define the role of the on-line moderator clearly: (1) to inform users about health issues without offering specific medical advice and (2) to create an on-line environment in which members are willing and able to help one another—in short, to build community. Both objectives are consistent with Kaiser's tradition of promoting a shared model for medical decision making.

Kaiser Permanente Online's experienced moderators have developed a set of guidelines that steer moderators toward these objectives:

▼ *Clarify, but don't edit or police.* The discussion groups are essentially free-speech areas. Moderators rarely delete postings unless they contain either personal attacks or advertising.

▼ *Understand participants' needs, even if it means reading between the lines.* The moderator's job is to find out what a community member really needs and what form the response should take—whether it is a direct answer to a question, a provider contact, a link to additional information, or simply feedback and support from the discussion community.

▼ *Keep the conversation going.* The role of the moderator is to stimulate conversation, not stifle it through excessive control. Kaiser moderators employ a range of approaches, such as starting new discussion threads, bringing in topical information from outside the site, or referring members to other relevant discussion groups.

▼ *Put members at center stage.* Kaiser moderators are expected to continually look for ways to turn the conversation over to the group. While this is a standard practice in on-line moderation of all kinds, it is particularly important in Kaiser's context, where peer support is a known success factor in managing chronic illnesses and diseases.

▼ *Show the human side.* Members can learn about moderators by clicking on their screen name, which calls up a personal profile and often a picture. Moderators also draw from their personal experience in answering questions, which helps promote a sense of intimacy and comfort.

▼ *Let them vent.* Kaiser considers unfettered conversation to be a valuable way to monitor member satisfaction. The fact that participants are anonymous—a necessity when people are revealing sensitive medical information—also contributes to an open discussion environment.

Moderators typically spend several hours a week monitoring their discussion groups. They are required to respond within forty-eight hours to every inquiry. Staff members conduct random audits that measure moderator response times and response appropriateness. (See box, The Doctor Is On(Line).)

ABOUT.COM: COMMUNITY SUPPORTS A VIRTUAL WORKFORCE

Headquartered in New York City, About.com is a news, information, and entertainment service that operates a network of more than six hundred topic-specific Web sites called GuideSites. Each

▼

The Doctor Is On(line)

Jack Chan is a California pediatrician whose work in developing electronic medical records brought him to the attention of the leadership at Kaiser Permanente Online. Today he serves as moderator of the Parenting and New Parents discussion groups.

Chan says the discussion groups offer a whole new experience to members and Kaiser professionals alike. He finds interacting with members on-line to be a welcome change from his office practice, where time constraints can sometimes limit the attention given to individual patients. He also enjoys the opportunity to draw from personal experience in his interactions with discussion group members.

"We made a conscious decision that the moderator would not be the medical answer man," he says. "Instead, much of what I post comes from my own experience. This makes people much more comfortable with me as a member of the community." Chan believes the asynchronous aspect of on-line discussion, which allows him to check the groups at his convenience, allows him to be more reflective in his comments. He spends up to twenty-four hours a month in discussion moderation.

site is managed by an expert "Guide," who combs the Internet for the best information available on his or her subject, gathering the prescreened links in a single place. Located in twenty countries around the world, the Guides also publish original content and manage discussion forums on their GuideSites.

About.com was founded by former executives of Prodigy Communications Corporation who believed search engines were ineffective at locating high-quality, relevant information on the Internet. The proliferation of self-published Web sites featuring links for specific topic areas substantiated their belief. About.com provided the platform and tools for the best of these Web sites to do what they already were doing and to reach a wider audience of information-seekers in the process.

The company recruited Guides by offering Web site creators a small fee to bring their sites under the About.com banner. By aggregating a large number of sites, About.com gained enough clout to attract advertisers, and a percentage of these revenues was passed on to the Guides. Since most of the Guides were already publishing their own Web sites without compensation, the major inducement to join About.com was the opportunity to reach a larger audience, not necessarily to receive a large financial return.

The Guides are geographically dispersed and are not employees of About.com. In managing this workforce, About.com is grappling with issues that are becoming increasingly common in an era of virtual organizations and freelance talent. The company has learned to manage and motivate a virtual workforce of independent contractors. A key element in this effort, the Community of Guides, is a forum that allows these independent agents to interact both with one another and with About.com staff members. These interactions help bind the Guides to one another and ultimately to the organization.

Prime the Pump with Communication

The Guide community is almost entirely virtual. From training sessions to performance appraisals, interactions take place via e-mail, chats, bulletin boards, or other computer-mediated communication. About.com conveys corporate goals and expectations to its Guides through an ongoing stream of Web communications. About.com continually updates Guides about corporate activities. They receive all press releases before they are issued to the general public. Conference calls twice a year bring Guides up-to-date on About.com news and provide answers to their questions about the company's direction. Such measures help Guides feel more like About.com members than outside contractors.

About.com's virtual community provides many means of support to Guides who work alone and frequently feel isolated and frustrated by the challenge of managing their Web sites. At the center of this community is a virtual water cooler in the form of a password-protected, Guides-only Web site called "the Lounge." The Lounge serves both a business and a social function. Announcements are posted there, as well as important Guide resources such as contracts, promotional packages, stationery, and archived newsletters. Guides convene in the Lounge and pose questions to staff members and one another. One full-time and several part-time About.com staff members manage the community, and all About.com editors and mentors participate in Guide community discussions.

Although most Guides visit the Lounge, About.com doesn't count on getting everyone to do so. Regular e-mail newsletters are sent to the Guides that repeat important messages found in the Lounge. Guides also receive continuous feedback from About.com managers as well as site visitors. Usage reports, which Guides can access in a private, password-protected area, tell them which pages on their own sites are most popular.

About.com seeks to create an intimate, friendly environment in which Guides feel comfortable interacting. The Lounge includes a section called "Photo Album," which contains pictures of About.com staff members and snapshots from face-to-face Guide events. Friday night chat sessions provide an opportunity to socialize with staff members in a party-like atmosphere.

Communication, of course, is a two-way street. About.com welcomes feedback from the Guides even if it comes in the form of rude complaints posted on Lounge bulletin boards. But not all complaints are as evident. Some Guides have formed private e-mail lists to exchange company scuttlebutt and gripes. One of the largest is Guidezone, a group of women Guides. Where some organizations might try to suppress such groups, thus driving them further underground, About.com's approach is to strengthen relationships between individual staff members and participants in these groups. This way, the group becomes an asset rather than a liability by keeping staff members aware of potential problems.

Help Members Help Each Other

About.com grew rapidly from a handful of employees in early 1997 to more than eighty when our study took place. At the same time, the number of Guides rose from six to nearly six hundred. How could the company maintain its relatively intimate feel and still be able to respond rapidly to the concerns of Guides? The solution became the Guide community itself. When Guides assist one another, it takes the burden off the About.com staff and is often far more effective.

About.com has instituted a peer mentoring program to help Guides who have just "gone live." In addition, staff members test new tools and design templates with a small group of Guides who then assist in "selling" the change throughout the Guide community. This "pyramid scheme" reduces the need for formal training.

Some 25 to 30 percent of conversation on the Lounge bulletin boards consists of Guides helping other Guides. The Lounge contains a "Bright Ideas" forum for exchanging best practices on topics such as community building, structuring content for optimal search engine results, and information design. About.com staff members scan GuideSites for fresh ideas and, when they find them, either ask the Guides to codify their approach in writing or offer to do it for them.

Acknowledge the Voluntary Nature of Participation

Participation in a community is generally a matter of choice: it draws on the discretionary energy that we often associate with volunteerism. Companies that try to compel participation find this rarely produces the desired results. At the same time, the motivations behind participation are far more complex than the desire for a reward, financial or otherwise. In the age of the knowledge worker, understanding how to inspire voluntary effort has relevance far beyond the management of on-line communities. In knowledge work, the work process itself is almost invisible: managers have to trust workers to apply their full talents to the task at hand.[3] Unlike the labor of the industrial age, knowledge work does not lend itself to measures such as defects per thousand or units per hour. Particularly in situations with talented workers whose skills are in high demand, employees today look a lot like volunteers—almost like the Guides at About.com.[4]

Tapping the Guides' discretionary energy depends on creating the right environment, which About.com achieves by treating its contractors as a combination of employee and customer: while insisting that Guides meet its standards of performance, the company also tries to be highly responsive to their needs.

About.com conducts surveys of the Guide community every three to four months, assessing everything from attitudes toward editors and marketing and technical support to satisfaction with the invoicing process and the tools available for site design. When management discovered that Guides were likely to be on-line at any hour of the day or night, they reorganized for around-the-clock technical support. Staff members carry cell phones, pagers, and beepers and are expected to respond to queries from Guides within forty-eight hours.

Guides are generally not shy about participating in About.com's virtual community. They understand that doing so has an impact. For example, the company's first survey on its editorial services resulted in a complete restructuring of that function. The

Lounge was also reorganized based on member suggestions. Staff members focus on identifying, promoting, and recognizing new ideas from the Guides, making it more likely that ideas will continue to emerge.

SUN MICROSYSTEMS: COMMUNITY AS AN ENGINE FOR THOUGHT LEADERSHIP

Sun Microsystems is a leading manufacturer of network computing systems, workstations, and software. The company employs 29,000 people worldwide. Among Sun's notable successes is the development of Java, a multiplatform, object-oriented programming language.

Created by Sun in 1995, Java is the focus of ongoing development efforts in many different organizations, including some of Sun's competitors. To maintain its thought leadership position, Sun must continue to stay ahead of its competitors, partners, and customers. The key lies in the organization's ability to share knowledge, code, and cases internally. According to Mark Bauhaus, director of worldwide Java and Internet consulting, "We can't continue to be the best Java architects in the world without sharing with one another."

Sun's Java Center Organization, which Bauhaus heads, works with end users, systems integrators, and groups within Sun on the design and implementation of Java application systems. The organization is growing quickly and now has managers, senior consultants, and architects in fifteen countries around the world. It is the host of the Java Center community, which consists of about 150 core community members and more than a thousand others who either work with the Java Centers or take advantage of their solutions and knowledge. The core community members are the "cream of the cream" of Java experts in Sun. They are involved in complex Java development efforts and get many requests for help from other consultants.

The Java Center Organization hosts the community, but not all participants are employed there. Participants work on many different projects and have many different roles, some internal to Sun, some external with Sun's clients and partners. The community is united by their shared practice as creators, developers, and architects of the Java programming language. They are, in fact, a "community of practice." Informal and voluntary by definition, communities of practice are thought by many to be the true seat of collaboration, learning, and innovation in organizations.[5]

Fit the Tools to the Community

One might expect Sun to use an advanced groupware product in its community-building efforts. In fact, the Java Center community relies on a relatively simple combination of e-mail and intranet Web sites. Although groupware and other discussion applications were considered, the dominance of e-mail as a communication mechanism at Sun and the low utilization of newsgroups led organizers to conclude that e-mail discussion lists would be the most effective solution. Perhaps wisely, they didn't try to encourage participants to form discussion groups. Instead, they met users where they lived—in their mailboxes.

Of course, storage and scale also matter, and these are addressed by the other place Sun employees "live"—on their intranet. Introduced in early 1994, SunWeb is one of the largest intranets in the world, containing more than five million documents. There are Web sites for all major divisions and groups in the company, including the Java Center. Users can drill down to lists of Java developers by region and specialty and, from those listings, can find developers' personal Web sites. It is a tradition in many groups at Sun that people who join the company send out an e-mail message introducing themselves. Eventually, they are expected to put up a Web site describing their work.

The interplay between the e-mail discussion lists and Web sites creates an effective medium for exchanging information when speed and easy access are critical and change is the order of the day.

Thanks to a simple, Java-based application on SunWeb, anyone at Sun can create a discussion list. Hundreds of lists have been created around groups, projects, and topics of interest. Some are relatively permanent; others have a life span that lasts as long as the related project or topic. The lists constitute a network of overlapping communities spanning the corporation, a virtual organizational structure that is constantly changing and evolving.

Mailing lists are used when timely communication is critical: announcements (often notifying users that something is now available on SunWeb), news, and requests for information are the most common occasions for posting to the discussion list. The Web is generally used to house information of more enduring value. However, like the e-mail lists, the Web also serves a collaborative purpose: the Java Center uses its site as an electronic whiteboard to display graphics during conference calls and e-mail discussions.

The discussion lists and the Web complement one another. When members of the Java Center Organization respond to information requests, they typically do it on a list, not via one-on-one e-mail. This makes for easy archiving of key conversations that are simply transferred to the Java Center's site on SunWeb. Messages sent to the list are also archived, so people searching the Web can see if a certain question has been asked before.

Play on All Motives for Participation

Despite the sophisticated tools and skills that make knowledge sharing easier at Sun, getting people to use the systems—and more important, contribute their knowledge—is still a challenge. According to Bauhaus, contribution at Sun remains a "culture in the making," not a finished product. Senior managers in the Java Center actively encourage people to participate. If they notice someone is not on the discussion list, they ask them to give it a try. This kind of nudge sends two messages simultaneously: (1) you should be participating and (2) I'm a participant and notice when others are not.

Participation can also be hindered by intercultural factors present in any global corporation. In some cultures, a face-to-face meeting is considered necessary before ideas or information can be freely shared on-line. Non-native speakers may be sensitive about their language skills and hesitant to risk committing a language error. In general, Sun managers believe that most people experience some inhibition the first time they participate in an on-line exchange. Getting people "over the hump" is considered a task for Java Center leaders, who provide members with informal coaching on how to participate effectively in an on-line setting. (See box, E-Mail Sun-Style.)

Java Center managers believe that only about one in seven people are really good about sharing and that this holds true at every level of the organization. Consequently, they also believe that, along with providing good tools and setting good examples, another element needs to be in place: a mandate to share. They are currently

E-Mail Sun Style

Sun recognizes that e-mail is not an optimal solution to the challenge of linking far-flung communities together. Daily e-mail traffic exceeds four million messages—an average of about 150 messages per employee per day. In addition to the problems of scale, e-mail is not an efficient use of the network infrastructure. Traffic increases needlessly when a message is sent out thirty thousand times instead of being posted once to a Web site. Storage also becomes a problem if users are not assiduous about filing or deleting their mail. But e-mail is a way of life at Sun. As one Sun employee noted, e-mail is often the fastest way to get an answer to your question: "I send out a question to one list, and if I don't hear back in five minutes, I send it to another list." So Sun is sticking to e-mail. But don't get comfortable if you work there and you've got a full inbox: A corporatewide policy ensures that e-mail a user has not filed for storage is not backed up. You therefore risk losing your mail if you don't manage it properly.

considering how to make contribution-related criteria part of every employee's annual performance review. They also plan to offer incentives to encourage people to share.

Mandates and encouragement are often combined to maximize the end result. Last year Stu Stern, senior manager of the North American Java Centers, decided to make it a priority for his employees to upload as much material as possible to SunWeb and make it available for reuse. The first step taken by Stern and his staff was to stipulate that everyone have a personal home page. They also required that everyone's home page provide one reusable item. People put up virtually anything that would be useful: proposals, project documents, design documents, links to other Web sites that have useful information, even links to source code. Other efforts are intended to keep the information flowing. Recently, the Java Centers declared an "international repository week" to encourage contributions.

Underlying all of this is another, more subtle influence. According to Bauhaus, leaders who want people to contribute their knowledge need to maintain a retribution-free environment. "People need to know that they won't be punished for what they say, even if they are wrong. If they don't trust you, they won't participate."

Reinforce the Community's Focus

Since the Java community is also a consulting practice, management's main objective is commerce, not community. Yet Bauhaus and his managers are able to articulate the link between the two. Business success requires the Java Center group to maintain thought leadership—to continue to be recognized by customers as having the best Java architects in the world. After all, its customers expect more because they know Sun invented Java. They are willing to pay a premium for Sun's unique authority and expertise.

Community enables thought leadership in two ways: by making a pool of resources available to members and by permitting specialization. For example, if someone needs information about a database access method, they can get it from the most knowledgeable person on the subject. In effect, the community provides a forum for people to take a thought-leadership role. When consultants have access to the expertise of others, they also realize they don't have to know everything themselves. This gives them the freedom to specialize, thus strengthening the entire organization.

The pace of development in the software industry is phenomenal, and no one group of people can possibly keep up by themselves. For the Java Center, the only way to maintain this thought leadership is both to share on a global basis and remain tightly focused. But maintaining focus is not a matter of intervening in community discussions or establishing rules for what can or cannot be discussed. Instead, it starts with a conscious effort to invite the right people to participate. This is one reason Sun's management limited the number of participants in the Java lists and kept the membership relatively small. According to Bauhaus, "Staying focused on the objective of the community is the most important thing. When the interest becomes muddy, the community falls apart."

FORD MOTOR CO.: COMMUNITY AIDS INFORMATION MANAGEMENT

In 1996, Ford Motor Co. set out two objectives for its internal Web efforts: to make its intranet a way of doing business and to create a single point of access for information. Community did not have a prominent place in this strategy, yet the strategy was clearly oriented toward collaboration, as suggested by the definition of intranet: "A network of networks . . . promoting information sharing among employees."

Ford's thinking here is more exceptional than it may seem. At its core is an insight that networks are fundamentally about people-to-people communication, not just network applications. The insight was prompted by surveys conducted by Ford's Enterprise Information Management (EIM) Group in 1994 and 1995, the purpose of which was to identify the information required by Ford employees to do their jobs and how much of it was then available. The results were an eye-opener. Respondents had access to only half of the information they needed. Perhaps more important, only 20 percent of the information that employees needed could be provided by the large corporate applications on which the company had focused its attention. Clearly, Ford's information management objectives could not be achieved without enabling many-to-many communication. "We tended to be application bigots," said Stevie Cote, head of the EIM, "but we realized that most of what people need is created by individuals using a PC."

Ford is just beginning its journey toward community, but it has done an excellent job of framing the issues and developing an infrastructure to make it happen.

Provide the Materials That Collaboration Requires

People don't collaborate in thin air. They collaborate around the artifacts of their work—documents, designs, diagrams, etc.[6] Thus, while in one sense collaboration completes information management, in another sense information management makes collaboration possible. As Cote says, "Our focus on growth requires innovation in order to achieve it. We think innovation occurs in the context of communities of practice, and the intranet can get the information to wherever these communities are happening."

The primary information repository at Ford is the Enterprise Knowledge Base (EKB), containing such items as engineering standards, test methods, and process descriptions used by program teams in designing new cars. Any kind of file, document (Microsoft Word, Excel, Adobe's PDF, HTML), or Web page can be added to the EKB, which now includes more than 500,000 items.

How was Ford able to convince people to contribute their files to the EKB? A major selling point was that the EKB made it easier to comply with ISO 9000 documentation requirements. Items in the EKB are managed in compliance with Ford's own document retention standards and features like version control, approval, and security greatly simplify document management. Previously, a program team spent days or even weeks to bring its documentation in line with ISO standards. That entire process was reduced in some cases to a mere day and a half.

Concentrate on Communities That Matter

A particular priority for information management at Ford is the Ford Product Development System (FPDS). Speed, quality, and cost efficiency in new product development are a primary source of competitive advantage in the automotive industry. Improvements in product design can also have a major impact on downstream costs in manufacturing and later in warranty repairs. At Ford, people involved in new product development have a special need for more effective information-management tools. Over the last five years, the company has set some extraordinary goals for the FPDS organization. As one interviewee noted, "We took away 40 percent of their time, 30 percent of their budget, 20 percent of their staff, and then we asked them to work better." In this environment, better information management is a survival tool.

Within FPDS, there are three Vehicle Centers: large cars, small cars, and trucks. Each Vehicle Center consists of multiple "program teams," which are groups of people responsible for taking a new car or truck all the way from the idea stage to production. They are also responsible for updates, or "freshenings," to existing models. The program teams are multidisciplinary, combining people from engineering, marketing, manufacturing, and supplier organizations—all those with a stake in the product development process.

When Vehicle Center structure was implemented in 1995, colocated functional groups like engineering and marketing were greatly reduced, and the personnel were redeployed to the new Vehicle Centers. While inefficient in many ways, colocation of functional specialists promoted an exchange of ideas and information that has become much more difficult under the new organizational structure. According to David Roggenkamp, manager of the FPDS Communications group, "You might call one of your functional colleagues to discuss an idea or to find out if a product problem has already been solved. But by the time you've left a few voice messages or e-mails and still haven't heard back, you whip out a blank piece of paper and figure it out yourself." Now Ford provides systems, tools, and processes that help functional specialists reconnect, not in physical space, but as on-line communities.

Form Communities Around People, Not Applications

The product development community at Ford does not have a single application or space where the community "lives" on-line. At Ford, the options include integrated e-mail, calendaring, corporate directory services; team and department home pages; the EKB; shared network storage; discussion forums (associated with each of the major sections of the EKB); corporate newsgroups; and other tools such as voice mail, videoconferencing, and whiteboarding. Ford's product development group relies most heavily on the Enterprise Knowledge Base, shared storage, Web sites, and voice mail.

Each program team has its own Web site. Links to the EKB from the template make sure that new team Web sites are effectively "preloaded" with the basic information members need. Instead of using the corporate directory, FPDS personnel are more likely to call the FPDS hotline, where staff members can often answer "whom to call about what" questions because of their frequent interactions with many parts of the organization.

Ford continuously modifies its plans in response to information it receives from users. In the early stages, EIM assumed community members would want to make information available for each other in Web page format. They later discovered that people preferred to share native files—spreadsheets, word-processing documents, and the like. Shared network storage was a compromise between the goals of information management and the messy realities of creativity and collaboration.

THREE KEYS TO CREATING AND SUSTAINING ON-LINE COMMUNITIES

As our four examples illustrate, on-line communities require a wide range of supporting activities, from making sure the enabling technologies are available and working to gathering and acting upon member feedback. Three kinds of activities appear critical to a community's continued viability: (1) member development, (2) asset management, and (3) community relations.

Member Development

Communities need critical mass to remain active and hold the attention of members. Because attrition always occurs, member development must be an ongoing effort. A clearly defined community focus helps coordinators conduct market research to identify potential members as well as the content, tools, and services that will draw them in. For example, are members and potential members technologically savvy? If so, sophisticated functionality will increase community activity; if not, it will merely cause frustration and turn people away.

Another effective approach is to work with individuals who influence community members or play leading roles in the community. They can become effective evangelists and a focal point for community formation. Community organizers need to know and cultivate such opinion leaders.

Finally, there's no substitute for one-on-one promotion among potential members. There are many approaches: direct e-mail, phone, or fax; on-line and off-line presentations to related groups or gatherings; and encouragement of recruitment activities by existing members. For communities of employees or business partners, training sessions and in-person meetings are also effective.

Asset Management

What are the assets of an on-line community? They range from content, both externally and internally generated, to alliances with other groups to the knowledge and experience of experts to the community infrastructure (hardware, software, interface, and other design elements). The commitment of members to the community is itself an asset. One way to sustain this commitment is to provide a blend of services, content, and relationships that is difficult to find elsewhere. This in turn creates the kind of virtuous cycle that drives a successful community.

The community coordinator is responsible for maintaining the community's assets. Start by identifying those assets and creating a plan to manage them. Among the communities that we studied, asset management activities included

▼ Creating member profiles and topic-specific subcommunities to make the expertise within the community more visible

▼ Maintaining a balance between experts and novices in the community

▼ Capturing the information members need and creating structures and taxonomies that make the information easily accessible

▼ Creating processes that facilitate discussion and other forms of contribution

▼ Creating a critical mass of functionality that encourages use of community spaces

Community needs, like those of individual members, are constantly shifting. Making sure that assets remain valuable to members involves a continual "ear to the ground." Community organizers must gather feedback from members about what they find most beneficial. This can be done through one-on-one interviews, surveys, electronic feedback forms, rating tools, or simply by monitoring discussion groups. Members can also share in asset management efforts. As a community matures, volunteers often come forward to help create and maintain assets that are pertinent to specific sub-groups. Organizers can harness this discretionary energy to build the value of the community.

Community Relations

Of course, the main reason people participate in communities—on-line or otherwise—is to interact with other people. Where there is little or no face-to-face interaction, nurturing and strengthening connections can be a delicate balancing act. It calls for both a solid structure of norms and guidelines and the flexible "reading between the lines" of on-line moderation and facilitation.

In many communities, conflict is welcomed as a spur to participation. Most communities have a strong element of self-policing; when conflicts arise or members behave inappropriately, other members step in. Explicit rules and guidelines provide a reference point for members who want to play this role. But formal moderation is often required, and it takes skills and experience to do it successfully. For communities where discussion is a core activity, moderators are usually experienced or rigorously trained.

Managing community relations involves tending to connections between people, rather than the assets the community creates. As such, informal or social interactions are typically valued and promoted. Some organizations, like About.com, hold real-time on-line events to celebrate important milestones in the community's life. Many communities take the activity off-line as well: face-to-face interactions help cement the relationships that have been established on-line.

As shown by Ford, Sun, About.com, and Kaiser Permanente, on-line community can be a powerful ally in confronting some of today's most challenging business issues. But success requires effective execution in member development, asset management, and community relations. By understanding and using these key elements, executives can begin to build communities that will support their business model, no matter what that model happens to be.

NOTES

1. The theme of this article is derived from *Four Ways of Being Human*, the classic anthropology textbook by Genevieve Hellen Lisitzky. Lisitzky's book illustrated the myriad ways of "being human" through four diverse examples.

2. The fifteen communities included Amoco, Awakening Technology, Buckman Laboratories, Fast Company, Ford Motor Company, Grand-Net, Hewlett-Packard, Kaiser Permanente, About.com, Monsanto, the Motley Fool, Snap-on Tools, Sun Microsystems, Swiss Re, and U.S. West. The research was conducted by a collaborative team led by Arthur Andersen's Next Generation Research Group and including representatives from the study's three co-sponsors: Shell Oil Company, Anheuser-Busch, and the Mutual Group. A representative from each of the fifteen communities completed a pre-interview questionnaire that provided such basic information as community origin, purpose, size, composition, support structure, and technologies. Hour-long telephone interviews were then conducted with individuals responsible for the day-to-day operations of the community, whom we refer to in this article as the "community coordinator." These individuals had a wide range of backgrounds and occupied many different levels of authority within their organizations. The interviews delved into such issues as frequency of contribution, personnel requirements to maintain community, the existence of formal roles, the use of on-line events, and how outcomes are measured. This phase resulted in a preliminary list of best practices that contributed to formulation of the lessons presented in this article. Four of the fifteen candidates were then selected for more in-depth study. This final phase included interviews with sponsors, managers, members, administrators, and technologists to obtain a broader perspective on the workings of the community. For each on-line community, we conducted up to eight hour-long interviews. Where possible, we performed an in-depth review of the community site as well as an assessment of the interaction among members and community moderators.

3. Steven Barley writes about the "invisibility" of today's work in his introduction to Julian Orr's classic of workplace ethnography, *Talking About Machines: An Ethnography of a Modern Job* (Ithaca, New York: ILR Press, 1994). Orr's book, which describes the work of copy-machine technicians, vividly describes the community interactions that effective work performance often depends upon.

4. Managing discretionary effort—not just from employees, but business partners and even customers—presents itself as one of the key management challenges of the twenty-first century. For a look at the customer dimension, see C. K. Prahalad and V. Ramaswamy, "Coopting Customer Competence," *Harvard Business Review,* January-February 2000, *78,* 79–87.

5. Key texts include E. Wenger, "Communities of Practice: The Organizational Frontier," *Harvard Business Review,* January-February 2000, *78,* 139–145; E. Wenger, *Communities of Practice: Learning, Meaning, and Identity* (New York: Cambridge University Press, 1998); J. S. Brown and P. Duguid, "Organizing Knowledge," *California Management Review,* Spring 1998, *40,* 90–111; and J. S. Brown and P. Duguid, "Organizational Learning and Communities-of-Practice: Toward a Unified View of Working, Learning, and Innovation," *Organization Science,* February 1991, *2,* 40–57.

6. As John Seely Brown and Paul Duguid point out, "Communities bound together by texts . . . predate not only the Net and the telephone, but even the printing press. Sharing and circulating documents, it seems, have long provided an interesting social glue." J. S. Brown and P. Duguid, *The Social Life of Information* (Boston: Harvard Business School Press, 2000), p. 190.

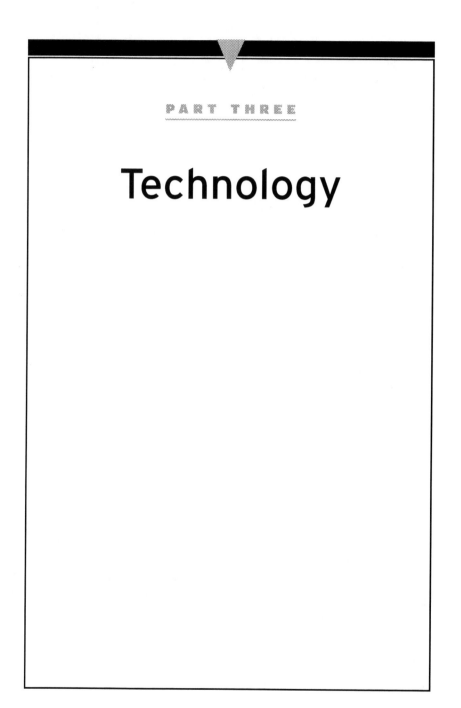

PART THREE

Technology

CHAPTER ELEVEN

Product-Development Practices That Work: How Internet Companies Build Software

ALAN MacCORMACK

Software is an increasingly pervasive part of the New Economy. As a result, today's general managers need to be aware of the most effective methods for developing and deploying software products and services within their organizations. Delegating such decisions to a technical staff, however skilled, can be a risky strategy. A study completed last year contains a surprising insight for managers: Dealing with the software revolution requires a process that is not revolutionary but evolutionary.

Evidence of the increasing importance of software abounds. In the United States alone, sales of software products and services exceeded $140 billion during 1998, a gain of more than 17 percent from the previous year.[1] In 2000, the software industry's contribution to the U.S. economy was expected to surpass that of the auto industry and overtake all other manufacturing industry groups for the first time.[2] Employment in software-related positions is growing, too. In 1998, the U.S. software industry directly employed more than eight hundred thousand people, with an average salary twice the national figure.[3] More than two million people are now employed as software programmers, a statistic that shows that software is not developed at a Microsoft or an Oracle but within the information-technology departments of large, traditional organizations.[4]

Software also is playing a larger role in the content delivered to customers in many industries. Nowadays, the average family sedan or high-end coffeemaker may contain more software than the first Apollo spacecraft. What's more, the software features in those products may be the most critical differentiating factors. And even in industries in which software is not yet part of the products, it is playing a greater role in the products' development. As companies adopt new computer-aided design technologies, the development processes for many products increasingly resemble those found in the software industry.

DEVELOPING PRODUCTS ON INTERNET TIME

Given the importance of software, the lack of research on the best ways to manage its development is surprising. Many different models have been proposed since the much-cited waterfall model emerged more than thirty years ago. Unfortunately, few studies have confirmed empirically the benefits of the newer models. The most widely quoted references report lessons from only a few successful projects.[5]

Now a two-year empirical study, which the author and colleagues Marco Iansiti and Roberto Verganti completed last year, reveals thought-provoking information from the Internet-software industry—an industry in which the need for a responsive development process has never been greater.[6] The researchers analyzed data from twenty-nine completed projects and identified the characteristics most associated with the best outcomes. (See box, Four Software-Development Practices That Spell Success.) Successful

▼

Four Software-Development Practices That Spell Success

Analysis of Internet-software-development projects in a recent study uncovered successful practices.

▼ An early release of the evolving product design to customers

▼ Daily incorporation of new software code and rapid feedback on design changes

▼ A team with broad-based experience of shipping multiple projects

▼ Major investments in the design of the product architecture

development was evolutionary in nature. Companies first would release a low-functionality version of a product to selected customers at a very early stage of development. Thereafter work would proceed in an iterative fashion, with the design allowed to evolve in response to the customers' feedback. The approach contrasts with traditional models of software development and their more sequential processes. Although the evolutionary model has been around for several years, this is the first time the connection has been demonstrated between the practices that support the model and the quality of the resulting product.

MICROSOFT MEETS THE CHALLENGE: INTERNET EXPLORER 3.0

Consider Microsoft and its development of Internet Explorer. In the Internet's early years, small, nimble competitors such as Netscape and Yahoo! established leading positions—in part, through highly flexible development techniques.[7] In late 1995, many analysts thought Microsoft would be another incumbent that stumbled when faced with a disruptive innovation in its core business. Microsoft had been slow to recognize the potential of the Internet and was considered at least a generation behind Netscape in browser technology. Yet in the course of one project, Microsoft succeeded in making up the ground and introducing a product—Internet Explorer 3.0—that many considered the equal of Netscape's offering. To a great extent, the achievement relied on the Explorer team's development process. (See Figure 11.1.)

Internet Explorer 3.0 (IE3) was Microsoft's first browser release with a major internal-development component.[8] The project started on November 1, 1995, with the white paper "How We Get 30 Percent Market Share in One Year." A small team started putting together the initial specifications, which were released to Microsoft's development partners on December 7. The project was designated a "companywide emergency." As one IE3 manager explained it, the designation meant that "if you were smart and had time on your hands, you should help out the IE3 team. Given that we have a bunch of people here who are incredibly smart, we got a lot of great help. People realized this was a group that was going to determine what their stock was worth."

During December, detailed coding of the individual modules started. But the IE3 team was still making decisions about the overall product architecture—decisions that would not only affect the features in the final product but also the development process itself. A team member explained, "We had a large number of people who would have to work in parallel to meet the target ship date. We therefore had to develop an architecture where we could have separate component teams feed into the product. Not all of these teams were necessarily inside the company. The investment in architectural design was therefore critical. In fact, if someone asked what the most successful aspect of IE3 was, I would say it was the job we did in 'componentizing' the product."

The first integration of the new component modules into a working system occurred in the first week of March 1996. Although only about 30 percent of the final functionality was included in IE3 at that point, it was enough to get meaningful feedback on how the product worked. It also provided a base-line

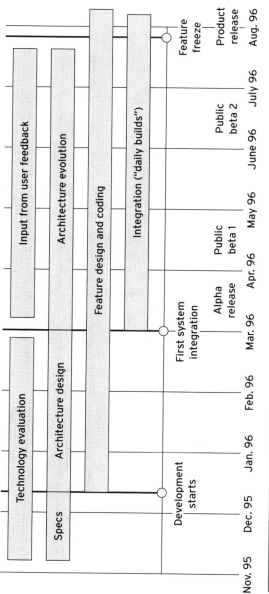

Figure 11.1. The Development of Internet Explorer 3.0.

product, or alpha version, that could be handed to Microsoft's development partners. From that point on, the team instituted a process of "daily builds," which integrated new code into a complete product every day. Once new code was "checked in" (integrated into the master version), getting performance feedback through a series of automated tests typically took less than three hours. With the rapid feedback cycle, the team could add new functionality to the product, test the impact of each feature, and make suitable adjustments to the design.

In mid-April, Microsoft distributed the first beta version of IE3 to the general public. That version included about 50 to 70 percent of the final functionality in the product. A second beta version followed in June and included 70 to 90 percent of IE's final functionality. The team used the beta versions (as well as the alpha version) to gather feedback on bugs and on possible new features. Customers had a chance to influence the design at a time that the development team had the flexibility to respond. A significant proportion of the design changes made after the first beta release resulted from direct customer feedback. Some of the changes introduced features that were not even present in the initial design specification.

The cycle of new-feature development and daily integration continued frenetically through the final weeks of the project. As one program manager said, "We tried to freeze the external components of the design three weeks before we shipped. In the end, it wasn't frozen until a week before. There were just too many things going on that we had to respond to . . . but, critically, we had a process that allowed us to do it."

MODELS OF THE SOFTWARE-DEVELOPMENT PROCESS

The Explorer team's process, increasingly common in Internet-software development, differs from past software-engineering approaches. (See box, The Evolution of the Evolutionary-Delivery

Model.) The waterfall model emerged thirty years ago from efforts to gain control over the management of large custom-software-development projects such as those for the U.S. military.[9] (See Figure 11.2.) The model features a highly structured, sequential process geared to maintaining a document trail of the significant design decisions made during development. A project proceeds through the stages of requirements analysis, specification, design, coding, and integration and testing—with sign-off points at the end of each stage. In theory, a project does not move to the next stage until all activities associated with the previous one have been completed.

The waterfall model, which has been compared to ordering a mail-order suit based upon a five-page text specification, is best for environments in which user requirements (and the technologies required to meet those requirements) are well understood. Its application in more uncertain environments, such as Internet-software engineering, is problematic. Uncertain environments call for interactivity that lets customers evaluate the design before the specification has been cast in stone.

▼

The Evolution of the Evolutionary-Delivery Model

Companies that develop software are constantly improving the development models.

- ▼ The Waterfall model (a sequential process maintains a document trail)
- ▼ The Rapid-Prototyping model (a disposable prototype helps establish customer preferences)
- ▼ The Spiral model (a series of prototypes identifies major risks)
- ▼ The Incremental, or Staged-Delivery, model (a system is delivered to customers in chunks)
- ▼ The Evolutionary-Delivery model (iterative approach in which customers test an actual version of the software)

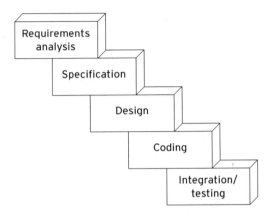

Figure 11.2. The Waterfall Model of Software Development Is the Traditional Approach.

To achieve that objective, several alternative models use prototypes that are shown to customers early in the development process. Some companies employ a rapid-prototyping model that emphasizes the construction of an early prototype to help establish customer requirements.[10] Similarly, the spiral model moves through a series of prototype builds to help developers identify and reduce the major risks associated with a project.[11]

In both those models, however, the prototypes are not part of the design itself but merely representations that are thrown away after fulfilling their function. The bulk of the design work carried out thereafter is performed in a similar manner to the waterfall model.[12] In contrast, the process used to develop Microsoft's IE3 browser had at its heart the notion that a product can be developed in an iterative fashion. Critical parts of the functionality were delivered to customers early in the process; subsequent work added to the core design and responded to customers' feedback. Although the core functionality was continually improved, the early design that customers tested was an actual working version of the product.[13]

One development model with similarities to the IE3 process is the incremental, or staged-delivery, model.[14] In its basic form, it involves a system that is delivered to the customer in discrete chunks. However, it is unlike IE3's iterative process in that it assumes that the entire product design is specified in the early stages of development. Staged delivery is used only as a means of partitioning work so that some functionality can be delivered to customers early. By contrast, an iterative process is founded upon the belief that not everything can be known up-front—the staged delivery of the product actually helps determine the priorities for work to be done in subsequent stages.

The iterative process is best captured in the evolutionary-delivery model proposed by Tom Gilb.[15] In Gilb's model, a project is broken down into many microprojects, each of which is designed to deliver a subset of the functionality in the overall product. (See Figure 11.3.) The microprojects give a team early feedback on how well the evolving design meets customer requirements. At the same time, they build in flexibility: the team can make changes in direction during development by altering the focus of subsequent microprojects. Furthermore, the number and length of the microprojects can be tailored to match the context of a project. In its most extreme form, each individual feature within a product could be developed in a separate microproject. To a large extent, the model mirrors the way IE3 was built.

RESEARCH ON THE INTERNET-SOFTWARE INDUSTRY

Our study of projects in the Internet-software industry asked the question: Does a more evolutionary development process result in better performance? The study was undertaken in stages. First, the researchers conducted face-to-face interviews with project managers in the industry to understand the types of practices being used.

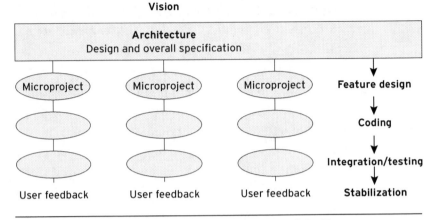

Figure 11.3. Evolutionary-Delivery Model of Software Development.

Next, they developed metrics to characterize the type of process adopted in each project. Finally, the metrics were incorporated into a survey that went to a sample of Internet-software companies identified through a review of industry journals. The final sample contained data on twenty-nine projects from seventeen companies.[16]

To assess the performance of projects in the industry, we examined two outcome measures—one related to the performance of the final product and the other to the productivity achieved in terms of resource consumption (resource productivity). To assess the former, the researchers asked a panel of fourteen independent industry experts to rate the comparative quality of each product relative to other products that targeted similar customer needs at the time the product was launched.[17] Product quality was defined as a combination of reliability, technical performance (such as speed), and breadth of functionality. Experts' ratings were gathered using a two-round Delphi process (in which information from the first round is given to all experts to help them make their final assessment).[18] To assess the resource productivity of each project, the researchers calculated a measure of the lines of new code developed per person-day and adjusted for differing levels of product complexity.[19] Analysis of the data uncovered four practices critical to success.

Early Release of the Evolving Product Design to Customers

The most striking result to emerge from the research concerned the importance of getting a low-functionality version of the product into customers' hands at the earliest opportunity. (See Figure 11.4.) The research provided data on the percentage of the final product functionality that was contained in the first beta version (the first working version distributed to external customers).[20] Plotting the functionality against the quality of the final product demonstrated that projects in which most of the functionality was developed and tested prior to releasing a beta version performed uniformly poorly. In contrast, the projects that performed best were those in which a low-functionality version of the product was distributed to customers at an early stage.

The differences in performance are dramatic. That one parameter explains more than one-third of the variation in product quality across the sample—a remarkable result, given that there are hundreds of variables that can influence the effectiveness of a development project, many of which are out of the project team's control.[21]

Consider the development of a simple Web browser. Its core functionality—the ability to input a Web-site address, have the software locate the server, receive data from the server, and then display it on a monitor—could be developed relatively rapidly and delivered to customers. Although that early version might not possess features such as the ability to print a page or to e-mail a page to other users, it would still represent the essence of what a browser is supposed to do.

Of course, getting a low-functionality version to the customer early has profound implications for task partitioning. For example, let's say the aim of a project called BigBrain is to develop a new software application encompassing ten major features. The traditional

If customers test products early in development, when the products have low functionality, the final products are likely to have higher quality.

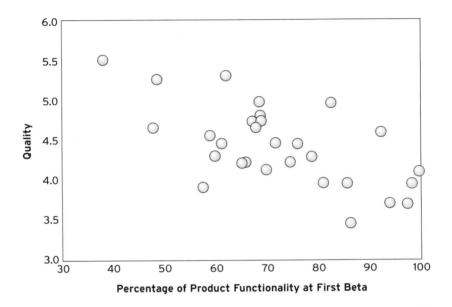

Figure 11.4. How the Product's Functionality at First Beta Affects Quality.

approach would involve dividing the team in such a way that all the features were worked on in parallel. Although progress would be made on each, the first opportunity to integrate a working version of the system would not occur until late in the project.

In an evolutionary process, however, the team might work first on only the three most important features—the essence of the system. Once those features were complete, the team would integrate them into a working version that could provide early feedback on how well the core modules interact. More important, the team would be able to distribute that early version to customers. As successive sets of features were completed and added to the product offering, their development would be guided by the customers' feedback.

The team might find that of the seven remaining features planned for BigBrain, customers value only five (something customers may not have realized prior to testing a working version). In addition, customers might identify several features that had not previously been part of the design, thus giving designers the opportunity to make midcourse corrections—and thereby deliver a superior product.

By allowing the team to react to unforeseen circumstances, an evolutionary approach also reduces risk. Suppose that during the first part of project BigBrain, problems emerge in getting the core technical components to work together. With the evolutionary approach, the team can reschedule later-stage work—perhaps by eliminating one or more features of the original design. If development had proceeded in a more traditional fashion, feedback on such problems would not have been received until all the various component modules were integrated—much later in the process. The flexibility to react to new information would have been lost, and BigBrain would have shipped late.

Given the marked benefits of early beta testing, we considered whether the number of separate beta versions released to customers contributed to a product's performance. The Netscape Navigator 3.0 development team, for example, released six beta versions to external customers, each one following two to three weeks after the previous one.[22] The process of distributing an early release, gathering feedback, updating the design, and redistributing the product to customers would seem an ideal way to ensure that the evolving functionality meshes with emerging customer needs. Surprisingly, however, the data showed no relationship between the performance of the final product and the number of beta releases. (See Figure 11.5.)

Our interviews revealed that the benefits obtained from the evolving product's early release to customers depended not upon the number of releases but on the intensity with which companies worked with customers after the first release. In general, the number

The number of beta tests an Internet-software-development group uses does not affect the quality of the end product.

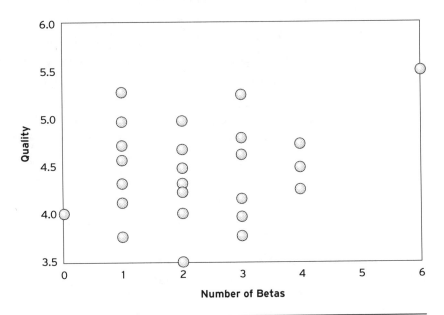

Figure 11.5. How the Number of Beta Tests Affects Quality.

of releases was not a good proxy for how well a company chose its beta customers or how well they subsequently worked with those customers.

Indeed, although the project that produced the highest-quality product in the sample—Netscape Navigator 3.0—released the largest number of beta versions, a member of its development team noted that multiple versions can create version-control problems: "The majority of beta testers who give us feedback don't necessarily tell us which beta version they have been working with. So the problem is they might be pointing out a bug that has already been fixed or one that manifests itself in a different way in a later release of the product. The result is we can spend as much time tracking down the problem as we do fixing it."

Daily Incorporation of New Software Code and Rapid Feedback on Design Changes

The need to respond to feedback generated through the release of early product versions to customers requires a process that allows teams to interpret new information quickly, then make appropriate design changes. In more than half the projects in the study, such changes were made through a daily build of the software code. In the same way that one checks books out of a library, developers working on the project would check out parts of the main code base to work on during the day. At the end of each day, they would take any newly modified code they had finished working on and check it back into the system. At check-in or overnight, a set of automated tests would run on the main code base to ensure that the new additions did not cause problems. At the start of the next day, the first task for each developer would be to fix any problems that had been found in his or her latest submissions.

Because daily builds have become an accepted approach to Internet-software development, they did not differentiate successful projects in the study. However, a measure of rapid feedback produced an intriguing result. (See Figure 11.6.) We looked at final product quality and plotted it against the time it took to get feedback on the most comprehensive set of automated tests performed on the design. None of the projects with extremely long feedback times (more than forty hours) had a quality level above the mean. The conclusion, supported by interviewees' comments, is that rapid feedback on new design choices is a necessary component of an evolutionary process. However, rapid feedback alone is not sufficient to guarantee that evolutionary software development will result in success. Indeed, projects with short feedback times were just as likely to perform poorly as to perform well.[23]

A Team with Broad-Based Experience of Shipping Multiple Projects

One might be forgiven for thinking that the value of experience is limited in a revolutionary environment such as the Internet-software

Rapid feedback on changes made to software facilitates better product performance.

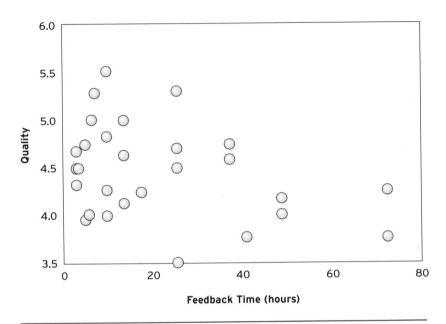

Figure 11.6. How Feedback Time Affects Quality.

industry. Much academic research has pointed out that in dynamic environments, experience may cause trouble, given that the knowledge of specific technologies and design solutions atrophy fast.[24] Indeed, the development ranks of many leading Internet-software companies often are filled with programmers barely out of college. Yet the view that a less experienced team is somehow better at developing products in such environments defies common sense—after all, a team with no experience at all would not know where to start. Even in a development process with the capacity to run thousands of design experiments, there is still a need to decide *which* experiments to run—and then to interpret the results. The question that must be asked therefore is, What *types* of experience have value in revolutionary environments?

To answer that question, we studied two different measures of experience. The first was associated with the more traditional view of experience—the average tenure of the development team in years. The second measure reflected a different form of experience—namely, the number of project generations a team member had completed (generational experience).[25]

Our thinking was that the experience of completing many different projects would give developers a more abstract approach—one that evolves over time as lessons are learned from successive projects. As a result, they would be better equipped to adapt to novel contexts and applications. In addition, the completion of each project would help developers see how their work fit into the system. The more projects completed, the greater their knowledge of how to design effectively at the module level while keeping the system level in view.

The results showed that the traditional measure of experience had no association with either product quality or resource productivity. The measure of generational experience had no association with product quality either, but it turned out to be a powerful predictor of resource productivity.[26] This suggests that the value of completing multiple projects in an evolutionary-development environment does not derive from an ability to predict specific customer requirements. Rather, such experience—by providing knowledge that helps developers analyze and respond to the data during development—allows greater efficiency in ongoing design activities.

The findings provide some insight into why a youthful development team is not necessarily one that lacks relevant experience. Given that many software-development projects have short lead times, it is possible for a developer to complete quickly a large number of projects, thereby gaining substantial generational experience. That experience benefits future projects by helping the developer frame and direct an experimentation strategy that can resolve design problems quickly, even when the problems faced are novel.

Major Investments in the Design
of the Product Architecture

In most development projects, the main design criterion for the product architecture is that it provide the highest possible level of performance. Often, the way that occurs is through an architecture that tightly links the various component modules. In an evolutionary process, however, there is another important criterion—flexibility in the development process. Designing the architecture so that a version of the product can be assembled at an early stage and distributed to customers requires explicit architectural choices. Building in the ability to accept additional functionality during late project stages adds further demands.

The key to an evolutionary process is to develop an architecture that is both modular and scaleable.[27] A more modular system is better at accommodating changes to the design of individual modules without requiring corresponding changes to other modules in the system. The loosely coupled nature of a modular system buffers the effect of changes. It is therefore suited to uncertain environments—at least, to the degree that the design isolates uncertainties within modules and does not allow them to affect the interfaces between modules. A more scaleable system allows initially unanticipated functions and features to be added at a late stage without disrupting the existing design. That requires a solid underlying infrastructure, such as that of the Linux operating system, one of the best examples of a modular and scaleable architecture. (See Table 11.1.)

When Torvalds released the original version of the code, he could not have predicted the functionality that would be added in subsequent years. So he based the design upon a modular architecture even though the inner core was monolithic. Developers around the world would be able to contribute to Linux without having to worry about the effect their code would have on other modules. Torvalds also made Linux scaleable—able to accept new functionality in a way that minimized changes to the existing core. Although the

Table 11.1. A Modular and Scaleable Architecture: The Linux Operating System.

The initial version of the Linux kernel, the core of the Linux system, was developed in 1991 as part of an open-source project to develop a freely available Unix-like operating system. (In open-source projects, the underlying code that makes the software work is distributed to users so they can improve upon or customize it.) At the time, the kernel comprised only ten thousand lines of code and ran on only one hardware platform—the Intel 386. However, as developers around the world began using the system and contributing to the project, its functionality expanded dramatically. By 1998, the kernel had grown to more than 1.5 million lines of code and was used on hardware platforms from supercomputers to robotic dogs. (See Evolution of the Linux Kernel.) Yet estimates of the amount of code added by the system's originator, Linus Torvalds, were typically less than 5 percent.

Evolution of the Linux Kernel

Year	Version	Lines of Code	Users
1991	0.01	10,000	1
1992	0.96	40,000	1,000
1993	0.99	100,000	20,000
1994	Linux 1.0	170,000	100,000
1995	Linux 1.2	250,000	500,000
1996	Linux 2.0	400,000	1,500,000
1997	Linux 2.1	800,000	3,500,000
1998	Linux 2.1.110	1,500,000	7,500,000

Source: Forbes, August 10, 1998.

Linux architecture owes much to the long heritage of Unix, it is also a reflection of the true genius of its author.

In lieu of being able to examine the details of each product's architecture for our study, we focused on the relative investments in architectural design that companies made.[28] Our assumption was that those investments reflected the degree to which companies were trying to resolve potential conflicts between a highly optimized architecture (one that is tightly coupled) and an architecture that facilitates process flexibility (one that is both modular and scaleable). Our analysis confirmed that a high level of investment in architectural design did indeed have a strong association with higher-quality products.[29]

PUTTING IT ALL TOGETHER

Although the study demonstrated that early customer involvement in an evolutionary process is vital, companies must take care to select suitable beta partners. We learned from the fieldwork that a valuable avenue for identifying beta partners is through exploring a company's customer-support database to identify customers who stretch the performance envelope. Customers who initiate numerous calls for support are good candidates for beta programs; however, it is the nature of those calls that is critical. The most effective beta groups include distinct customers for each performance dimension (say, reliability, speed, or functionality) rather than customers who make demands on many fronts. Asking support employees which customers experience the strangest problems is one way of identifying those who are using the product in novel ways and who therefore might provide useful insights on performance.

With regard to the number of beta customers involved, we noticed that some companies emphasized a broad release of early versions to the entire customer base, whereas others employed a narrower distribution to a select group. The former strategy seemed most useful for product segments in which the software was meant to operate on a variety of different hardware platforms and alongside other software products. In such situations, mass distribution helped identify bugs related to the interactions among systems and products. In contrast, enterprises with sophisticated products that placed greater demands upon users preferred to work with a smaller group, given the extra support that such users required.

The benefits of an evolutionary approach to software development have been evangelized in the software-engineering literature for many years. However, the precise form of an evolutionary model and the empirical validation of its supposed advantages have eluded researchers. The model has now been proved successful in the Internet-software industry. When combined with the insights gained in fieldwork, our research suggests a clear agenda for managers: get a low-functionality version of the product into customers' hands at the earliest possible stage and thereafter adopt an iterative approach to adding functionality. The results also underscore the importance of having a development team with experience on multiple projects and creating a product architecture that facilitates flexibility.[30]

The usefulness of the evolutionary model extends beyond developing software in environments with rapidly changing markets and technologies. By dividing tasks into microprojects, a company can tailor the process to reflect any particular context. Uncertainty in the Internet-software industry dictates short microprojects—down to the level of individual features. Traditional market research has limited value here, so companies need an early working version to gain feedback on the product concept.[31] In more-mature environments, however, companies can specify more of the product design up-front, use longer microprojects, and develop greater functionality before needing feedback. In a world where customer needs and the underlying technologies in a product are known with certainty, only one large microproject is necessary, and the waterfall model suffices. An evolutionary-delivery model represents a transcendent process for managing the development of all types of software, with the details tailored to reflect each project's unique challenges.

ADDITIONAL RESOURCES

Readers interested in the general topic of managing product development are directed to a popular textbook, *Revolutionizing Product Development,* by Steven Wheelwright and Kim Clark, published in

1992 by the Free Press (New York). The most practical publication specifically on software development may be the 1996 Microsoft Press (Redmond, Washington) book *Rapid Development* by Steve McConnell.

A deeper discussion of the open-source approach can be found at www.opensource.org/. To read more about Linux and one of the companies involved in its distribution, see the Harvard Business School case "Red Hat and the Linux Revolution," by Alan MacCormack, no. 9-600-009.

For a discussion of Microsoft's approach to developing software, see *Microsoft Secrets,* by Michael Cusumano and Richard Selby, a 1995 Free Press book. Harvard Business School's multimedia case "Microsoft Office 2000," by Alan MacCormack, illustrates that approach in detail (case no. 9-600-023), and the accompanying CD-ROM contains interviews with team members and a demonstration of Microsoft's Web-based project-management system.

A new model of software development with similarities to the evolutionary model is "extreme programming." Details can be found at www.ExtremeProgramming.org/. The Software Engineering Institute at Carnegie Mellon University is a useful source of research on software-engineering management. See www.sei.cmu.edu/.

NOTES

1. "Forecasting a Robust Future," www.bsa.org/statistics/index.html?/statistics/global_economic_studies_c.html.
2. Measured in terms of value added. "Forecasting a Robust Future."
3. "Forecasting a Robust Future."
4. "A Survey of the Software Industry," *Economist,* May 25, 1996, p. 14.
5. See, for example, M. A. Cusumano and R. Selby, *Microsoft Secrets* (New York: Free Press, 1995); and F. P. Brooks, *The Mythical Man-Month* (Reading, Massachusetts: Addison-Wesley, 1995).
6. A. MacCormack, R. Verganti, and M. Iansiti, "Developing Products on Internet Time: The Anatomy of a Flexible Development Process," *Management Science,* January 2001, 47(1).

7. M. Iansiti and A. MacCormack, "Developing Products on Internet Time," *Harvard Business Review,* September-October 1997, 75, 108–117.

8. The first two versions of Internet Explorer relied extensively on licensed technology.

9. W. W. Royce, "Managing the Development of Large Software Systems: Concepts and Techniques" (Procedures of WESCON [Western Electric Show and Convention], Los Angeles, August 1970).

10. J. L. Connell and L. Shafer, *Structured Rapid Prototyping: An Evolutionary Approach to Software Development* (Englewood Cliffs, New Jersey: Yourdon Press, 1989.

11. B. Boehm, "A Spiral Model of Software Development and Enhancement," *IEEE Computer,* May 1988, 21, 61–72.

12. For example, in Boehm's spiral model, the outer layer of the spiral contains the activities of detailed design, coding, unit testing, integration testing, acceptance testing, and implementation. Those activities are carried out sequentially.

13. That does not preclude the fact that "throwaway" prototypes are used in such a process. Indeed, they are likely to be extremely important in establishing a direction for the initial design work.

14. See, for example, C. Wong, "A Successful Software Development," *IEEE Transactions on Software Engineering,* November 1984, pp. 714–727.

15. T. Gilb, *Principles of Software Engineering Management* (Reading, Massachusetts: Addison-Wesley, 1988), pp. 84–114.

16. The survey was distributed to thirty-nine firms, of which seventeen responded with data on completed projects. The resulting sample of products is quite diverse and includes products and services targeted at both commercial and consumer users.

17. Quality was assessed on a seven-point scale, with level four indicating the product was at parity with competitive offerings.

18. H. A. Linstone and M. Turoff, eds., *The Delphi Method: Techniques and Applications* (Reading, Massachusetts: Addison-Wesley, 1975).

19. Projects in our sample differed significantly with regard to the number of lines of code developed. We therefore normalized the resources consumed in each project to reflect the development of an

application of standard size. We adjusted the resulting measure for scale effects (larger projects were found to consume relatively fewer resources) and complexity effects (projects to develop Web-based services were found to consume relatively fewer resources, because of the specifics of the programming language used).

20. A beta version, as defined, is not a throwaway prototype. It is a working version of the system. The measure of the percentage of product functionality contained in the first beta was adjusted for scale effects.

21. We also examined the relationship an early beta release has with resource productivity. One might have imagined that in an evolutionary process there is a penalty to pay in terms of productivity, given the possibility that some early design work will be thrown away as customer requirements become clearer. However, our results showed no association between an early release to customers and lower productivity. The benefits from an early release appear to overcome the potential drawbacks of multiple iterations.

22. M. Iansiti and A. MacCormack, "Developing Products on Internet Time," *Harvard Business Review,* September-October 1997, 75, 108–117.

23. As a result, the correlation between feedback time and product quality is not statistically significant.

24. See, for example, R. Katz and T. J. Allen, "Investigating the Not-Invented-Here (NIH) Syndrome: A Look at the Performance, Tenure, and Communication Patterns of 50 R&D Project Groups," in *Readings in the Management of Innovation,* M. Tushman and W. Moore, eds. (New York: HarperBusiness, 1982), pp. 293–309.

25. We used the term "generations" to distinguish between major "platform" projects (that is, those in which major changes were made to the previous version of a product) and minor derivative-incremental projects.

26. The measure of generational experience we used in our analysis was the percentage of the development team that had previously completed more than two generations of software projects. Note that the variation in generational experience explains more than 24 percent of the variation in resource productivity.

27. Note that there is a relationship between those two characteristics. Namely, a scaleable architecture is likely to be modular. A modular architecture, however, is not necessarily scaleable.

28. The measure we used, adjusted to control for scale effects, was a ratio of the resources dedicated to architectural design relative to the resources dedicated to development and testing.

29. Those investments explain more than 15 percent of the variation in product quality. We found no significant association between them and differences in resource productivity.

30. In our sample, measures of the parameters in combination explain almost half the variation in product quality and a quarter of the variation in resource productivity.

31. For example, consider attempting back in early 1996 to conduct market research into the features that a browser should contain. Most people would have had no clue what a browser was meant to do. Hence traditional market research techniques (focus groups, surveys, and the like) would have had less value.

CHAPTER TWELVE

What Makes a Virtual Organization Work?

M. LYNNE MARKUS
BROOK MANVILLE
CAROLE E. AGRES

In his 1998 article "Management's New Paradigms," Peter F. Drucker argues against the traditional view that the essential managerial task is to tell workers what to do.[1] In fact, managing a workforce increasingly made up of knowledge workers has very different demands. Managers today, Drucker tells us, must direct people as if they were unpaid volunteers, tied to the organization by commitment to its aims and purposes and often expecting to participate in its governance. They must lead workers instead of managing them.

Drucker's view of knowledge workers as volunteers seems to be on target with today's economic, business, and workforce trends. A number of industries have seen the breakup of large traditional organizations and the emergence of new, networked organizational forms, in which work is conducted by temporary teams that cross organizational lines. With a booming economy, there is a shortage of skilled labor, exacerbated by an aging population and fewer new workforce entrants. High-tech companies in particular are facing a war for talent, while people increasingly value personal time and autonomy over greater income and advancement. Consequently, companies seek to harness the talents and energies of dispersed "communities of practice." At the same time, a record number of knowledge workers are self-employed freelancers, and more people choose periods of less than full-time work. If those trends continue, managers will increasingly face a workforce of volunteers—at least in spirit if not in fact.

How will the traditional management tasks of motivating and directing employees have to change in the face of these new realities? One way to answer that question is to examine an example of an economic enterprise that acts in many ways like a voluntary organization: the open-source software movement. Open-source software, such as the Linux operating system, is licensed as a public good—in other words, it is essentially given away for free. And many open-source software products are built, at least in part, by people who are neither employees nor contract workers and who receive no direct compensation for their participation. Nevertheless, open sourcing has become an increasingly popular way of doing business in the software world, and many entrepreneurs and investors are making considerable money from companies involved with open-source software. (See box, About the Research.)

What motivates people to participate in open-source projects? And how is participation governed in the absence of employment or fee-for-service contracts? The answers to those questions reveal some important lessons for organizations—whether or not they develop software products—about both the challenges of keeping and motivating knowledge workers and the process of managing various types of virtual organizations, such as ad hoc project teams, virtual teams, communities of practice, and multicompany collaborations.

First, money is only one, and not always the most important, motivation of open-source volunteers. Although professional contributors may value a possible share in the collective wealth a successful new software project generates, they also are motivated by the personal benefit of using an improved software product and by social values such as altruism, reputation, and ideology. In many cases, several motivations operate together and reinforce one

About the Research

We became interested in the open-source movement during the course of our work with a knowledge-based organization (not in the software business) that was facing a crisis of governance. Traditional principles and practices that had served the organization well through its long history no longer seemed to work. People felt distanced from organizational governance, and employee retention began to be a problem. It was generally agreed that a new model of organizational governance was needed.

After hearing open-source proponent Eric Raymond speak at a public forum, we began to think that the movement might offer just the model the organization needed. We decided to undertake a case study focusing on the motivation of open-source participants and the coordination of their software-development work. We examined the extensive literature on the open-source phenomenon, filled in a few gaps through e-mail correspondence with a small number of open-source developers, and triangulated those sources with the academic literature on management, virtual organizations, and "public goods" phenomena, in which people jointly produce a benefit they all can share. The literature suggested the concepts we used to describe our findings, although we sometimes relabeled them.

another, suggesting that traditional organizations should plan for a broader array of work motivations than they often do today. (See box, Why Virtual Organizations Work.)

Second, despite the clear potential for chaos, open-source projects are often surprisingly disciplined and successful through the action of multiple, interacting governance mechanisms. Membership management, rules and institutions, monitoring and sanctions, and reputation build on the precondition of shared culture to self-regulate open-source projects. The implication is that traditional organizations should consider ways to shift from the management of knowledge workers—an oxymoron, some say—to the self-governance of knowledge work.

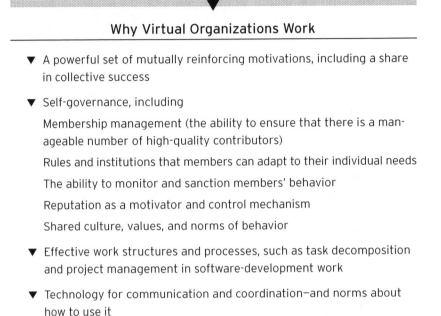

Why Virtual Organizations Work

▼ A powerful set of mutually reinforcing motivations, including a share in collective success

▼ Self-governance, including

Membership management (the ability to ensure that there is a manageable number of high-quality contributors)

Rules and institutions that members can adapt to their individual needs

The ability to monitor and sanction members' behavior

Reputation as a motivator and control mechanism

Shared culture, values, and norms of behavior

▼ Effective work structures and processes, such as task decomposition and project management in software-development work

▼ Technology for communication and coordination—and norms about how to use it

MOTIVATING CONTRIBUTORS TO OPEN-SOURCE PROJECTS

There are many different types of contributors to open-source projects: organizations and individuals; initiators and those who help with other people's projects; hobbyists and professionals. Each has different needs. Our primary focus is on the many participants who are not employees or contract laborers of the companies that are directly involved with initiating or managing an open-source project. Such volunteers may play a significant role in open-source software product development, or they may simply participate in maintenance and enhancement work by reporting and fixing the bugs they encounter while using the software. Because they have access to the source code, volunteers can actually make changes to open-source programs, whereas users of proprietary software products (such as the Microsoft Office Suite) cannot.

Most professional volunteers have multiple, reinforcing reasons for participating in open-source projects. And there are both social and economic benefits.

The Social Benefits of Open-Source Participation

The social benefits of participating in open-source projects—altruism and gift giving, reputation and ideology—interact with the sheer joy and challenge of "hacking" to motivate professionals to volunteer their time and skill to open-source projects.

Although open-source software has been around since the 1960s, much of the buzz was created in 1997 by Eric S. Raymond's influential online publication, "The Cathedral and the Bazaar,"[2] which triggered Netscape's decision to open its Navigator browser. In "Cathedral" and subsequent papers, Raymond forcefully argues for the benefits of open-source software development and describes the motivations of participants. Carefully distinguishing between "hackers," who build software, and "crackers," who destroy it, Raymond waxes lyrical about the joys of hacking.[3] Writing software can be challenging and fun. But why would hackers give their software away?

Altruism and reciprocity undoubtedly play a role in open-source participation, as they do with other volunteers. Open-source contributors have told us that they enjoy the sense of "helping others out" and "giving something back." But just as philanthropists can bask in public esteem, open-source volunteers can benefit from enhanced reputations among their peers. Participating in open-source projects can be a highly visible activity: much of it is coordinated over the Internet, where one's performance can be monitored by other members of a particular open-source community. As an example, the Mozilla public Web site, which actively solicits volunteers, posts the names of individuals responsible for various parts of the project.

Consequently, participating in open-source projects is one way that software workers can develop a name for themselves or enhance their reputations. For example, in "How to Become a Hacker,"[4] Raymond notes that writing open-source software and helping test and debug it are two critical ways to earn the respect of "alpha" hackers. Elsewhere, Raymond explains that gaining a reputation for one's work is an important reward for participating in open-source projects: "We do keep score in the open-source world. . . . Our scoreboard is the 'credit list' or the 'history file' that's attached to every open-source project. . . . If you see somebody's name on several credit lists, then you know that person is doing lots of good work."[5]

Gaining or enhancing reputation through participation in open-source projects can lead to such tangible rewards as employment opportunities or access to venture capital.[6] But in "reputation cultures" such as academia and the open-source world, reputation serves as a coin of the realm in its own right. Raymond describes the hacker culture as a "gift" culture or "potlatch" culture, in which reputation is the only measure of success: "Gift cultures [unlike exchange cultures such as our society] are adaptations not to scarcity but to abundance. . . . In gift cultures, social status is determined not by what you control but by what you give away. . . . It is quite clear that the society of open-source hackers is in fact a gift culture. Within it, there is no serious shortage of the 'survival necessities'—disk space, network bandwidth, computing power. Software is freely shared. This abundance creates a situation in which the only available measure of competitive success is reputation among one's peers."

As important as reputation is as a motivation for open-source participation, ideology also undoubtedly plays a role. The belief that giving software away is the right thing to do is not uncommon in university computer-science research labs, where much open-source software originates. The corollary is the belief that proprietary ownership of software is evil. In the public Web site of the open-source

GNU project, one page asks, "Is Microsoft the Great Satan?"[7] The page gives the strong impression that the answer is yes. A similar impression is gained from reading the "Halloween documents," which are edited versions of what are alleged to be confidential Microsoft documents discussing the open-source "threat."[8] In essence, some of the fuel for the open-source movement is the almost anarchic glee of hackers hoping to destroy what they regard as Microsoft's evil empire—as evidenced by their enthusiasm for the Justice Department's move to break up the company.

The Economic Benefits of Open-Source Participation

Although altruism, reputation, and ideology are certainly powerful motivators of open-source participation, professionals cannot afford to be indifferent to economic issues. Self-employed professionals must earn a living somehow, and employed professionals must convince their superiors that working on open-source projects during company time is valuable. If volunteers' labor provided economic benefits to someone else but not to the volunteers, contributions to open-source projects would likely not occur very often. As one developer explained: "My development contributions could possibly earn you money, but I would not contribute my time and programming effort solely for you to profit. I would be contributing to your source code because it would benefit me directly in some other way."[9]

In other words, many professional developers worry about their own ability to benefit economically from participating in open-source projects. One benefit would be having a better software product to use.[10] Another would be sharing in the collective wealth generated by successful commercialization of an open-source software product.[11]

The appeal of the better mousetrap underlies much open-source participation. Individuals and companies can benefit by enhancing the products they have already decided to use. For example, Linus Torvalds was a university student when he initiated the development of the Linux operating system. He liked the Unix operating system but couldn't afford a workstation to run it, so he decided to use a version of Unix that would run on his PC. (See Table 12.1.)

Similarly, individual professionals and organizations can often benefit from participating in open-source projects when their volunteering enhances the products they use. One open-source contributor was motivated to participate when he ran into problems with a 3Com card he was using. "I've been a Linux user for years," he wrote, "but I'm only just now beginning to fully appreciate open source. Using open source is like getting dozens of detectives to work together to solve a good mystery. . . . With open source, everyone shares the clues they find. And . . . a dozen other detectives are there to confirm or poke holes in the theory."[12]

In that instance, the fix the developer submitted was rejected by the software's primary author because it might have caused problems elsewhere, but the author was able to solve the problem differently. Then the author published the revision so that others could benefit from it.

The 3Com example illustrates an important dynamic of the open-source world: the results of volunteer labor are provided as a public good, free of charge. The rights and obligations associated with open-source software are spelled out in licenses, as is the case with proprietary software. Open-source rights include the right to make copies and the right to access the source code, which is necessary to modify it. Open-source obligations may include the obligation to check enhancements with lead developers (called "checking in") or to make all enhancements available to others. Although there are variations in open-source licenses and some are more favorable than others to the interests of commercial developers, the features of open-source licenses differ markedly from the licenses of proprietary software products.[13]

Open-source licenses prohibit the sale (collection of license fees) of open-source software and serve to ensure that no one party can unfairly monopolize the commercial rewards from others' voluntary

Table 12.1. A Brief History of the Open-Source Movement.

The open-source movement has been around for a long time. Quite a number of software products have been licensed as a public good. Examples include Sendmail, Apache, and Perl. The Internet itself is widely regarded as the largest and best-known example of open-source development.

But the open-source movement as we know it today largely grew out of an influential 1997 online publication by Eric S. Raymond, *The Cathedral and the Bazaar.* Raymond contrasted the way in which software products such as the Linux operating system are built with the way in which proprietary software products are developed by companies such as Microsoft. Raymond claimed that opening software development to the efforts of many volunteer developers resulted in products that are technically superior to those produced under closed development conditions.

In recent years, the open-source movement has been gathering momentum. In January 1998, influenced by publication of *The Cathedral and the Bazaar,* Netscape announced the launch of its Navigator browser with open-source code. In November 1998, the Open Source Initiative was formed. By late 1999, open-source software had become a household word with the IPO of Red Hat Software, a company that provides support for the Linux operating system and other open-source products. That event was pivotal to the acceptance of open-source software by businesses, which have traditionally shunned so-called freeware. Today some analysts suggest that Linux is poised to rival Microsoft's operating systems.

Date	Event	Description
1969	Development of Unix was initiated.	Bell Labs researchers Ken Thompson and Dennis Ritchie completed the Unix operating system in 1973. When AT&T was forbidden to enter the computer business, Thompson and Ritchie offered tapes of source code for Unix to anyone willing to pay a small copying fee.
1981	Sendmail was developed.	A University of California, Berkeley, graduate and Unix guru, Eric Allman, developed Sendmail. Sendmail is an e-mail transfer agent that today moves at least 75 percent of Internet service provider data traffic.
1984	Free Software Foundation (FSF) was founded, and GNU project was initiated.	Richard Stallman, recognized as the father of free software and the ultimate hacker, founded the Free Software Foundation (FSF) and started the GNU (GNU's Not Unix) project. Stallman developed FSF in part to fight the injustices associated with proprietary software triggered by the legal battles of AT&T; University of California, Berkeley; and software developers over licensing copyrights for Unix. The goal of the GNU project was to create a comprehensive—and free—Unix-compatible operating system.

(continued)

Table 12.1. Continued.

▼

Date	Event	Description
1986	Perl (Practical Extractions and Report Language) was released.	Larry Wall released the Perl language to the Internet, and collaborative development by interested programmers ensued. Perl's capabilities include the ability to scan text files, create HTML files from text files, and navigate the Net.
1989	Cygnus Solutions was founded.	The first commercial venture built on open-source or freeware products was founded. Cygnus provides consulting, engineering, and support services for open-source software, including GNU development tool kits.
1991	Development of Linux began.	Linus Torvalds, then a twenty-one-year-old computer science student at the University of Helsinki, began working on a Unix kernel to run on a PC. The kernel was the one piece of the Unix operating system that the GNU project had not yet successfully produced. When he had the kernel working, he announced his project on the Internet, essentially asking for assistance in debugging it. The response was terrific, and a powerful community evolved as people everywhere began fixing bugs and enhancing the software. Today Linux is considered a stable operating system of higher quality than Windows NT. Linux International, a nonprofit organization, distributes information about Linux and accepts donations to support its work.
1994	Additional companies joined Cygnus to rally around the open-source business model.	Red Hat Inc. and Caldera Systems Inc. were formed. The companies use open-source support-revenue models to distribute, brand, train, consult, undertake custom development, and provide post-sales support.
1997	Eric S. Raymond wrote and posted an on-line version of *The Cathedral and the Bazaar.*	Raymond had been involved in the GNU project, but his experience with the Linux style of development was an epiphany. In his influential article, later published in book form, he contrasts the traditional proprietary model of development (such as that used by Microsoft) with the "bazaar" style of the open-source model, claiming that the latter produces a higher-quality product by exposing the source code to many codevelopers who will see bugs and suggest fixes.
Jan. 1998	Netscape "opened" its Navigator source code.	In an unprecedented move influenced by Raymond's article, Netscape announced that it would release the source code for Navigator 5.0, thereby establishing a prescription for other software

Date	Event	Description
		companies to change their business-as-usual revenue model. The software, renamed Mozilla (after the original code name for the Navigator project), was released after a licensing team wrote the software licenses, posted them on the Web, and incorporated the public's responses in less than one month. Mozilla.org was formed to organize, coordinate, arbitrate, and act as final authority for Mozilla changes. The Web site is overseen by Netscape employees and contains the entire process framework for Mozilla, including a mission statement and how others can participate. The Web site also describes the lessons learned in one year of operating in the open-source mode.
Feb. 1998	The term *open source* wins over *freeware* and *shareware*.	*Open source* was selected to replace the terms *freeware* and *shareware* in a brainstorming session attended by key open-source champions. The advantages of using the term *open source* are that the business world usually tries to keep free technologies from being installed and commercially oriented developers want to distance themselves from Stallman's ideological philosophy regarding the free-software movement.
Nov.-Dec. 1998	Confidential Microsoft documents about open source end up on the Web.	Internal memos written by Vinod Valloppillil of Microsoft identifying the open-source movement as a threat to Microsoft's proprietary software-development model were leaked to Raymond. Raymond named them the "Halloween documents" and annotated and republished them.
Nov. 1998	*The Open Source Revolution, Release 1.0* was published.	Esther Dyson devoted an issue of her highly influential newsletter to the open-source movement. The issue refers to the Halloween documents and describes the licensing arrangements and business models for making money in the open-source world.
Nov. 1998	The Open Source Initiative (OSI) was formed.	Influenced by the Mozilla release, Eric Raymond and Bruce Perens launched the Open Source Initiative as a research and educational association whose mission is to own and defend the Open Source trademark. In June 1999, OSI abandoned its trademark initiative because the U.S. Patent and Trademark Office ruled that the term was too descriptive. OSI is now pursuing a certification mark.

labor. The approach removes powerful reasons professionals might have for not contributing to an open-source project. ("I would not contribute my time . . . solely for you to profit.")

At the same time, open-source licenses may appear to remove a powerful motivator to contribute—the ability to commercialize the product. And in fact, proponents of the open-source movement readily acknowledge that making money from open-source software is "nonintuitive."[14] Nevertheless, a number of different open-source business models, proposed or tried, can give volunteers economic rewards from their participation. The most prominent example is that of Red Hat Inc., which sells support for open-source software. Other business models include selling educational materials and using open-source software as a loss leader or as a hardware add-on. (See Table 12.2.)

The opportunity to benefit commercially from open-source software—albeit in nontraditional ways—provides a powerful incentive for many individuals and companies to collaborate in the development of a product that none of them can own. Open-source business models can provide a level playing field—giving each open-source participant a fair chance to benefit from the common effort, while licenses prevent any participant from unfairly monopolizing all the benefits. Open-source licenses and business models provide incentives for individual companies to band together to challenge dominant software products. Of course, the dynamics of network marketplaces are such that the open-source movement could deflate rapidly if the products lose popularity.

The open-source example tells us that money as a motivator is not likely to go out of style—and that should be reassuring for traditional organizations. But a closer look at the social and economic benefits of open-source participation suggests some areas that traditional organizations will need to reflect on. (See box, The Open-Source Challenge to Conventional Software Companies.) Financial compensation in the open-source world usually takes the form of a

Table 12.2. Open-Source Business Models.

Model	Description	Examples
Support Sellers	Revenue comes from media distribution, branding, training, consulting, custom development, and post-sales support.	Red Hat Inc. Caldera Systems Inc.
Loss Leader	An open-source product is used as a loss leader for traditional commercial software (similar to practices in retailing).	Sendmail Inc.
Hardware Add-Ons	Industry-related companies, such as computer hardware companies, use the open-source model to enable software such as printer drivers and operating-systems interface code.	Corel Corporation VA Linux Systems
Accessories	Companies obtain their revenue through sales and support for products related to open-source software, such as educational books, CD-ROMs, and computer hardware peripherals.	O'Reilly & Associates Inc.
Service Enabler	This model develops or distributes (or both) open-source software to enable the creation of revenue from on-line services.	Netscape Communications Corporation • Netscape's Netcenter Services • Netscape Communicator
Brand Licensing	Brand-licensing organizations obtain revenue by creating brand names for open-source software and then charging other companies to use the brands and trademarks to create derivative products.	Netscape Communications Corporation • Netscape Communicator (only Netscape can use that name; others must use Mozilla name)
Sell It, Free It	Companies initially create and sell proprietary products but convert to open-source products. It is the extended loss-leader model.	Netscape Communications Corporation has some elements of the model
Software Franchising	In this model, a company exploits its dominance—for example, its brand name—and creates other companies from which it provides services such as training. It receives franchise fees in return.	None known, but sourceXchange and Cosource.com have business models that possess such characteristics

▼

The Open-Source Challenge
to Conventional Software Companies

Many believe that software is a winner-take-all industry that produces natural monopolies. It is often the case that a single software product, such as the Microsoft Office Suite, comes to dominate competitors so completely that it drives them out of the market. Eventually, a better product may come along to challenge the monopolist. But the new product will succeed only if it becomes dominant in its turn. That involves building market share quickly and inexorably against the incumbent.[1]

A small entrepreneurial company with a proprietary software product faces formidable challenges in competing with a well-entrenched and well-funded monopolist. Even if the product has innovative features that are valued by the market, the dominant company will often be able to imitate the innovation, and the start-up may lack the resources to continue improving its product in a competitive race. Furthermore, because the product is proprietary, other companies have little incentive to help the start-up succeed. If anything, they may oppose it with their own proprietary products.

The open-software movement lets companies that could never challenge an incumbent on their own do so as collaborators. If companies codevelop or comarket a common product, that product may have a fighting chance of becoming the next monopoly. But for companies to be willing to cooperate in that way, they need to be sure they will have a fair chance of benefiting from the cooperative effort and that no other company will be able to monopolize or appropriate all the benefits of their efforts.

[1] S. J. Liebowitz and S. E. Margolis, *Winners, Losers, and Microsoft* (Oakland, California: The Independent Institute, 1999).

share in collectively produced wealth, rather than wages or contract fees. That type of compensation is more similar to the stock options that high-tech firms distribute widely to their knowledge workers than to the compensation practices of most traditional firms. Furthermore, credit and reputation may be equally important motiva-

Open-source participants prevent monopolies through open-source software licenses. As source proponent Bruce Perens, cofounder with Eric Raymond of the Open Source Initiative, explains: "The volunteers who made products like Linux possible are only there, and the companies are only able to cooperate, because of the rights that come with Open Source. The average computer programmer would feel stupid if he put lots of work into a program, only to have the owner of the program sell his improvement without giving anything back. Those same programmers feel comfortable contributing to Open Source because they are assured of these rights:

- ▼ "The right to make copies of the program, and distribute those copies.
- ▼ "The right to have access to the software's source code, a necessary preliminary before you can change it.
- ▼ "The right to make improvements to the program."[2]

Perens goes on to explain that those rights are important to open-source volunteers because they level the playing field, allowing many participants, not just a single proprietary software owner, to benefit from the commercialization of open-source software. But because open-source licenses generally prohibit the sale (collection of license fees) of open-source software, participants need alternative commercialization strategies. Several successful business models have been tried, including the sale of support for open-source software (Red Hat Inc.) and the sale of educational resources (O'Reilly & Associates Inc.).

[2] B. Perens, *Open Sources: Voices from the Open-Source Revolution, Freeing the Source, the Open Source Definition* (Sebastopol, California: O'Reilly & Associates, 1999).

tors to open-source participants. Such benefits are more rarely bestowed by today's traditional organizations. To the extent that credit and reputation are becoming a coin of the realm in knowledge work, managers should consider them essential to motivating employees.

GOVERNING OPEN-SOURCE PROJECTS

The potential for chaos in open-source projects appears great. First of all, open-source volunteers are neither employees nor contractors. They can defect at any time, and the threat of job loss or wage cuts is largely ineffective as a management tool. Second, large numbers of people may participate in some open-source projects. There may be as many as 750,000 open-source developers; organizing the contributions of even a tiny fraction of that number would challenge any project leader's skills. Third, some projects welcome all comers. For example, Netscape's Mozilla site, which is updated regularly, at one point read: "So you want to help? Great! Please read the rest of the introductory documents on this web site. . . . After that, it would be a really good idea for you to join the appropriate mailing lists and to get a feel for how the community works together. Before you actually start coding up a project, we'd strongly recommend that you let us know about it. If you like, we can publicize the fact that you're working on it, and perhaps someone else will want to work with you on it. If you don't want it publicized, that's fine too, but it would help us . . . to know how many different people are tackling the same kinds of problems. . . . Active contributors can be given write access to our CVS repository. Consult the guidelines . . . to learn about our build process and to find out how to get access."[15]

Since anyone can join some open-source projects, project leaders would seem to lack that important mechanism of quality control—the ability to select people and assign them to particular tasks. In general, open-source projects have conditions that tend to promote freeloading, unstable membership, or low-quality contributions.

In fact, however, many open-source projects work remarkably well, despite such management challenges. As a rule, open-source projects have well-structured governance models with clearly identified leadership. Often the initial software developer maintains a lead role in the ongoing development and distribution of open-source products. Examples include Larry Wall's leadership in Perl and Linus Torvalds' in Linux. But it is usually the case that formal authority for an open-source project is vested in a team. For example, FreeBSD is managed by a fifteen-person team called the Core. In a few cases, project leaders are elected by the membership. (See Table 12.3.)

As with proprietary-software-development efforts, work on open-source projects is partitioned by lead architects or designers into smaller units or modules, which can be tackled by individuals or teams. The architects also manage issues that require coordination across teams. The same pattern of deconstruction may occur within each module. Although module owners solicit (or receive) input from members, they have final authority for decisions in cases of disputes.

Open-source projects exhibit four interrelated coordination mechanisms, all in the context of the shared hacker culture: managed membership, rules and institutions, monitoring and sanctions, and reputation. By means of the interaction of such governance mechanisms, open-source projects can stay on track despite their obvious potential for chaos.

Managing Membership in Open-Source Projects

Anyone can get involved in a particular open-source project by identifying a bug or contributing a fix using Internet-based reporting systems. But achieving a responsible position in an open-source project requires a more formal process of vetting and quality control. For example, Apache volunteers are allowed to work on a project for a number of months, during which time the quality of their work can be assessed. After a probationary period, formal membership—the ability to remain in a particular role—is determined by a consensus vote of core Apache Foundation members.[16]

The Debian development effort (GNU-Linux, GNU-Hurd) is less democratic when it comes to accepting members. Project leaders (or delegates) have total authority over who works on their projects: they can admit or expel members. Project leaders are elected by developers; project leaders in turn appoint technical committees.

Table 12.3. Open-Source Governance Models.

▼

Project	Governing Body, Leadership	Dispute Resolution
Apache	The governing body is the Apache Foundation (formerly called the Apache Group). It is a core group of about twenty members formed from the founders of the project, who vote on decisions by committee. The members elect a board of directors (currently nine members) who manage organizational affairs per the bylaws. The board appoints officers to oversee day-to-day operations, and officers assign project leaders to specific projects.	Changes to products are proposed on a mailing list and voted on by active members. Three yes votes and zero no votes are needed to agree to a code change for any given release cycle.
The Debian Project (GNU-Linux, GNU-Hurd)	According to the Debian Constitution, "Each decision in the Project is made by one or more of the following: "1. The Developers, by way of General Resolution or an election; "2. The Project Leader; "3. The Technical Committee and/or its Chairman; "4. The individual Developer working on a particular task; "5. Delegates appointed by the Project Leader for specific tasks; "6. The Project Secretary." For the Linux product, Torvalds is the universally accepted leader who delegates responsibility for the major components or modules to trusted subordinates. Raymond refers to this as the "benevolent dictator" model of leadership.	Resolutions are placed on a discussion list for review and vote. The voting process is well defined in the Debian Constitution: http://www. debian.org/devel/constitution.
Perl	The Perl Institute was established to oversee and support Perl projects. It consists of six core members, including Perl creator Larry Wall. The Perl model for leadership is a rotating dictatorship, but the model is in the process of being redefined to reflect its grass-roots approach to product development. Recently, the board voted to dissolve the	Project leaders, or "pumpkins," are responsible for the projects' decision making and conflict resolution.

Project	Governing Body, Leadership	Dispute Resolution
	institute and combine its resources with Perl Mongers Inc. (more of a high-level user group than a decision-making body). There is significantly less structure than in the Apache, Debian-GNU-Linux or Mozilla projects. Project leaders have a high degree of autonomy in decision making.	
Mozilla	Mozilla.org was created in 1998 to organize and manage the Mozilla development community. It is led by a small group of Netscape employees to oversee operations. Module owners are viewed as benevolent dictators who arbitrate what happens in a module. The majority of module owners are Netscape employees.	Mozilla.org has the final say in any dispute.

If a developer does not agree with the actions or behavior of the project leader or technical committee, he or she can challenge those actions by following a documented resolution process.[17]

These examples show that those working on open-source projects find ways to restrict a potentially large and possibly unqualified workforce to one that is small enough to be manageable and of high enough quality to get the job done. But they also show that managing the membership of open-source projects works in conjunction with rules and institutions (such as how members and leaders are chosen) and with monitoring and sanctions (such as dispute-resolution processes and the ability to expel members).

Rules and Institutions

In well-functioning, cooperative efforts, community members participate in making and changing the rules, and the rules they adopt fit their unique needs.[18] An example of the adaptability of open-source rules is the variety of open-source licenses. For example, the

Berkeley Software Distribution (BSD) license poses no limits on the commercial use of open-source software, whereas the General Public License (GPL) prevents the release of proprietary derivative products through its "copyleft" (as opposed to copyright) provisions. In other words, some open-source licenses are more compatible with the interests of developer communities that want to commercialize open-source software. A drawback of so much variety is that some open licenses are incompatible with others. It is impossible, for example, to create—legally—an open-source product that combines elements of products licensed under GPL and Mozilla Public License (MozPL).

Another interesting aspect of rules and institutions in open-source communities is their procedures for discussing and voting on important issues. Most voting takes place over the Internet. For example, the Perl project uses a phased discussion-group process: request for discussion (RFD), first call for votes (CFV), last CFV, and results. (Each phase of the process is conducted during a specific, limited time period.) An example of the process at work is documented online. When Perl's central electronic discussion group got bogged down with issues unrelated to product development, core members proposed a moderated discussion group for general discussions. The RFD related to that change included the rationale for creating the group, its charter, specifics of administration, and the names of the action's proponents. After two CFVs (including detailed instructions for the electronic voting process), an unbiased, third-party volunteer tabulated and posted the results. In total, approximately 1,200 members of Perl newsgroups participated in the vote, in which a two-thirds majority was required for the motion to pass.

Linux uses a similar voting process. When community members believed that the existing newsgroup, comp.security.unix, was aimed at Unix administrators rather than at home and small-business users of Linux, they voted to create a new newsgroup to complement the other newsgroup.[19] The first call for discussion refers the reader to the online Introduction to Usenet Voting, which reveals another important aspect of open-source governance—it is not a democracy: "Understanding this principle is necessary to understanding how Usenet operates. You, the user, have absolutely no rights regarding Usenet as a whole, and you cannot complain about anything being 'undemocratic,' 'violating your civil rights,' 'un-Constitutional,' etc. . . . The final arbiter of which groups are created and which ones are not is not the voting system! The one person who can overrule the voting system is the moderator of news.announce.newgroups. Currently this job is held by David 'Tale' Lawrence, occasionally known as the 'Thousand-Pound Gorilla' thanks to the old joke (Q: Where does a 1,000-pound gorilla sit? A: Anywhere he wants to.). Jokes aside, while Tale has overturned voting results on occasion, he has done it only very, very rarely and even then only after lengthy deliberations."[20]

Monitoring and Sanctions

Rules and institutions are vulnerable to decay if members have no means of observing behavior and ensuring compliance. Successful communities must have access to graduated sanctions against those who violate group norms and to low-cost mechanisms for resolving conflict.

Sanctions and conflict-resolution mechanisms appear to be reasonably well developed in open-source communities. There are strong social pressures against noncompliance with norms in open-source communities. Flagrant or continued noncompliance results in flaming (sending someone angry or hostile e-mail), spamming (flooding someone with unsolicited e-mail), and shunning (deliberately refusing to respond). Faced with such sanctions, members often leave the community on their own initiative; leaders don't always have to expel offending members. Even leaders are not immune to social sanction when community members are incensed by their behavior. At one point, a "flame war" erupted between open-source leaders Eric Raymond and Bruce Perens. When details of the interaction were posted online, community members responded with sharp criticism.[21]

Although not always resolved to everyone's satisfaction, conflict is generally not considered detrimental for open-source projects, because deliberation is a valued principle of community behavior. Sometimes, of course, conflicts end badly for some or all participants. One developer explained how a badly handled conflict destroyed motivation to work on an open-source project: "I now have such bad feelings associated with the whole affair that I don't like to think about [it], much less work on it. I've stopped working publicly on it."[22]

In the conflict, the same tools that support collaboration were used to destroy it: "Mr. J proceeded to mail me back and tell me that he would do whatever he pleased (again, putting it mildly). He also added a text description offering to let me perform an obscene act on him to his sig file [signature file, appended to the end of e-mail messages], which he used publicly on mailing lists and whatnot. Completely appalled at this point, I e-mailed his providers for web space and connectivity, threatening them and him with lawsuits if he didn't remove my name from his postings. This got another nasty response from Mr. J, but eventually did get him to remove my name from his sig file."

The Importance of Reputation

Monitoring and sanctions work because people care about what others think of them. While the opportunity to build a reputation may be an important motivation for joining an open-source project, the desire to maintain a good reputation is a key mechanism in making sure that open-source projects continue on track. The fear of exclusion can be a motivational factor. Performance and behavior in the open-source world are always visible: All members can see whether a volunteer has done a good job or whether a manager has followed accepted norms of behavior or the results of a vote.

Of course, it is important to realize that the same things that make communities strong also can make them narrow-minded, self-deluding, and contentious.[23] As in any other community, the open-source movement occasionally exhibits political behavior, lack of fairness, work stress, and burnout.

The Shared Culture of Open Source

An essential precondition for the operation of all four governance mechanisms—membership management, rules and institutions, monitoring and sanctions, and reputation—is a set of shared values and assumptions about how things work.[24] "Hacker culture" grows from, and is maintained by, direct and indirect interactions among open-source community members, which in turn are enabled by the Internet.[25] Shared cultural knowledge and enabling technology make it possible for open-source participants to collaborate successfully, often without face-to-face interaction or prior personal acquaintance.

To leaders of traditional organizations, the findings may at first glance appear to be a bit troubling. Although the importance of organizational culture is often stressed in traditional organizations, much less emphasis has been placed on building self-control (to preserve one's reputation) and social control (for peers to monitor and sanction others' behavior) into formal organizational control systems. And the idea of voting procedures for key business decisions may unsettle more than a few managers. However, the specific forms that the governance mechanisms take in open-source projects are probably less important to traditional organizations than the fact that they exist. Managers should give careful thought to the categories, the relationships among them, and how they can be applied in different contexts.

THE OPEN-SOURCE MOVEMENT AND THE ORGANIZATION OF THE FUTURE

The open-source movement exhibits many of the qualities said to characterize new organizational forms. But those characteristics are tempered by mechanisms and processes ensuring that order reigns despite the potential for chaos:

▼ The intrinsic motivation and self-management of autonomous knowledge workers play important roles in open-source projects. Economic rewards and management processes are also important. Still, the types of economic rewards and management behaviors observed in open-source projects differ quite substantially from those observed in traditional organizations. For example, open-source rewards emphasize collective performance (the successful commercialization of an open-source product) and individual benefit (benefit in use) as much as they emphasize an individual's performance. And the development and maintenance of personal reputation figure prominently in both motivation and control when it comes to open-source projects.

▼ Membership in open-source projects is fluid, but only to some extent. Open-source projects maintain a stable core of participants while capitalizing on the temporary efforts of numerous volunteers. Membership in particular open-source communities is an important part of members' professional identities.

▼ Control in the open-source world is maintained through autonomous decision makers following a few simple rules. The key rules, defining appropriate conduct and fair play in benefiting from the collective effort, are embodied in software licenses, rules of membership, and voting procedures. Different open-source projects adopt somewhat different rules, showing adaptability to unique circumstances.

▼ Self-governance, both formally through discussion and voting and informally through social control, is evident in open-source projects. At the same time, project initiators and "alpha" hackers can retain a powerful influence on a project's direction—as long as they maintain their reputations for high-quality work and appropriate social behavior.

▼ Information technology is a key enabler of the open-source movement. Technology is required both for product development and support and for project coordination. Communication technology makes behavior highly visible to the community, which in turn permits enforcement of the rules. Many open-source governing bodies hold occasional face-to-face meetings to make decisions, but day-to-day decision making occurs almost solely through the Internet.

In short, there is a relatively high degree of correspondence between the open-source movement and popular depictions of the organization of the future and the virtual networked organization. Therefore, the open-source movement provides some suggestions about how management must change in the years ahead. At the same time, care should be taken in attempting to apply the lessons of the open-source movement to other contexts, because many of its characteristics are unusual or unique:

▼ A precondition for the open-source movement is a large "community of practice" with a strong, shared culture of technical professionalism. Whether open-source motivation and governance principles would work in other settings may depend on the existence of an active community of talented practitioners.

▼ Successful open-source projects have involved work that is intrinsically challenging. Whether the open-source model would work for routine activities, such as basic customer service or projects such as developing a new word processor, remains to be seen.

▼ The open-source movement is evolving rapidly. Whether current rules and processes will retain their character in the face of such rapid change is unknown.

▼ Software developers enjoy using technology for communicating and decision making. Other types of workers might prefer traditional communication and decision-making practices and fail to adapt to electronically mediated self-governance.

▼ Finally, self-governance is essential to the success of the open-source movement. Without self-governance, perceptions of fairness would diminish and the motivation of the volunteers would erode. Without volunteers, the movement would collapse. Furthermore, self-governance in the open-source movement is heavily reinforced by business models that offer the possibility of economic benefit and by legal arrangements designed to ensure fairness. It is not clear how well this style of self-governance would work in the absence of such strong reinforcing conditions.

Although managers in industries other than software development may prefer more traditional styles of management, they should remember that the world is changing and workers are changing along with it. In a labor force of volunteers and virtual teams, the motivational and self-governing patterns of the open-source movement may well become essential to business success.

Acknowledgments

The authors would like to thank Les Gasser of the University of Illinois, Alexander Hars of the University of Southern California, John Ferejohn of Stanford University, and Josh Ober of Princeton University for their valuable suggestions about the research.

Carole E. Agres, In Memoriam

After raising her children, author Carole Agres started a career in information systems, combining work and family life with active community service and the pursuit of higher education. She had reached the senior ranks of IT management in an aerospace company—one of the few women to do so—and was well on her way to completing her Ph.D. in information science when she died suddenly in fall 1999 at the age of fifty. She was an active participant in this project. She is missed.

ADDITIONAL RESOURCES

Readers might find helpful *The Economics of Online Cooperation*, a 1999 Routledge book edited by P. Kollock and M. Smith. Also, the Internet site First Monday has an interesting article by K. Kuwabara called, "Linux: A Bazaar on the Edge of Chaos," http://firstmonday.org/issues/issue5_3/ kuwabara/index.html.

NOTES

1. P. F. Drucker, "Management's New Paradigms," *Forbes*, October 5, 1998, pp. 152–177.

2. E. S. Raymond, *The Cathedral and the Bazaar* (Sebastopol, California: O'Reilly & Associates, 1999).

3. E. S. Raymond, "Homesteading the Noosphere," http://www.tuxedo.org/~esr/writings/homesteading/homesteading.html.

4. E. S. Raymond, "How to Become a Hacker," http://www.tuxedo.org/~esr/faqs/hacker-howto.html.

5. W. C. Taylor, "Inspired by Work," *Fast Company*, November 29, 1999, p. 200.

6. J. Lerner and J. Tirole, "The Simple Economics of Open Source," working paper, Harvard Business School, Boston, Feb. 25, 2000.

7. "Is Microsoft the Great Satan?" http://www.gnu.org/philosophy/microsoft.html.

8. E. S. Raymond, "The Halloween Documents," http://www.open-source.org/halloween/.

9. J. Corbet, "Letters to the Editor," *Linux Weekly News*, March 25, 1999, http://www.lwn.net/ 1999/0325/backpage.phtml.

10. N. Bezroukov, "A Second Look at the Cathedral and the Bazaar," *First Monday*, December 9, 1999, http://firstmonday.org/issues/issue4_12/bezroukov/index.html.

11. C. Shapiro and H. R. Varian, *Information Rules: A Strategic Guide to the Network Economy* (Harvard Business School Press: Boston, Massachusetts, 1999); and "The Business Case for Open Source," http://www.opensource.org/for-suits.html.

12. N. Petreley, "It Takes a Village of Detectives to Solve the Case of the Faulty 3Com," *Infoworld*, May 4, 1998, p. 4.

13. F. Hecker, "Setting Up Shop: The Business of Open-Source Software," http://www.hecker.org/ writings/setting-up-shop.html; and T. O'Reilly, "The Open-Source Revolution," *Release 1.0*, November 1998, http://www.edventure.com/ release1/1198.html.

14. L. Radosevich and B. Zerega, "Free Money Model," *Infoworld*, June 8, 1998, pp. 102–110.

15. "Getting Involved," http://www.mozilla.org/get-involved.html.

16. "Apache HTTP Server Project," http://www.apache.org/ABOUT_ APACHE.html.

17. "Debian Constitution," http://www.debian.org/devel/constitution.

18. Our thinking in this section has benefited from a governance-research collaboration involving McKinsey & Company's Organization Practice, Josh Ober of Princeton University, and John Ferejohn of Stanford University.

19. J. Billones, "First Call for Votes," *Linux Weekly News*, March 15, 1999, http://lwn.net/ 1999/0318/a/cols.html; and J.Billones, "Results of Vote," *Linux Weekly News*, April 11, 1999, http://lwn.net/1999/0415/ a/cols.html.

20. J. Patokallio, "An Introduction to Usenet Voting," http://www.hut.fi/ ~jpatokal/uvv/intro.html.

21. L. Kahney, "Open-Source Gurus Trade Jabs," *Wired*, April 10, 1999, http://www.wired.com/news/news/technology/linux/story/19049.html.

22. N. Bezroukov, "Open Source Software Development as a Special Type of Academic Research," *First Monday*, October 12, 1999, http://first-monday.org/ issues/issue4_10/bezroukov/index.html#b5.

23. J. S. Brown and P. Duguid, "Organizing Knowledge," *California Management Review*, Spring 1998, 40(3), 90–111.

24. C. Jones, W. S. Hesterly, and S. P. Borgatti, "A General Theory of Network Governance: Exchange Conditions and Social Mechanisms," *Academy of Management Review*, October 4, 1997, 22, 911–945.

25. S. Turkle, *The Second Self: Computers and the Human Spirit* (New York: Simon & Schuster, 1984).

Ron Adner is assistant professor of strategy and management at INSEAD, where he teaches courses on strategy, innovation, and technology. His research on these topics has been published in *Management Science,* the *Sloan Management Review, Financial Times,* and in edited book chapters. He holds a Ph.D. in strategic management from the Wharton School of Business as well as master's and bachelor's degrees in mechanical engineering from the Cooper Union for the Advancement of Science and Art. His current research examines the emergence of competition and the onset of commoditization in high-technology industries. Previously, he was engineering consultant for Allegheny Power Systems and engineering researcher for the U.S. Environmental Protection Agency.

After raising her children, the late *Carole E. Agres* started a career in information systems. She had become director of systems implementation development at Boeing and was working on completing her Ph.D. in information science at Claremont Graduate University when she died in fall 1999. She had coauthored articles for leading publications including *Sloan Management Review,* the *Information Society,* and the *Journal of Business Management.*

Erik Brynjolfsson is codirector of the Center for eBusiness at MIT, professor at the MIT Sloan School of Management, and founder, director, or advisor of several technology-intensive firms. He was among the first researchers to measure the productivity contributions of information technologies, and his research has been recognized with six "best paper" awards by fellow academics. He lectures worldwide on e-business strategy, pricing models, and intangible assets, including keynote addresses at the *BusinessWeek* CEO Summit in 2000 and the *BusinessWeek* CIO Summit in 2001. He is the co-editor of the *Ecommerce Research Forum* and several books including *Understanding the Digital Economy.* He has served on the editorial boards of numerous academic journals as well as *Time Magazine's* board of economists.

Brynjolfsson created and co-directs the Sloan School's Executive Education program on eBusiness Transformation and is an associate member of the MIT Laboratory for Computer Science.

Previously, he was a visiting professor at Stanford Business School and on the faculty at Harvard University. He holds bachelor's and master's degrees from Harvard University in applied mathematics and decision sciences and a Ph.D. from MIT in managerial economics.

Clayton M. Christensen is professor of business administration at Harvard Business School, with a joint appointment in the technology and operations management and general management faculty groups. His research and teaching interests center on the management of technological innovation, developing organizational capabilities, and finding markets for new technologies. He has won numerous awards for his papers and articles and for his book *The Innovator's Dilemma.* His writings have been published in the *Wall*

Street Journal, Harvard Business Review, and *European Management Journal,* among others. He advises many leading corporations concerning their management of technological innovation.

Previously, Christensen co-founded and served as chairman and president of Ceramics Process Systems Corporation, a leading developer of products and manufacturing processes using high-technology ceramics materials. He also worked as a consultant and project manager with the Boston Consulting Group, where he was instrumental in founding the firm's manufacturing strategy consulting practice. In 1982 he was named a White House Fellow, and has served on numerous nonprofit boards and in the local government of Belmont, Massachusetts. He holds a B.A. from Brigham Young University, an M.Phil. from Oxford University, and an M.B.A. and D.B.A. from Harvard Business School.

Joseph Cothrel is vice president of research at Participate.com, a company that creates and manages on-line communities for Global 1000 companies such as AT&T, Cisco Systems, IBM, Microsoft, and SAP AG. His current research focuses on emerging technologies for community interaction, return on investment and other measures of community performance, and best practices in community management. Previously he spent five years at Arthur Andersen's Next Generation Research Group, where he served as research director and senior researcher in the Global Best Practices Group, as well as playing a guiding role in the firm's early Internet efforts.

Cothrel is a frequent speaker on topics related to on-line community in business and has written for such publications as *Sloan Management Review, Knowledge Directions,* the *Journal of Knowledge Management, Strategy and Leadership, InteractiveWeek,* and *Digitrends.* His work has been cited in many publications including the *Wall Street Journal,* the *New York Times,* and *Forbes.* Joe holds a master's degree from the University of Michigan and a bachelor's degree from the University of Toledo.

Thomas H. Davenport is director of the Accenture Institute for Strategic Change and a Distinguished Scholar in Residence at Babson College. He is a widely published author and acclaimed speaker on the topics of information and knowledge management, reengineering, enterprise systems, and electronic business and markets. He has a Ph.D. from Harvard University in organizational behavior and has taught at the Harvard Business School, the University of Chicago, Dartmouth's Tuck School of Business, and the University of Texas at Austin. He has also directed research centers at Ernst & Young, McKinsey & Company, and CSC Index.

Davenport has written or edited nine books, including *The Attention Economy* and the first books on business process reengineering, knowledge management, and enterprise systems. He has also written over a hundred articles for such publications as *Harvard Business Review, Sloan Management Review,* and the *Financial Times.* He also writes a monthly column for *CIO Magazine* and another for *Darwin* magazine on information technology and organizational change. He was recently named one of ten "Masters of the New Economy" by *CIO* and one of twenty-five "E-Business Gurus" by *Darwin* magazine.

John M. de Figueiredo is assistant professor of strategic management at the Sloan School of Management at MIT and a faculty research fellow at the National Bureau of Economic Research. His research focus is twofold: first, he examines the regulatory politics and economics of telecommunications and Internet technologies and how companies frame their "nonmarket" strategy; second, he examines the applicability of strategic management tools to electronic commerce ventures to determine the profitability of e-commerce firms. At MIT, he is affiliated with the E-Business Research Center, the Internet and Telecommunication Convergence Consortia, and the Industrial Performance Center. Before coming to academia, he worked at Monitor Company as a strategic management consultant. He has an A.B. *magna cum laude* in economics from Harvard University, an M.Sc. in economics from the London School of Economics, and a Ph.D. in business administration from the University of California, Berkeley.

David Feeny is a fellow of Templeton College, University of Oxford, and director of the Oxford Institute of Information Management. His teaching and research interests center on the connections among strategy, organization, and information technology. He contributes to a large proportion of the college's programs for senior executives, whose participants are drawn from a wide range of industries. His work has won international recognition, and he has published a number of articles in the *Sloan Management Review* on CIOs, IT sourcing, core IS capabilities, CEOs for the information age, and e-business opportunity.

Feeny is a fellow of the Royal Society of Arts and Commerce. He holds an M.A. from Oxford University and an M.B.A. from Harvard Business School. He was vice president of Templeton College from 1995 to 1999 and is currently an advisory board member of two new venture companies. Before returning to Oxford in 1984 he was a senior marketing manager with IBM.

Jeanne G. Harris is associate partner and senior research fellow at the Accenture Institute for Strategic Change. She is currently leading research projects dealing with personalization and customer intimacy in mCommerce, customer relationship management, customer insight, and human performance. Her past research has focused on knowledge management strategies, development of executive management capabilities, and how organizations can build more effective analytic capabilities. She holds a dual degree in English and art history from Washington University and an M.S. in information science from the University of Illinois.

Prior to joining the Institute, she led Accenture's knowledge management, executive intelligence, and data warehousing global consulting practices. In her years as a consultant, she worked extensively with clients in many different industries to help enhance their managerial information, customer analytic, and knowledge management capabilities. She has published articles in many publications, such as *Sloan Management Review, California Management Review,* and *CIO* magazine.

Ajay K. Kohli is the Isaac Stiles Hopkins Professor of Marketing at Emory University's Goizueta Business School. He has also taught at the Harvard Business School, University of Texas at Austin, Koblenz School of Corporate Management in Germany, and at the Norwegian School of Management. His research interests include defining, measuring, and developing a market orientation, sales management, and industrial marketing. He has published in many journals including the *Journal of Marketing, Journal of Marketing Research, Journal of the Academy of Management Science, Journal of Business Research, Sloan Management Review,* and *Journal of Market-Focused Management.* He serves on a number of editorial review boards, and has received several research and teaching awards including the Alpha Kappa Psi award, the Jagdish N. Sheth Award, and the Jack Taylor award. He has worked with a number of companies including 3M, Accenture Institute for Strategic Change, Anderson, Dow Chemical, Eastman Kodak, Halliburton, IBM, Texas Instruments, the Forum Corporation, and the World Bank, and has led executive education seminars in the United States, Europe, Asia, and Latin America.

Alan MacCormack is assistant professor in the technology and operations management area at the Harvard Business School. His research explores the management of technology and product development in high-technology industries, such as the Internet software industry and the computer workstation and server industry. His work has appeared in a number of books and journals, including the *Harvard Business Review* and *Sloan Management Review.* Before coming to Harvard, he worked for five years as a management consultant with both Ernst & Young and Booz Allen & Hamilton, focusing on manufacturing- and operations-related issues for clients in the automotive and aerospace industries. He received his D.B.A from the Harvard Business School, where he was a recipient of the George S. Dively Award for distinguished research. He holds an M.A. in management from MIT's Sloan School of Management and a B.Sc. in electrical and electronic engineering from the University of Bath in England. He currently teaches the elective curriculum course "Managing Technology Ventures," which explores the factors that influence success in high-technology venturing.

Brook Manville is chief learning officer and customer evangelist of Saba, the leading provider of human capital development and management solutions. He has responsibility for Saba's learning programs and processes and a variety of external programs related to the development of Saba's knowledge and customer assets. He is also the publisher of the independent Web-based magazine *Learning in the New Economy* (www.linezine.com).

Previously, he held various positions at McKinsey & Co., including director of knowledge management, CIO, and partner. He has written articles on organizational learning and knowledge management in *Fast Company, Datamation, Leader to Leader,* the *Harvard Business Review, Sloan Management Review,* and industry publications such as *Knowledge Management Review.* He also speaks frequently to conferences and industry groups.

Trained as a historian, Manville was originally on the faculty of arts and sciences at Northwestern University (Chicago) and later entered business as a freelance journalist and then a business-technology analyst at CBS. He also helped launch the first on-line medical information service for physicians. He holds a Ph.D. in history from Yale and undergraduate degrees in classics from Yale and Oxford.

M. Lynne Markus is professor (chair) of electronic business at the City University of Hong Kong. She is on leave from the Peter F. Drucker Graduate School of Management, Claremont Graduate University, where she is professor of management and information science. Her research focuses on electronic commerce, enterprise systems integration, and knowledge management. She was formerly a member of the faculties of the Anderson Graduate School of Management (UCLA) and the Sloan School of Management (MIT), and has also taught at Warwick Business School (United Kingdom), Nanyang Business School (Singapore), and the Universidade Tecnica de Lisboa (Portugal).

She has written three books and numerous articles for journals such as *MIS Quarterly, Management Science, Organization Science, Communications of the ACM,* and *Sloan Management Review.* She serves on the editorial boards of several leading journals in the information systems field. She has served as AIS Council member for the Americas and as vice president for academic community affairs for SIM International. She holds a B.S. in Industrial Engineering from the University of Pittsburgh and a Ph.D. in organizational behavior from Case Western Reserve University.

Gil McWilliam is associate professor of marketing at London Business School. Her current research and writing interests focus on the strategic use of branding, on-line consumer behavior, and on-line communities and their relevance for brand strategy. She is part of the Future Media Research Program at London Business School and also researches and writes on brand development processes and corporate and marketing communications.

Throughout her academic career, she has kept close links with commercial organizations, working at board and senior executive level with a number of companies throughout Europe in the consumer goods arena, and also in the pharmaceutical, high-tech, and media industries. Formerly, she taught at the School of Management, Imperial College London and the Cranfield School of Management. She was also senior account planner for the Leagas Delaney Partnership and account planner at J. Walter Thompson.

Robert Plant is associate professor at the School of Business Administration, University of Miami. He obtained his Ph.D. in computer science at the University of Liverpool, England, having previously studied computation at Wadham College, Oxford University. He is a Microsoft certified systems engineer (MCSE), a chartered engineer, and European engineer. He holds visiting teaching and research positions at Universidad Gabriela Mistral (Santiago, Chile), Templeton College, Oxford University (England), and Victoria University of Wellington (New Zealand). In addition, he has taught in executive M.B.A. programs at IBM, Motorola, Pratt & Whitney, Office Depot, American Express, W. R. Grace, Siemens, and other Fortune 500 companies.

His consulting and research interests are centered on the role of information systems in strategic management. He is the author of *eCommerce: Formulation of Strategy* and has published over eighty articles in such leading journals as *Sloan Management Review, Communications of the ACM,* and *Information & Management.*

William J. Qualls is the first African-American tenured professor of business administration and director of the Industrial Distribution Management program at the University of Illinois at Urbana-Champaign. Previously, he was associate professor of marketing at MIT's Sloan School of Management and the University of Michigan. He has also been a visiting professor at the Helsinki School of Economics, Nanyang Technological University (Singapore), Auckland University (New Zealand), and Universidad Gabriela Mistral (Chile), among others.

Qualls has been published in such journals as the *Journal of Marketing, Journal of Marketing Research, Journal of Consumer Research,* and *Journal of Business Research,* and sits on several editorial boards. His current research examines the role of trust in distribution channel relationships, performance measurement in supply chain management practices, and new product development.

Qualls has consulted with numerous firms, including KPMG-Peat Marwick, IBM, BellSouth, General Motors, TI, and Becton-Dickinson. He has been an active contributor in numerous capacities with the NBMBAA and was a member of the board

1996–1997. He has also worked with the KPMG Ph.D. Project to increase the flow of doctoral students of color into the college classroom.

Subramanian Rangan is associate professor of strategy and management at INSEAD. He received an M.B.A. from the MIT Sloan School of Management and a Ph.D. from Harvard University. His research and teaching have focused on strategy and management challenges confronting multinational firms. He was the 1998 winner of the Academy of International Business's Eldridge Haynes Prize (awarded biennially to a scholar under forty for the best original essay in international business) and the 1995 winner of that academy's Best Dissertation award. Coauthor of two books, *Manager in the International Economy* and *A Prism on Globalization,* he has written in journals such as the *Brookings Papers on Economic Activity,* the *Journal of International Business Studies,* and the *Academy of Management Review.* He also serves on the editorial boards of *JIBS, Journal of International Management,* and *Strategic Management Journal.* He is working currently on the topic of global teamwork in multinational firms.

Fareena Sultan is associate professor of marketing at Northeastern University. Previously, she has been a visiting scholar at Columbia University, visiting associate professor at UC Berkeley, associate professor at Golden Gate University, and assistant professor at Harvard Business School. She obtained her doctoral degree in marketing from Columbia University, and has master's degrees in operations research (MIT) and applied mathematics (University of Karachi). She has won awards for both her teaching and her research.

Her research interests include e-commerce, Internet marketing, and marketing innovations, particularly trust issues on the Internet and adoption and diffusion of innovations. Her current research includes business-to-customer and business-to-business trust issues on the Internet, diffusion of the Internet, and new product development.

Sultan has worked with companies such as IBM, Zenith, Philips, Mitsubishi, SONY, Matsushita, Arthur Andersen, and Texas Instruments, and done executive training and consulting in the United States, Argentina, and Pakistan. She has also worked as a senior research associate with the Marketing Science Institute in Cambridge, Massachusetts. She has published articles in numerous journals, including the *Sloan Management Review, Journal of Marketing Research,* and *Marketing Management.*

Glen L. Urban is professor of management at the MIT Sloan School of Management and codirector of the Center for eBusiness at MIT. He has been on the Sloan School faculty since 1966, including a stint as dean. His research focus is on management science models that improve the productivity of new product development. He devised a methodology called Information Acceleration that uses computer technology to simulate future sales of products; this methodology emerged from his ground-breaking work in premarket forecasting for frequently purchased consumer goods. Currently, he is working to develop a trust-based marketing system on the Internet.

Urban is coauthor of five books, including *Design and Marketing of New Products, Advanced Marketing Strategy,* and *Essentials of New Product Management,* and has published over twenty articles. His writing and research have won prestigious awards including two O'Dells and prizes from the American Marketing Association, the *Journal of Marketing,* and the Wharton School. He has founded or cofounded a number of consulting and high-tech companies and is currently chair of Experion. He earned a B.S. in mechanical engineering and an M.B.A. from the University of Wisconsin and a Ph.D. in marketing at Northwestern University.

N. Venkatraman is the David J. McGrath, Jr. Professor of Management at Boston University School of Management. His work is at the interface between business and IT strategies. Previously, he served on the faculty at MIT Sloan School of Management and was a lead researcher in the Management in the 1990s Project. He has also served as a visiting professor of management at London Business School. Currently he coordinates a multiuniversity research project among Boston University, London Business School, and INSEAD on the global impact of the mobile Internet. He has won many awards for his academic work and was recognized by *BusinessWeek* as one of the outstanding educators of 1999.

Venkatraman speaks at leading conferences throughout the world and his research has been featured in the *Economist, Financial Times,* and *ComputerWorld.* He has published extensively in academic and management journals; his articles on the strategic impact of information technology published in the *Sloan Management Review* have been widely influential. He is working on a book tentatively titled *Winning in the Networked Era: Breakthrough Business Models That Deliver Distinct Value.*

Leslie P. Willcocks is Andersen Professor of Information Management and E-Business at Warwick Business School, United Kingdom, and associate fellow at Templeton College, University of Oxford. He is also visiting professor at Erasmus University, Rotterdam, professorial associate at the University of Melbourne, and distinguished visitor at the Australian Graduate School of Management. He holds a doctorate in information systems from the University of Cambridge and is editor-in-chief of the *Journal of Information Technology.* He is also a nonexecutive board director of Mainpass Technologies.

Previously he worked in accounting and management consultancy for Touche Ross and several smaller firms. He is coauthor of nineteen books, including *Global IT Outsourcing, Moving to E-Business,* and *Building the E-Business Infrastructure,* and has been published in journals such as *Harvard Business Review, Sloan Management Review, MIS Quarterly,* and *Journal of Management Studies.* He is a regular keynote speaker at international practitioner and academic conferences, has extensive consulting experience, and is regularly retained as adviser by major corporations and government institutions. In

2001 he was awarded the PriceWaterhouseCoopers–Michael Corbett Associates World Outsourcing Achievement Award.

Ruth L. Williams is a senior manager with PriceWaterhouseCoopers' Unifi Network where she is responsible for integrating knowledge management expertise and solutions into client projects that focus on maximizing the value of human capital. Her areas of focus include identification of mission-critical knowledge, knowledge strategy, and knowledge harvesting. Previously she was a member of PwC's Intellectual Asset Management practice where she designed approaches for inventorying, articulating, and protecting intellectual assets. Prior to joining PwC, she was a founder and codirector of Arthur Andersen's Next Generation Research Group, which helped client organizations understand topics of emerging importance to global businesses, including new forms of leadership, online communities, and knowledge measurement. Her research in knowledge management culminated in coauthorship of *The Knowledge Management Fieldbook*. She holds a dual degree in English and Psychology from the University of Pennsylvania and an M.B.A. from the University of Pennsylvania's Wharton School.

INDEX